THE MYSTICAL IMAGINATION OF
PATRICK KAVANAGH

Best wishes from
Una Agnew
Nov 28th 2004

Tues. — Fri
—
—

www. amaravati.....

For my mother, Gretta,
and in memory of my father,
John Agnew

Una Agnew SSL

The Mystical Imagination of Patrick Kavanagh

Can a man grow from the dead clod of failure
Some consoling flower
Something humble as a dandelion or a daisy,
Something to wear as A buttonhole in heaven?

(*From Failure Up* by Patrick Kavanagh)

the columba press

First published in 1998
This revised paperback edition first published in 1999 by
ᴄhe ᴄoʟumʙᴀ pʀess
55A Spruce Avenue, Stillorgan Industrial Park, Blackrock, Co Dublin

Reprinted 2003

Cover by Bill Bolger
Origination by The Columba Press
Printed in Ireland by Colour Books Ltd, Dublin

ISBN 1 85607 276 2

Author's Note

I wish to express my sincere appreciation for the advice and encouragement received from the late Professor Augustine Martin, UCD, during
the early stages of this research 1985-1991. His help was invaluable and
I deeply regret his passing. I would like to thank members of the
Kavanagh family, Peter and the late Mary and Josephine, who afforded
me much helpful co-operation during the early stages of my work. For
Peter's 'sacred keepership' of his brother's writing I, along with fellow
researchers, owe an enormous debt of gratitude. My gratitude also goes
to my brother Art Agnew, Carrickmacross, an expert on Patrick Kavanagh in his own right, and Margaret Agnew SSL, my sister, both of
whom made helpful comments and advised on early and later drafts of
this book. My thanks to Mr Ray Leonard, Claremorris, who read chapters six and seven and made helpful suggestions. I owe a great debt of
gratitude to those who gave me long and short loans of books: Gretta
Agnew, the late John Jordan, Bishop Duffy of Clogher, Eilis Gallagher,
Muirhevna, Dundalk, and Peter Murphy, Inniskeen. A special word of
thanks to all members of my family who helped with phone-calls,
checked references, helped with proof-reading, and made contributions
to this work too numerous to recount. Thanks finally to the Sisters of St
Louis, collectively and individually, who supported me in making this
book a reality.

Contents

Acknowledgements

The author and the publisher gratefully acknowledge the following:
Quotations from the poems and prose of Patrick Kavanagh are reprinted
by kind permission of the Trustees of the Estate of Patrick Kavanagh,
c/o Peter Fallon, Literary Agent, Loughcrew, Oldcastle, Co Meath. The
Library Staff of The National Library of Ireland, Kildare St, Dublin 2;
The Library staff at Milltown Institute, Milltown Park, Dublin 6; Norma
Jessop and assistants, UCD Special Collections, The Library, Belfield,
Co Dublin; The staff at The National Archives, Four Courts and Bishop
Street, Dublin 2; Ann Duff and staff, Irish Messenger Office, 37 Lower
Leeson St, Dublin; Richard Riordan, 4 Fortfield Gdns, Dublin 6; Patrick
Duffy and the staff of Inniskeen NS, Co Monaghan; Mary Butler, Local
History Dept, Tullamore County Library; Michael Byrne, Historical
Society, Tullamore; Fr Mc Guinness, Parochial House, Inniskeen, Co
Monaghan; Presentation Sisters, The Generalate, Monasterevan, and
the Isle of Wight; Srs of Mercy, Tullamore, Galway and Downpatrick,
Co Down; Hugh Mc Fadden, Rathmines, Dublin, for material relating
to John Jordan; The late Michael O'Reilly, Stephen Cahill and Finian
Lynch, Moynalty, Co Meath, for information pertaining to Miss
Cassidy. Riana Lohan and the staff of UCD Archives, Belfield, Co
Dublin; Sr Francis Lowe, formerly of Carysford College Library, Gretta
Agnew, Courtbane, Dundalk, Annie McEnaney, Shelagh, Dundalk, the
late Katie Kirk-Compbell, Ballykelly, Dundalk, Eddie Filgate, Louth vil-
lage and John Gallagher, Muirhevna Nua, Dundalk for their assistance
in identifying and providing schoolbook sources. Mrs Minnie Gorman
and her brother Philip McArdle, Ballybinaby, for material relating to
their grand-uncle Fr Pat McConnon. Jennie Uí Chléirigh, Beechwood
Avenue, Dublin, for material relating to her uncle Fr Bernard Maguire.
Mrs Quinn (Secretary), of the Patrick Kavanagh Society, Inniskeen; Cllr
Peter Murphy, Kednaminsha, Inniskeen, for verifying data on numer-
ous occasions; Gene Carroll and the staff of Inniskeen Rural and
Literary Centre; Mrs Mary Mulholland, Thornfield, and her son Patrick,
Gortin, Inniskeen, for items of local history pertaining to the Inniskeen
area. Art and Helen Agnew of the Kavanagh Yearly Committee,
Carrickmacross (1984-1992). Sr Margaret Agnew, St Mary's Training
College, Belfast, for consultation on matters theological. John
Kavanagh, the late Michael McHugh, Mary Jo Feeney and the
Keveney/Kevany families of Easkey for information pertaining to
Patrick Kevany. Sr Fionnuala Keveney, Gortnor Abbey, Crossmolina,
and Mrs Mary Kelly, Tubbercurry, for photographic material relating
to the Keveneys. Thanks to the Sisters of Mercy, Tullamore Convent,
the Sisters of Jesus and Mary, Gortnor Abbey, Anne Keveney,
Castletown, Easkey, and the Sisters of Mercy, Kinvara, Co Galway, for
their generous hospitality during the research for this book.

Patrick Kavanagh 1904-1967:
A Brief Chronology

1904 Patrick Kavanagh was born 21/22 October, baptised at St Mary's Church, Inniskeen, 23 October.

1909 Admitted to infant class at Kednaminsha School.

1915 Fr Maguire appointed PP of Inniskeen (1915-1948d).

1918 Left school and became an apprentice shoemaker.

1926 Purchase of Reynolds' farm by Kavanaghs.

1929 Death of James Kavanagh. Patrick's first poems published.

1930 Walked to Dublin to meet with AE (George Russell).

1936 *Ploughman and Other Poems* published by Macmillan.

1937 Went to London to write *The Green Fool*. Met G. B. Shaw, Seán O'Casey, Gawsworth, etc.

1939 Went to live permanently in Dublin.

1941 Worked intermittently for *The Standard* until 1949 and as a columnist for *The Irish Press*.

1942 Wrote *The Great Hunger*, published by The Cuala Press, and 'Lough Derg' published posthumously by his brother Peter.

1943 Moved to a flat at 62 Pembroke Road.

1945 Death of his mother, Brigid Kavanagh.

1947 *A Soul for Sale* (poems) published by Macmillan.

1948 Completed *Tarry Flynn* (novel), published by Pilot Press.

1952 Wrote, edited and published, along with Peter, *Kavanagh's Weekly*, 12 April until 5 July.

1954 Libel case, 3-12 February: Kavanagh *v The Leader*.

1955 Experienced a spiritual rebirth while convalescing from lung cancer surgery. Received a stipend for life through the intervention of John A. Costello, Michael Tierney, UCD, and Archbishop J. C. McQuaid.

1958 *Recent Poems* published by Peter Kavanagh Hand Press.

1960 *Come Dance with Kitty Stobbling* (Longmans).

1963 *Self-Portrait* produced by RTÉ, published 1964 by The Dolmen Press.

1964 *Collected Poems* published by Martin Brian and O'Keeffe.

1967 *Collected Pruse* published. Married Katherine Moloney in Rathgar Church, 19 April 1967. Died 30 November, Merrion Nursing Home, Dublin, buried in Inniskeen.

Patrick Kavanagh at Inniskeen in October 1963

Introduction

For we must record love's mystery without claptrap,
Snatch out of time the passionate transitory.
(The Hospital)[1]

These lines summarise Patrick Kavanagh's gospel of life. Whatever touched him deeply, he considered eternal, and therefore worthy of immortalisation. More and more he became fluent in the simple language of things held in mystery. The light that radiated from the commonplace, from ordinary life around him, frequently caught him in its stare, transfixing him with wonder. He allowed himself to be susceptible to this Beauty beyond beauty, 'a beauty that the world did not touch'. 'God must be allowed to surprise us' was the creed to which he strongly subscribed.

It is difficult to write about Kavanagh's mysticism without doing him an injustice. Those who are devoted to his poetry may accuse me of killing him with comment. His work is best read as he might himself say: 'without comment from the scholar'. And yet more and more people today feel the need to invoke Kavanagh's work, to read it and explore its spirituality. Exploring the mystical dimension of his work is something I have wanted to do for some time. I have always felt that Kavanagh has important things to say as a Christian and as a human being. His voice is part of what Joyce called the 'uncreated conscience' of his people. He speaks to the heart of every townland and to the 'important places' of our lives. He speaks for the holiness of the earth in danger of being despoiled by the pollution of modern living. Above all he speaks to the soul of a people which may be in danger of being jostled by a rampant modern economy.

I have also felt, without any logical foundation, that I owe something to this poet of my childhood country. I come from a few townlands away, from the parish of Creggan next to Inniskeen. I too have lived within sight of Slieve Gullion and the landscape Kavanagh loved. The purpose of this book is to explore the mystical vision he experienced in this south-east Ulster/ north Leinster environment. Kavanagh's claim that 'poetry is a mystical thing and a dangerous thing' begs examination. The poet's roots, like my own, are in the Catholic faith and in a rural Catholic upbringing. He was a contemporary of my parents and followed the same programme at school and in church. My grand-aunt Brigid Agnew taught him at Kednaminsha school. There is therefore an element of self-interest in my work. As I read and reread his poems and prose I cannot avoid the feeling that this writing also 'reads me' and tells me who I am.

Kavanagh, I believe, had a strong sense of his mission as poet in society. He was druid-like in his demeanour, feeling that he was born to make a poetic contribution to society and that society should support him. In this he was disappointed, being born too late to benefit from any rich patron. Nevertheless he pursued his mission as a holy vocation. 'The poet,' he believes, 'is a theologian' whose duty it is to build 'a new city' which he unashamedly calls the 'city of God'. A sense of priesthood went along with his sense of being a poet. Wearing the vestment of poetry, he uses his mystical wizardry to spill 'magic' on 'the living road' of life. (*A Wreath for Thomas Moore's Statue*)

'Choose life, so that you and your descendents may live,' says the sacred writer of the Book of Deuteronomy.[2] Kavanagh chose the life of commonplace things where he found an abundance of 'ordinary plenty'. He took the lilies of the field, bluebells, primroses, violets and common weeds and saw in them aspects of the life of God. He sought to capture, often with superb technique, the beauty of everyday things. He found 'at every turn of the living road' a magic that enraptured him. He knew that by celebrating the ordinary he was fulfilling his true vocation. This vocation to communicate 'God's truth' was so simple it almost seemed banal:

God's truth was such a thing you could not mention
Without being ashamed of its commonness;
First there is
A dark lane between a garden wall and a gable
A vegetable garden too, for yellow cabbage leaves
Sometimes are caught on the jutting spikes of masonry
And on top of nettles.
(Common Beauty)

Because he was in love with life, nothing was too mean to be noticed and transformed by him. His official role was that 'of prophet and saviour' called to 'smelt in passion the commonplaces of life'. This role involves being 'a god in a new fashion' who would release people through the medium of poetry from the meanness, sordidness and materialism of life. He wished to free them from 'the fog' which clogged their footsteps and give them apertures into a land of the imagination, 'chance windows of poetry and prayer'.

Few who knew him by sight were likely to regard Patrick Kavanagh as a mystic or a prophet. He did little to inspire confidence in his general public either in his native Inniskeen or in the Dublin circles he frequented. People moved away from him in pubs, buses and trains. He frightened young girls with his loud language when they passed him in the street. Yet his work stands as a monument to a nobility and gentility of soul that surprises even as it inspires. His poetry above all challenges us not to be deceived by appearance – that beneath the coat of a beggar there may lurk a hidden mystic.

Kavanagh's poetry is the principal vehicle of his spirituality. At times it exudes such delicate beauty and strong religious sense that he commands our careful attention, not only as a moral poet but as a mystical one as well. Though his poetry has immortalised his native Monaghan landscape with its whitethorn hedges, it is also true that he has gained entrance to the halls of literature through his concern for what pertains to the soul. His visionary qualities bestowed on him 'fields that were part of no earthly estate'. And yet he ruled as 'king of banks and stones and every blooming thing', cherishing ordinary everyday realities. His earthly and unearthly estate gave depth and scope to the literary legacy he has left us.

Kavanagh speaks prophetically of building 'a new city', 'a city of God'. Despite his limited formal education he was aware that he was using a heavily-laden metaphor. St Augustine's *City of God* illustrated the fact that God's ultimate purpose was being worked out in history. He promulgated his message through his metaphor of the two cities, the City of God rooted in the love of God, and the City of Earth which finds its radicle in love of self. Thus Augustine succeeded in establishing an enormous chasm between 'the city of the world' and 'the city of God'.

Kavanagh sought to bridge the gap between God's kingdom and the earthly kingdom. He was closer to the gospel notion that the kingdom of God is among you than many preaching the gospel at this time. His God was in the fields and in the ditches and in the hedgerows. The pessimism that clung to Augustinian thinking still permeated the Irish church of Kavanagh's time. A sharp distinction between the world of God and the 'tarnished' world of humanity pertained.

Kavanagh wanted to live in both worlds. For him the created world was as God-filled and radiant as the heavenly city of God. Kavanagh was instinctively holistic. His poetry, became a radical affirmation of life, of earth, of the human condition and of God's presence everywhere. He became the forgotten voice of the sacred 'commonplaces of life'. Unlike Augustine, the poet promised a transformed vision of the world. He undertook to build 'a new city'. Instead of concentrating on making one place, the church building for example, holy, the poet spills his magic and mystery everywhere.

Here was an attempt, long before the official theologians proclaimed it openly, to break old moulds of secularism versus religion and preach a new life-affirming theology of faith and vision. Kavanagh was expressing a sophisticated theology of incarnation well ahead of the official church of his time. For him, the fields as well as all humankind were involved in the miracle of the Word made flesh. Mystical vision alone was capable of such insight:

> The old cranky spinster is dead
> Who fed us cold flesh.
> And in the green meadows
> The maiden of spring
> Is with child by the Holy Ghost. *(April)*

Kavanagh's capacity to comprehend the involvement of earth in the mystery of Incarnation is prophetic. For the first time in twentieth-century Irish literature, a writer consistently baptises the rural landscape in a way that has not been done before in English. Earth and common things are redeemed by the poet ahead even of theologians, so that a new graced landscape with which people can identify is established. We will see how Kavanagh undertook this work and how he was fitted for the task.

Structure of the book

My method of dealing with the question of Kavanagh's mystical imagination is straightforward. Chapter One addresses the question of what is meant by 'mystical'. It poses questions that influence the ground-plan of the remainder of the book: What is mysticism? and does Kavanagh's writing give evidence of the criteria established by experts in this field? The ancient mystical stages: Awakening, Purification, Illumination and Transformation, outlined by Evelyn Underhill, serve as a frame of reference for examining Kavanagh's life and writing.

Chapter Two broaches the question of the poet's first mystical stirrings in the home, at school and in his neighbourhood. The gradual awakening of the imagination is seen to have roots in folktales and fairylore as well as the drumlin landscape of South Monaghan. His sacramental initiation into the Catholic faith owes much to the influence of his parents, teachers and local wisdom figures. Religious influence could also be attributed to a learned parish priest, Fr Maguire, who unknowingly gave his young altar-boy food for thought.

Chapter Three describes how Kavanagh's literary roots stemmed from the many schoolbooks he cherished. He was awakened to the beauty of poetry especially through the poems of James Clarence Mangan, Tennyson, Longfellow and Harte. The local Bard of Callenberg demonstrated that verse could earn a few shillings weekly in the *Dundalk Democrat* and so the door to writing was open. Later it was William Carleton, with his *Traits and Stories of the Irish Peasantry,* who inspired his allegiance and awakened him to the possibility that ordinary peasants were worthy of a place in literature. It was his eventual introduction to George Russell (AE) which gave Kavanagh the impetus he needed.

Chapter Four shows Kavanagh's mystical imagination being continually harrowed and purified. This occurred not only through the religious and social ethos of his time, whose anti-life mentality sorely cramped his vision, but also through his intense suffering at being misunderstood even within his own family. When he left home to live in Dublin he was confronted there by hardship and poverty, especially during the war years (1939-1945). Because of his strong mystical propensities, Kavanagh succeeded in transforming material poverty into 'poverty of spirit' which helped somewhat to sublimate his misery.

Chapter Five outlines the sources of personal purification that continued to dog Kavanagh's footsteps throughout his life. Dealing with poverty, joblessness, stigma and deprivation was Kavanagh's lot. This ongoing purification of his vision is seen to play a key role in the achievement of his poetical-mystical technique. Little has been known until now concerning the humiliating effects of his father's illegitimacy and the needless loss of his paternal lineage. This story of tragedy and romance is documented for the first time in this chapter. Despite his suffering and sense of being 'a holy fool', of experiencing repeated failure as a poet and as a person, Kavanagh was able to turn purification to good effect.

Chapters Six and Seven look at the accumulated fruits of awakening and purification. This is Kavanagh at his most memorable. Darkness invariably breaks open, just as, biblically speaking, 'the earth breaks open and buds forth a Saviour' (Is 27:6) Kavanagh is the poet of numerous epiphanies, where an inner radiance breaks into the outer world and Kavanagh adorns these moments with fitting lyrical expression. Whether he describes Christ as 'a January flower' or notices 'fantastic light' that 'looks through the eyes of bridges', Kavanagh is a competent recorder of his moments of illumination. There follows a necessary and not completely unexpected transformation of the poet's life and work. His earthly estate becomes radiant with a suffused inner mystical light. Kavanagh, at his best, is capable of making this radiance visible.

By way of conclusion, I identify in the movement from Monaghan to the Grand Canal an intensely idiosyncratic inner journey. The poet pursued his mystical pathway awkwardly but with painstaking perseverance. The persistent subtraction of all that is *not* God, leaves the poet with a solid poetic kernel corresponding to a firm intuition of God. Kavanagh's contribution to poetry must therefore be seen as both thoroughly Christian and essentially mystical. It is, I believe, a worthy 'buttonhole' which he can proudly wear in the heavenly place where he undoubtedly finds rest.

CHAPTER 1

Patrick Kavanagh:
A Mystical Writer?

There is, of course, a poetic movement which sees poetry material-
istically. The writers of this school see no transcendent nature in
the poet; they are practical chaps, excellent technicians. But some-
how or other I have a belief in poetry as a mystical thing, and a dan-
gerous thing.
(*Collected Poems*, Martin, Brian and O'Keeffe, 1964, p.xiii.)

PART ONE

KAVANAGH: A MYSTICAL POET?

When Patrick Kavanagh announced his belief in poetry as 'a
mystical thing and a dangerous thing', no one seemed to pay attention. This unusual declaration, which appeared in the introduction to his first major poetry collection (1964), went largely
unnoticed by scholars and critics alike. Indeed, Kavanagh's
strong roots in the Catholic religion and his life-long pre-occu-
pation with eternal questionings, give credence to his claim. But
how serious is his assertion that poetry, of its essence, is mystical? And does his work demonstrate this? To test the validity of
his statement, it is necessary to bear with me while I examine
with some care what mysticism is, and if it can fittingly describe
Kavanagh's work.

What is Mysticism?
Evelyn Underhill (1875-1941) outlines the principal characteristics of the mystic in her classic work, *Mysticism*.[1] She is helpful in
that she is herself a poet as well as a spiritual writer. The mystic,
she holds, is firstly a seeker who passionately follows the pursuit of beauty, goodness or truth. The lifelong quest for the Holy
Grail is the object of mystical love. St John of the Cross's quest

17

for his 'Beloved' is immortalised in his famous 'Spiritual Canticle',
a poem of delectable but painful longing:

> Where have you hidden,
> Beloved, and left me moaning?
> You fled like the stag
> After wounding me...[2]

Mystical knowledge belongs in a category of its own. The mystic
stands in sharp contrast to the empirical scientist who generally
regards mystical knowledge as unreliable and unworthy of con-
sideration. The mystic, on the other hand, holds to have seen, or
at least glimpsed, a vision of beauty beyond the veil of custom or
calculation. This revelation is authentic knowledge, but can be
grasped only in images and symbols.

Once the vision of beauty, truth, or goodness has been
glimpsed, the mystic is smitten with desire for this cherished
goal. In St John's case, he has been 'wounded' at the deepest centre of his soul. He relentlessly seeks a 'way out' or a 'way back',
restlessly yearning to be at home in the heart of Essential Being.[3]

Restless and uneasy with platitudes, the mystic seeks to
know things in their essence. This desire for knowledge is part
of the quest for perfection. And, for the mystic, knowing goes
beyond mere rational knowledge. It is coupled with a desire for
union with reality, and often consists in a direct intuition of
truth. The mystic frequently knows, without being able to explain why.

The mystic above all seeks to love. The lover, the poet and the
mystic experience the joy of 'seeing into the heart of things'.
With the writer St Exupéry they affirm that it is with the heart
that one sees. To love with one's whole being, intellect, emotions
and volition, is intrinsically mystical. Through love, doors fly
open which logic has battered on in vain.[4] Reason can speak, but
it is only love that sings.[5] The mystic is well aware that there exists a life beyond reach of the senses.

More and more, the mystic experiences a level of consciousness beyond the ordinary. The awakening of the hidden faculty
of the soul opens up a level of awareness which produces exper-

iences of great joy, alternating with profound desolation. The mystic encounters life with greater intensity and sensitivity than most. As is the case with poet and mystic William Blake (1757-1827), one becomes periodically 'drunk with … vision' or, as in the Christian tradition, 'inebriated' with Christ.[6]

Single-mindedly the mystic follows the hidden Paradise of Love. Once the glory of transcendent beauty has been glimpsed, he remains dissatisfied with anything less. Those who become 'drunk with God' through visions or ecstasy, find it more difficult to return to mundane realities. The mystic gone astray is in danger of seeking compensatory substances such as drugs or alcohol as substitutes for the exquisite 'Bread of Angels'. At best, the mystical life is one lived in a kind of limbo, always seeking paradise yet attaining little but its merest glimpse.

At certain points along the way, there occur periods of darkness and disillusionment. This experience may seem to overwhelm the subject with deprivation of light and solace. Darkness, however, can be interpreted as a time of gestation or purgation, during which the soul is drawn even closer to its beloved object:

Oh night that was my guide!
Oh darkness dearer than the morning's pride,
Oh night that joined the lover
To the beloved bride
Transfiguring them each into the other.[7]

This purgation is aptly described by T. S. Eliot, who resonates deeply with the mystical darkness of St John of the Cross. Darkness, for Eliot, is a time of waiting:

I said to my soul, be still, and let the dark come upon you
Which shall be the darkness of God…[8]

Emerging from a period of purification, the mystic is prepared for further awakenings of spirit.

The mystic's secret knowledge[9] cuts him or her adrift from ordinary people, and imposes a kind of involuntary exile. The pursuit of vision requires complete dedication. One becomes impatient with all that is false in oneself and in one's world. The mystic is not simply a dreamer, but one who is engaged energetically with life, tirelessly discerning what is true from what is false. Periodically the mystic skirts a mental state akin to madness, a state of psychic openness which brings blessing and torture in its wake. Thus, the mystical state can be dangerous in that it can unhinge the mind, drive it to the edge of sanity or carry it to unbidden heights only to sink it once more into troughs of darkness.

The poet's claim to be a mystic lies in the fact that he or she 'has achieved a passionate communion with deeper levels of life than those with which we usually deal'.[10] Such a poet is Walt Whitman, admired greatly by Patrick Kavanagh. Above all, the poet-mystic is a visionary. The mystical soul sees beyond the surface of the ordinary and penetrates the mystery at the heart of all things. This was particularly obvious in the Celtic mystical tradition, where the veil between earth and heaven is thin. Joseph Mary Plunkett (1887-1916) was possessed of a mystical awareness of God's presence in the created world around him. He saw Christ traced on elements of the natural world:

I see his blood upon the rose
And in the stars the glory of his eyes,
His body gleams amid eternal snows,
His tears fall from the skies.[11]

In summary, Underhill states that the emergence of the mystic in society is a recurring phenomenon. Life for the mystic becomes a mysterious search, guided and inspired by an innate 'spiritual spark' or transcendent faculty. Such powers remain dormant in many, and yet are available to all. Speaking of this 'divine spark' she sees it emerge from 'the still point' or 'apex of the soul' and gradually become dominant in the mystic's life. Possessed of a secret knowledge, the mystic wends a solitary path through life, sometimes elated by vision, oftentimes living in a dark, abandoned contemplation. The 'inner eye of love' is a Zen Buddhist expression for this mystical faculty, which gradually leads to enlightenment.[12] Mystical vision is little understood in our modern world. It can evoke admiration, but also irritation and ridicule, when others fail to understand it.[13] In this the poet and mystic have much in common.

The Poet and the Mystic

Henri Bremond points out that the poet and mystic share a common ground.[14] Both have an instinct for the transcendent and enjoy fleeting glimpses of the mystery that surrounds everyday life. This is made clear in the poetry of Francis Thompson:

O world invisible, we view thee,
O world intangible, we touch thee,
O world unknowable, we know thee,
Inapprehensible, we clutch thee!

Experiences of poetry and mysticism belong to the same order of knowledge, a knowledge of the heart.[15] The mystic, Bremond says, is 'graced with an immediate intuition of God'. Poet and mystic alike rely on intuition, that immediate grasp of the truth, beyond reason or analysis. The essential difference between them is principally one of communication. The poet trades in the magic of words as a vehicle for expression, while the mystic takes refuge in contemplative silence. While both may have a profound experience, one is greater in communication, the other in interior communion. In terms of communication, the mystic is 'less' than the poet. One is greater by experience, the other by expression. Though they share the same terrain, their goals differ. The 'mystical state' of the poet cannot be said to be identical with the 'state of grace' experienced by the mystic. Yet they are not mutually exclusive. Both share parallel moments which spill over onto the terrain of the other, making it sometimes impossible to tell them apart.

For the religious mystic, a glimpse of the glory of God demands a rigorous *ascesis* of bringing one's life into conformity with the graces gratuitously received. The poet-mystic, on the other hand, assumes the discipline of bringing experience to birth in poetry, and is often consumed with a prophetic mission to restore for mankind the integrity of the universe. A margin of incommunicability, nevertheless, generally lingers in the experience of both.

The mystic who is *also* an artist will attempt to describe in images and symbols what is seen and heard. 'Painting, poetry and music,' argues Blake, are 'the three powers in man of conversing with Paradise.'[16] The poet longs to capture the elusive beauty of Eden. Martin Heidegger sees the poet as the one who senses the banishment of 'the gods' from the earth. Poets, he believes, detect 'the trace of the fugitive gods' and 'stay on (their) tracks'. Their mission is seen to be that of leading fellow mortals back to the path of 'the holy'. The artist acts, then, as prophet for the people, seeking to grasp their dreams and echo their aspirations. Yeats, echoing Blake, clearly envisions a spiritual role for the artist when he exhorts his fellow Irish poets to 'learn their trade':

> Poet and sculptor do the work
> Nor let the modish painter shirk
> What his great forefathers did,
> Bring the soul of man to God ...[17]

Poet and mystic together experience intermittent states of light and darkness, sunshine and shadow, agony and ecstasy: all of which, from Blake's standpoint, are 'eternal'.[18] The poet and mystic are close to one another in their mutual quest for beauty, which 'tends of itself to unite us to God'.[19] Poetry and mysticism, then, have similar sources and can, in certain cases, be synonymous. Although they may express themselves differently, they reflect and illumine one another.

The Mystical Path

Strangely, it is the mystic who teaches us to better understand the poet.[20] Mystical development can help us comprehend the development of the poet's mystical imagination. It provides us with a 'rough sketch' of the poetic mind. Among all those writing about mysticism, Underhill best outlines the process.[21] Mystical development involves *three* main stages: Awakening, Purification, and Illumination. This schema originated with the Neo-Platonists and is valid for all metaphysical systems.

Awakening constitutes the first opening of the eyes of the mystical sense. This can occur gradually from childhood, as in the case of the French mystic Madame Guyon, or suddenly on the roadside, as in the case of St Paul. An experience of acute pain or pleasure can be instrumental in the awakening process. Nature mystics are possessed of a high degree of perceptive vision. Like Blake and the Celtic mystics, they can 'see a world in a grain of sand / And heaven in a wild flower'. The mystic has a sense of awakening from sleep to a world that is new.

Purification can accompany or follow upon awakening. Each new level of insight and self-understanding causes the mystic to shed superficial ways of being. Illness and suffering can be instrumental in the purification process, as was the case with Julian of Norwich and St Ignatius of Loyola. Poverty and destitution, loneliness and rejection can frequently be sources of purification. Inner cleansing takes place through letting go of the ego. This is often called the *via negativa* or the negative experience of God. These dark passages of the mystic's formation are ascetical in nature. Self-denial, penance and exile were frequently chosen by Celtic monks of the early Irish church who embraced the search for God. The interior suffering of Gerard Manley Hopkins and T. S. Eliot was the refining fire of their souls. Hurt, ridicule and disparagement were instrumental in the soul-formation of mystical poets and artists, not least among them Patrick Kavanagh, for whom poverty and rejection were part of a life-long purification.

Illumination occurs when mystical consciousness, no longer clouded by custom, becomes lucid and awake. Wordsworth best evokes this stage in his 'Tintern Abbey', when he experiences the quieting of bodily sense and awakening of spiritual vision: 'we are laid asleep in body and become a living soul'. The soul, alive and fully awake at last, is illumined, so that 'we see into the life of things'. This mystical seeing occurs in a specifically religious context for Hopkins when he becomes dazzled by a transformed vision of the world. 'God's Grandeur', he sees, is an energy that 'charges' the universe with splendour:

The world is charged with the grandeur of God
It will flame out, like shook foil;
It gathers to a greatness, like the ooze of oil
Crushed.[22]

Here illumination takes on a sacramental character which is of interest when we come to consider the poet Patrick Kavanagh. The radiance of God's presence is the fruit of an expanded consciousness. This radiance is all-pervasive; it becomes 'resplendent in the meanest things'.[23]

A similar view of sacramentality is described by Eliade when he speaks about primitive man's capacity to converse with the sacredness of the cosmos. 'Tilling ... the clay put(s) primitive man into a universe steeped in the sacred'.[24] The mountain or the tree are not simply items on the horizon but sacred places linking earth and heaven. Primitive man was unconsciously a symbolic thinker. He preserved a sense of the sacred amid daily life. Modern technology has, for the most part, robbed humankind of a sense of the sacredness of matter. Thus the cosmos has become de-sanctified. In the words of Heidegger, 'the gods have fled' ... and 'the divine radiance has become extinguished in the world's history'.[25] The poet and mystic can recover, in moments of illumination, a sense of the cosmos as hierophanic. Poetry can reconstitute the earth as sacred. This radiant vision, or sacramental presence of God, is experienced as illumination in the Christian mystical tradition.

Ecstasy is a degree of illumination where the mystic is seized by an awareness so total, so absorbing that he experiences himself outside time and space. In this state, one remains momentarily freed from the constraints of time and space. Experience of this kind usually leads to further purification. In some cases, there is a total dying to self in what St John calls the 'Dark Night' of the soul. Some mystics reach a state of surrender so complete that there ensues 'a mystical marriage'; an intense union with God.

Transformation is the natural outcome of mystical life. A person becomes changed inwardly because of the intensity of this personal inner journey. There is a gradual 'rebirthing', sometimes dramatic, sometimes barely perceptible in the personality. What is most obvious is that the person achieves inner peace; is at one within the self, radiating a deep, imperturbable inner joy.

The equanimity that ensues is not the end, but the beginning of new levels of enlightenment.

Summary

This brief examination of mysticism, along with the distinctions between the poet and the mystic, help clarify what is meant by the mystical dimension of poetry. Underhill's description of mystical states and stages is particularly helpful. She especially, among all those writing on mysticism, presents the clearest pattern of mystical development: Awakening, Purification, Illumination and Transformation.[26] Bremond has drawn useful parallels between mysticism and poetry, showing that sublime mystical states shed light on what happens in the poetic process.[27] Together these experts present us with a useful set of guidelines to apply to Patrick Kavanagh's work as a poet and writer.

In view of Kavanagh's claim for poetry as mystical and John Jordan's assessment of him as 'an instinctive theologian', it is necessary to attempt to evaluate these statements and settle the question once for all.[28] Is there a mystical dimension to Kavanagh's work? The mystic regularly undergoes scrutiny from both theology and psychology, to test every 'spirit' against self-delusion.[29] Poetic states must likewise surrender to investigation. Mystical science sheds light on the workings of the mystical imagination. It is reasonable to suggest that a poet such as Kavanagh be tested, with advantage to poetry and mysticism alike.

PART TWO

MYSTICAL ELEMENTS IN KAVANAGH'S WORK

The questions now to be asked are: Does the poet Patrick Kavanagh fulfil any or all of the characteristics typical of the mystic? Was he gifted with a level of consciousness above the ordinary? Was he a seeker of Beauty and of God? Was he gifted with intuitive knowledge and did this knowledge stretch beyond the confines of rational knowledge and common sense? Did he, in the course of his life, achieve illumination or, in Underhill's words, 'sacramental expansion'?[30] Did he succeed in piercing the veil and disclosing the eternal? Did he follow the traditional mystical path of Awakening, Purification, Illumination and Transformation?

Mystical Awareness
The Green Fool portrays Kavanagh as a young man, emerging self-consciously as a dreamer and seer. He seems to be possessed of certain visionary tendencies at least. He is often perplexed by what he sees; for example 'the strange beautiful light' on 'the Drumgonnelly Hills':

'Do you see anything very beautiful and strange on those hills?' I asked my brother as we cycled together to a football match in Dundalk. 'This free-wheel is missing,' and he gave it a vigorous crack with the heel of his shoe. 'Is it on Drumgonnelly Hills?'
'Yes?'
'Do you mean the general beauty of the landscape?'
'Something beyond that, beyond that,' I said.
'Them hills are fine no doubt.'
'And is that all you see?'
'This free-wheel is missing again,' he said. 'I'll have to get down and put a drop of oil on it.'
We got moving again. 'What were we talking about?'
'Beauty', I said.[31]

In this short passage, the awakening of an early mystical consciousness can be discerned. Mystical imagination is juxtaposed with the rather bald realism of 'This free-wheel is missing' or the even more vision-damping analysis: 'Do you mean the general beauty of the landscape?' Patrick Kavanagh is gradually becoming aware of the lonely world of the poet, whose experience is not understood, not even by his brother. No earth-bound eye can reach this place which, in biblical terms, 'no eye has seen nor ear has heard' (1 Cor 2:9). The 'strange light' mentioned in his early autobiography is converted later into religious coinage as 'the Holy Spirit on the hills'.[32]

At home in Inniskeen, it dawns slowly on Kavanagh that the world he inhabits is different. At moments of heightened awareness he receives meanings and messages that come from the 'hills of the imagination, far beyond the flat fields of common sense'.[33] He finds within himself the 'half-god' who can 'see the immortal in things mortal'; a kind of mythological god-man brooding over the ancient territory of Farney and the Fews. During his High Court proceedings of February, 1954, when he sued *The Leader* for allegedly libellous remarks and defamation of character, he stated unambiguously that his reference to going 'over the fields to the City of Kings' was mystical by implication. Emphatically he proclaimed: 'I am speaking mystically of God, of the City without Walls' and not of any 'mortal city'.[34]

His early period of development he called an 'angelhood' or 'the angel while...' when, with typical Kavanagh originality, he experienced God as 'unstirred mud in a shallow pool'. His vision was clear and open to possibilities. He guarded this gift jealously, refusing to expose 'moments innocent with revelation' to the vulgarity of 'the market-place'. The market-place was ignorant of his 'transfigured hills' his 'Edenic landscape'. To speak of them was to risk losing them forever. Kavanagh's Eden is where, like Blake, he sings his 'Songs of Innocence' in a mood of rapt 'starriness'.

The penalty for sharing his treasure was severe. His spirit was shocked by those who neither saw nor understood what he saw. He was both angered and hurt at being misunderstood, feelings which contributed to a life of on-going purification:

… I told of that beatific wonder to clods and disillusioned
lovers. I asked if they didn't see something beyond the hills
of Glassdrummond. They laughed and said I was mad.[35]

His Eden, or 'garden of the golden apples', becomes occasionally
sullied by twisted thinking of people who distrust what he considered to be 'innocent and lovely'. Sadly, these people 'twist
awry' the original blessedness of life, and perceive only guilt
and sinfulness in 'the dark places of soul':

We are a dark people,
Our eyes are ever turned
Inward
Watching the liar who twists
The hill-paths awry.
O false fondler with what
Was made lovely
In a garden!
(*Dark Ireland*)

Even though he moved away from his 'childhood country', he
retains his 'Eden-flowering mind' which, though prone to disen-
chantment by falsehood and hypocrisy, is still allowed blossom.
Kavanagh is one of Bremond's 'elite' among the poets and mystics who 'penetrate the lost paradise'.[36] He recaptures once more
his sense of 'fields that are part of no earthly estate'. At such
times his world, as in 'A Christmas Childhood', becomes 'won-
derful', 'magical' and capable of being distilled into a symbol of
mystical prayer: white, wordless, iridescent, transcendent … 'a
white rose pinned/ on the Virgin Mary's blouse'.

His 'garden of the golden apples',[37] a strip of garden 'between a railway and a road' is transformed into a paradise
where miracles are commonplace and time eternal. Here mystical knowledge is bestowed on the poet by the strange light of the
new moon. The structure of the lines yields happily to 'the expanded voltage' of the experience. Kavanagh is rapt as he re-
members:

And when the sun went down into Drumcatton
And the New Moon by its little finger swung

From the telegraph wires, we knew how God had happened
And what the blackbird in the whitethorn sang.
(The Long Garden)

He feels he had, at this moment, an insight into God and God's earthly revelation. This world was neither worn nor pedestrian but magical and mystical. Nothing is soiled or sordid or out of tune with the harmony experienced. Here paganism and Christianity intermingle, united in primeval innocence. In Kavanagh's imaginative landscape, Slieve Gullion is a 'sacred mountain' and 'place of mystery', exuding pagan splendour, yet blending harmoniously with the simple radiance of the newly built Catholic church in its foothills. This is 'Glassdrummond chapel', a place of brightness, contrasting favourably with the dark north-facing beauty of Shancoduff.

Little wonder that he envisioned his life as being on a different plane from others, his rhyme in 'Come Dance with Kitty Stobling', 'cavorting on mile-high stilts'. Bewildered, 'the unnerved crowds' looked up 'with terror in their rational faces'. The poet in this instance may appear contemptuous towards the non-poetic. Is he arrogant, a victim of spiritual pride? Or is he rather like Yeat's 'Malachi Stilt-Jack', metaphorically stalking 'the terrible novelty of the night' 'like a barnacle goose/ Far up in the stretches of night'. Kitty Stobling and Malachi Stilt-Jack are both outrageous characters, which present a comic view of the awkward, vulnerable position of the poet vis-à-vis society. The essential loneliness and exile of the poet is made abundantly clear.

Ironically, Kavanagh longed for the ordinary sense of belonging to mundane activities of town and country:

And sometimes I am sorry when the grass
Is growing over the stones in quiet hollows
And the cocksfoot leans across the rutted cart-pass
That I am not the voice of country fellows
Who now are standing by some headland talking
Of turnips and potatoes or young corn… *(Peace)*

He wished to live on the plane of farming, football, horse-racing and everyday commonalities, but he could not survive without the vision that transported him 'on mile-high stilts' above 'the timorous paces' and the tediousness of the crowd who lacked imagination. Often he portrays the arrogance and impatience of one who sees a different vision and hears 'a different drummer'. Occasionally he begs compassion for his own eccentricity and vulnerability from those whom he loved and trusted and asks a prayer for one 'who walked apart on the hills'. Too well he knew the price of 'loving life's miracles of stone and grass...' That price was loneliness and isolation.

Mystical Seeing

Kavanagh sees beyond the surface of everyday life. He senses, like William Blake and Elizabeth Barrett-Browning (1806-1861), a radiance in life around him. His earth too is 'crammed with heaven'. Herein lies, perhaps, the greatest proof of his mystical imagination. In his early work he is almost intoxicated by vision. He celebrates this early clear-sightedness in words that point to veritable glimpses of heaven. He is the darling of whatever God he worships:

> The gods of poetry are generous: they give every young poet a year's salary which he hasn't worked for; they let him take one peep into every tabernacle; they give him transcendent power. While he is learning the craft of verse and getting ready his tools, they present him with wonderful lines which he thinks are his own. In those days I had vision. I saw upon the little hills and in the eyes of small flowers beauty too deli- cately rare for carnal words.[38]

From the common experience of ploughing and harrowing in spring he sees into the mystery of quickening life. At this early stage of his career, he also analogously envisions the first seeds of his poetry. He foresees the mystical fruitfulness of clay when he leaves 'the check rein slack' and surrenders to 'the harrow('s) play'. Already he has become wise to the role of 'the worm's opinion' and the 'pointed harrow-pins' of life. His vision has be- come capable of penetrating the potency of 'seed' scattered 'on the dark eternity of April's clay':

This seed is potent as the seed
Of knowledge in the Hebrew Book.
So drive your horses in the creed
Of God the Father as a stook.
(To the Man After the Harrow)

Mystical vision reaches farther than the human eye, and acquires a dark knowledge, a wisdom learned only in the mystical 'cloud of unknowing'.[39] For Kavanagh, a spiritual journey as well as a poetic one has been initiated. He is entering 'the mist where Genesis begins'. The symbols of sower and seed propel him deeply into Biblical territory: 'unless the grain of wheat falls to the ground and dies it remains only a single grain' (Jn 12:24). Does he foresee the harrowing of his own soul as a prerequisite for a harvest of poetry? Symbolically and mystically he is being transformed by the land that bore him, by the landscape that enshrines his spirit. He is being made into 'a carbon copy' of his surrounding hills:

O Monaghan hills when is writ your story
A carbon copy will unfold my being.
(Monaghan Hills)

Ploughing for Kavanagh becomes real contemplation as well as a symbol of his poetic art. His instrument, the swing-plough, though crude and clumsy by modern standards, provides an ideal opportunity for the two activities he so often pursues in tandem: 'poetry and prayer'. As a young poet, he has unabashed confidence in his ability to do both:

I find a star-lovely art
In a dark sod.
Joy that is timeless! O heart
That knows God!
(Ploughman)

With considerable assurance of his visionary powers, he sets about learning his poetic art, with only the most rudimentary education at his disposal. He asserts unambiguously in an early poem, 'Plough Horses' (1938), that he owes his clarity of vision to the unsealing of his eyes by the power of the Holy Spirit. Yet, ne surprises his reader by asserting that the visionary form he contemplates has been shaped at the hand of Phidias, the celebrated fifth-century BC Greek sculptor. This knowledge, undoubtedly gleaned from schoolbook sources, serves to strengthen Kavanagh's natural mystical ability.[40] He masters the classical allusion with remarkable ease. Meanwhile, his 'third eye', or 'inner eye',[41] sees beyond the animal shape. In Eliade's terms, he had easy access to the sacred dimension of the cosmos,[42] the prerogative of primitive man:

> The cosmos being a hierophany and human existence sacred, work possessed a liturgical value which still survives, albeit obscurely, among rural populations of contemporary Europe. What is especially important to emphasise is the possibility given to primitive man to immerse himself in the sacred by his own work as a *homo faber* and as creator and manipulator of tools.[43]

As a simple ploughman, and not a very skillful one by all accounts, Kavanagh's poetic genius sees two ordinary farmyard 'nags' transformed under his gaze. He has experienced something of the power of the Holy Spirit in this early epiphany:

> Seeing with eyes the Spirit unsealed
> Plough-horses in a quiet field.
> *(Plough Horses)*

Not only does Kavanagh see beneath the surface of life but he shows himself to be Celtic in mind-set, by attributing life to the fields and trees themselves. He not only finds 'the immortal in things mortal' but knows that the fields in turn have witnessed 'the immortal' within him. They speak to his spirit in a wordless conversation – a mystical communion:

> There was I, me face black, sitting on the sate-board, me legs crossed, letting the fields look at me. Ah, the fields looked at me more than I at them, at this moment they are still staring at me.[44]

In an even more compelling way, his hawthorn ditches 'smile at (him) with violets', and the bluebells 'under the big trees' think of him with lovers' delight. The items in Kavanagh's landscape are as alive as those of the ninth century Celtic monk:

> A wall of woodland overlooks me.
> A blackbird sings me a song (no lie!)
> Above my book, with its lines laid out,
> The birds in their music sing to me.[45]

By the time he writes 'Primrose' (1939), he has established him-self as a poet with visionary powers. This 'one small primrose', bearing the signature of the Holy Spirit at its centre, speaks elo-quently to him of the transfigured Christ. Vision has become in-teriorised for the poet and reaches towards a Being who is God:

> I look at Christ transfigured without fear
> The light was very beautiful and kind,
> And where the Holy Ghost in flame had signed
> I read it through the lenses of a tear.

Kavanagh as a poet is by now advancing on the road of mystical knowledge.

Secret Knowledge

As a boy, Patrick Kavanagh loved to rummage in the 'thalidge', a sort of semi-loft over the kitchen of his maternal grandfather, Oul' Quinn's, thatched cottage. Here he glimpsed hints of a world of mystery and romance. He delighted in his 'museum that never had known a curator' – a place 'rich with ancient smells' where one might expect to find an old pike or a Fenian gun…'[46] This descriptive passage from his autobiography pre-sents a boy innocently in love with secret knowledge, and show-ing a predilection for the hidden, the obscure, the unsophisticated. He learned to relish 'dark truths' which generally went un-noticed. He was extraordinarily precocious in realising that in remote rural places there existed 'the secret archives of peasant minds of which no official document has ever been made'. The travelling workmen, 'journeymen cobblers', who brought these 'dark truths' into view were the delight of his boyhood.[47]

In his early teens Kavanagh listened intently to the conversa-tion of neighbours around his father's work-bench. He read and learned by heart chosen texts from old schoolbooks and from the newspaper bought daily by his father. Following the trend of the current educational system, there was an undue emphasis in the Kavanagh home on the accumulation of facts: local history, mythology, politics and folklore. His father, Peter said, wished to fill Patrick's head with lore which he had collected from *Titbits* and *Answers*.[48]

Patrick, however, soon learned to trust his own 'animal-remembering mind' which he discovered is superior to much of the knowledge which is more academic or merely informational. He may have compensated a little, at first, for his secretly felt lack of educational opportunity. So-called intellectual knowledge, he says, taught him 'far too many things', endangering thereby his mystical song and vision. He complains in his address 'To Knowledge' that he is angry at his loss of 'the speech of mountains', and at falling victim to the false promise of erudition. He who could once steer 'by night unstarred' and 'pray with stone and water' has placed his 'lamp of contemplation' in jeopardy by aspiring to worship knowledge. It was a long road ahead to come to accept his mystical gifts or to own his poetic predispositions:

> It wasn't considered manly to feel any poetic emotion. If a scene was beautiful you didn't say so. A man in love with anything was daft.[49]

True to his mystical instinct, he knew that analysis, explanation or reason were inadequate tools for the spirit. His poem 'Advent' expresses the need to be purged of cerebral excesses and of the temptation to be over-analytical:

> … and please
> God we shall not ask for reason's payment,
> The why of heart-breaking strangeness in dreeping hedges
> Nor analyse God's breath in common statement.
> (*Advent*)

For Kavanagh, the rational, the superficial and the sophisticated belonged to 'secular wisdom' and to the 'secular city'. They belonged also to every 'tedious man' who lacks imagination, deprived of consort with the gods. Illumination, enlightenment, vision, are given only to those prepared to surrender forever the glamour of ego-titillating knowledge:

> We have thrown into the dustbin the clay-minted wages
> Of pleasure, knowledge and the conscious hour–
> And Christ comes with a January flower.

'Revelation', Kavanagh admits, 'comes as an aside.' It comes unbidden in an essentially non-academic way but, nevertheless, as
compelling as is the appearance of an early spring flower.
Kavanagh boldly claims that mystical knowledge, though difficult of access, soars higher than reason and attains its goal with
precision:

> And I have a feeling
> Through a hole in reason's ceiling;
> We can fly to knowledge
> Without ever going to college.
> (To Hell with Commonsense)

The chink in reason becomes the sacred threshold of a knowledge that 'passeth understanding'. St John of the Cross's description of a moment of high contemplation has certain marked
likenesses to that experienced by the poet:

> He who truly arrives there
> Cuts free from himself;
> All that he knew before
> Now seems worthless,
> And his knowledge so soars
> That he is left unknowing
> Transcending all knowledge.[50]

The mystic, in the language of St John, soars to an unknowing
transcendent knowledge. True enlightenment, or that 'flash of
Divine Intelligence',[51] is the moment of genuine insight and illumination. Waiting in a state of unknowing is often a preliminary
to mystical insight. Given to occasional outward rapt behaviour,
neighbours presumed Kavanagh to be unsound of mind.
Nevertheless, lost in reverie, he continued to plough his mystical furrow. He remained faithful to hidden knowledge, paying
ultimate homage as an accomplished poet in 'Canal Bank Walk'
to 'arguments that cannot be proven'.

'Remote places', 'ancient smells', 'secret archives of peasant-minds'; these attracted the poet towards the contemplation of mysterious things. He felt at home in this strange, unchartered territory.

Mystical Loving
Revelation, though normally gratuitously bestowed on the poet-mystic, can sometimes be facilitated by contemplation:

> To look on is enough
> In the business of love   *(Is)*

Ultimately Kavanagh sees loving contemplation as the supreme activity of the poet. Kavanagh loves secretly, passionately, constantly and universally. 'For,' he says 'nothing whatever is by love debarred.' *(The Hospital)* He loves 'girls in red blouses', 'dandelions growing on headlands', buckets 'with half-hung handles', weeds, a gate 'bent by a lorry', bits of road and up-turned carts.[52] Everything he loves becomes transformed. The intensity of love reaches mystical proportions when he contemplates a scene from the Rialto Hospital in March 1955:

> This is what love does to things: the Rialto Bridge,
> The main gate that was bent by a heavy lorry,
> The seat at the back of a shed that was a suntrap.
> Naming these things is the love-act and its pledge;
> For we must record love's mystery without claptrap,
> Snatch out of time the passionate transitory.
> *(The Hospital)*

It must be remembered that this was the Kavanagh who had undergone surgery for lung cancer and had survived!

Some years previously (1950), while 'in exile' in London, memory of details from his past re-awaken his slumbering 'god of imagination'. The names of almost-forgotten farmyard harness, names hidden 'in the unrecorded archives of rural minds' become transformed through the poet's naming ritual:

> The winkers that had no choke-band,
> The collar and the reins...
> In Ealing Broadway, London Town
> I name their several names

Until a world comes to life –
Morning, the silent bog,

And the God of imagination waking
In a Mucker fog.
(Kerr's Ass)

Naming in this case belongs to the creative act of God described in the Book of Genesis. To be named, biblically speaking, is a pledge of immortality. It is a supremely mystical and creative event, since naming can invoke the hidden power of the named. Recalling and reciting the names of beloved objects and place-names can resemble the repetition of the mystic's mantra which gradually induces a heightened state of consciousness akin to inspired poetic activity.[53] For Kavanagh in particular, naming evokes a realisation of divine presence. Thus, memory plays an important role in the creative process. 'On the stem of memory' he insists, 'imaginations blossom'. *(Why Sorrow?)* The mystic ritually re-members the object of love and recreates a new state of being-in-love:

And remembering you
O Sion, whom I loved,
In that sweet memory
I wept even more.[54]

In summary, Kavanagh was undoubtedly a self-styled lover. Love, requited and unrequited, rendered him vulnerable. The 'lovers that (he) could not have', inflicted on him a purification designed by the 'agonising pincer-jaws of heaven'. *(Sanctity)* Kavanagh knew only the language of Christian sanctification to describe his painful condition. But for this very reason, his love became mystical, capable of transforming the banalities and failures of life into shining radiances.

Mystical Time

One of the striking gifts of the mystic is his sense of the timeless. He can see the past in the present, and be simultaneously transported by a sudden flash of intuition into a timeless synthesis. For Kavanagh, local history and folklore provided foundational data which awakened his imagination and allowed him to see beyond recorded facts. He developed this habit in youth, as is seen in a fragment of juvenilia written about the Land Agent, Stuart Trench, who was alleged to have treated his tenants, and Kavanagh's ancestors in particular, with cruelty and disdain. Unable to pay their rent, the Callans, his grandmother's people, had had their land confiscated and succeeded only with difficulty in retaining a roof over their heads. The Agent's residence at Essex Castle, Carrickmacross, had, since 1888, become a convent-school where Kavanagh's contemporaries, including his sister Lucy, went to school:

> Today I see in my mind's eye
> A shadow of the Trenche's (*sic*) great
> Pass slowly through the convent gate,
> Those haters of the Celtic race
> Who lived to see their own disgrace
> And lived to see a convent grand
> Beneath the roof where oft they planned
> Destruction for the weak and small
> Who dared to break the landlord's thrall.[55]
> (*Juvenilia*)

This was one of Kavanagh's earliest attempts at poetry. Whatever its technical defects, it is clear that his intuitive faculty is already active. Time barriers crumble, nearness and distance intermingle as, in a mood of contemplation, he peers through the corridors of history and finds the 'mills of God' which grind slowly but 'grind exceedingly fine'. The rent-offices of the great Stuart Trench are slowly replaced by 'a convent grand', signalling a new era for this locality. A once-detested landlord's den, which repeatedly 'planned destruction' for the small farmers of the Bath Estate, is transformed. Kavanagh may intuitively have sensed something of Trench's harsh decisions that touched his ancestors, not merely when their land was taken from them, but more poignantly still, when his grandfather Patrick Kevany, the local schoolteacher, was banished from the area.[56]

Kavanagh's sense of mystical time becomes more explicit in

his contemplation of the poplar trees which grow on Mucker lane. He recalled helping to plant these, selecting the straightest saplings with his father who imagined their future possibilities:

My father dreamt forests, he is dead –

And there are poplar forests in the waste places

And on the banks of drains. *(Poplars)*

The trees, now fully grown, appear to the poet to link heaven and earth, past and present. The evocations of sun and earth link these trees with the Celtic underground gods, the mythological Tuatha Dé Danann who share the earth with mortals. Mention of his dead father evokes the world of the mortal and immortal Kavanaghs. 'These straightest spears of sky.' Are they trees? Or are they Kavanaghs? Throughout the poem our gaze is focused on his dead father, even now 'peering through the branched sky'. These trees will endure. They have, like other trees, 'caught him in their mysteries', since it is here 'among the poplars' that the spirit of his mother also walks:

I do not think of you lying in the wet clay

Of a Monaghan graveyard; I see

You walking down a lane among the poplars

On your way to the station…

(In Memory of My Mother)

Father, mother and offspring are symbolically metamorphosed in a row of poplar trees. Once again, the poet transcends the barriers of chronological time.

An incident recounted by Kavanagh's nephew, Kieran Markey, recalls how in the 1950s, when his uncle Patrick took him, then a young boy, out of doors to play football in the garden, he became easily tired of the youngster. He would say, 'Leave me alone now, I want to do a bit of dramin' to myself,' whereupon he would lean against a tree and look off into the distance towards 'Cassidy's hanging hill', or towards Woods' fields, the setting of 'The Great Hunger', or Rocksavage and the 'triangular field' he loved. Kieran Markey had no idea that his uncle was even then caught in the grip of his 'fantasy soaring mind' or mystically communing with his hidden paradise.[57]

Kavanagh was frustrated, in youth, by the ceaseless round of farming chores which violated the rhythms of his poetic soul. As a farm-hand, working for a neighbour, he found the incessant pace of life irksome; the constant 'nag of jobs waiting to be done', a vicious circle, 'a wheel without a spoke of time missing'.[58] The much-needed 'spoke of time' was essential to the contemplation he needed as a poet. 'To get to know one small field or the corner of one is a life-time's experience'.[59] This is the language of the contemplative, as well as that of the poet. 'It's what the imagination does to things that makes them big.' At another time he speaks of 'moments as big as years', making one aware that time and space expand immeasurably in the mind of the poet and mystic.[60]

Kavanagh can occasionally appear to be outside time, contemplating his life from the standpoint of history. To his friend Tarry Lennon[61] (Eusebius Cassidy) he would say, as they worked together digging or sowing potatoes, 'Some day, people will say that you dug this ground with me.' Later in Dublin, he is even more confident that his name will survive:

On Pembroke Road look out for my ghost,
Dishevelled with shoes untied,
Playing through the railings with little children
Whose children have long since died.
(*If ever you go to Dublin Town*)

Time past, present and future mingle uncannily, producing a deliberately eerie effect. A sense of ghostliness is achieved by blending the more permanent elements of life with the transitory ones: railings, children, a well-known Dublin street (Pembroke Road), and his own ghost wandering there 'dishevelled with shoes untied'. Prophetically he was correct. His loneliness, his humour, his eccentric cantankerousness, his spirituality and unfulfilled ambition still haunt Pembroke Road and vindicate the poet's 'trick of time' that makes the past present and sees the future now!

Dark Knowledge
As well as experiencing moments of mystical radiance, Kavan-

agh also underwent periods of spiritual darkness and painful emptiness. Vague murmurings of inner anguish can be detected in early lines which hint at some hellish experience:

Child do not go

Into the dark places of soul

For there the lean wolves whine,

The lean grey wolves. *(To A Child)*

It is difficult to interpret the sadness and rejection which surrounds some of the poet's earliest attempts at verse. In his 'Address to an Old Wooden Gate' he depicts himself as 'the scorn of women,' rejected, laughed at, abused, like the 'old wooden gate'. He and the gate are kindred spirits:

But you and I are kindred, Ruined Gate,

For both of us have met the self-same fate.

(Juvenilia)

He fluctuates between seeing himself as the darling child of the gods and as their persecuted servant. He often sounds the most sorrowful and rejected of mortals. He knows personal hurt from his native surroundings where 'the worm's opinion' and 'pointed harrow pins' cut deeply into his poetic sensibilities. His religious scruples, his 'monsters of despair', threaten him in a dark church while waiting for confession. Sexual confusions tortured the delicacy of his conscience. These were, no doubt, the 'uncouth monsters', 'the nightmare of the soul and the fathers of remorse'[62] inflicted by a harsh religious teaching. He refers scathingly to 'a childhood perverted by Christian moralists'. But is there not something more that weighs on the poet's mind? The story of his lost genealogy will be discussed fully in Chapter Five.

The greatest exorcism of despair in Kavanagh, and perhaps the most complete expression of his 'dark night', was undoubtedly 'The Great Hunger'. Spectre-like, the inhabitants of 'The Great Hunger' groan with the anguish of unlived life. Physical, mental, emotional and spiritual famine stalk the land, bringing not death but half-life to these rural people. Kavanagh's personal nightmares are perhaps best expressed in such lines as:

Life dried in the veins of these women and men:
The grey and grief and unlove,
The bones in the backs of their hands,
And the chapel pressing its low ceiling over them.

Kavanagh is as powerful in his dark imagery as he is radiant in his spiritual seeing. His apocalypse of clay screams not only throughout 'every corner of this land' but also into the soul of every sympathetic reader. Its hysterical laugh is that of the defeated. One suspects that this dark dream emanated from the depths of his own psyche, where life was experienced at times as 'sad, grey, twisted, blind, just awful'.[63] Clay, often experienced as fruitful, is also experienced as dead and infertile as 'putty spread on stones' (Lough Derg). The poet's cry to 'the stony grey soil of Monaghan' is that of one robbed, forsaken, abandoned – even raped. His sharp Jansenistic upbringing frequently pruned life that is budding, green and full of promise. There remains for him only, on occasion, the sterile life of current pieties and religious hypocrisy which degenerated into a claustrophobia of popular devotion.

In religious terms Kavanagh's purification is endless. Though vigorously expressed in 'The Great Hunger', his despair, disillusionment and felt absence of God, is often suppressed and only given expression through the less worthy medium of angry, satirical verse.

Conclusion

At the beginning of this chapter we noted the general characteristics of the mystical path. It is seen to follow a spiral or maze-like movement, moving forward towards an unknown goal, yet frequently returning back on itself toward the point of departure. Kavanagh began with a springtime of poems written out of a vision of ordinary life in his Monaghan landscape. He returned, towards the end of his life, in 'Canal Bank Walk', to the belief that, all along, this had been God's will for him. His pursuit of poetry may not exactly match the classical mystical pattern, but he did seem to be possessed of a desire to pursue a spiritual goal. The object of his desire, he knew, would be costly in personal terms. It would cost him 'something not sold for a penny/ In the slums of the Mind'. For the desired prize he would be tireless in his efforts to 'climb the unending stair'. (*Ascetic*)

Though this poem 'Ascetic' was written as early as 1930, its idealistic and self-conscious sentiments alert us to the truth that Kavanagh is a seeker in a mysterious territory – 'in the other lands'. He is not interested in poetry as a technician; it is the hidden spark of the Divine that he seeks. He is prepared to work in difficult and lonely circumstances to pursue his goal. In the 1940s he renews his resolution and, though momentarily tempted to renege on his dream, as suggested in 'Temptation in Harvest' (1945-46), he follows unflinchingly the beckoning 'wink' of his vocation. Though struggling with a series of failures in the early 50s, he is resolved to start again: 'I at the bottom will start.' This is the resolute promise he makes to himself in 'Auditors In' (1951). It is not surprising that towards the end of his life, in spite of the many vicissitudes endured, Kavanagh can claim his inheritance before the final day of reckoning – 'the opening of that holy door'. By then he knows that he will endure only because he has scorned interest in 'anything but the soul'.

Scant attention has, until now, been paid to Kavanagh's mystical propensities, yet there is abundant evidence of their existence. His visionary seeing, loving, knowing and his genuine insight into God's presence in everyday life is evident throughout his work. The sacramentality of ordinary life becomes the special focus of his attention, though he does not discount 'the dark places of the soul' as sources of purifying knowledge. Mystically, he crosses barriers of time and space as he embarks on his spiritual quest. On arrival in the dangerous territory of the mystic, he has, on his own admission, both taken fright and flight. Poetically speaking he 'became airborne', a flight that culminated in his 'hegira' on the banks of the Grand Canal in 1955.[64] The frightful element in his development involved an on-going purification, almost to the point of despair.

Kavanagh was undoubtedly a dreamer and a visionary, despite his outer cantankerous behaviour both in Inniskeen and Dublin. He told of his 'beatific wonder' to people whom he thought would understand but they laughed and thought he was mad.[65] Nevertheless, in his own intensely idiosyncratic way, I believe that he underwent the classic mystical pathway, outlined by Underhill, of Awakening, Purification and Illumination. Only a chosen few could see that his life was transformed towards the end. The nature of his personal encounter with God was hidden from most. This intensely personal aspect of his life he reserved for intimate friends, but above all for expression in poetry.

CHAPTER 2

Awakening I

... And the God of imagination waking
In a Mucker fog.
(Kerr's Ass)

Early Educational Influences

Although he received a limited formal education, Patrick Kavanagh came from a family where learning was appreciated, and where song, story and good conversation were part of daily life. His father, James Kavanagh, the local shoemaker, was accustomed to conversing at length with his customers while they waited for their shoes to be mended or new boots fitted. He was proficient in current affairs, in local history and dabbled in the vast oral tradition of ghost and fairy-lore of south-east Ulster and north Leinster. Kavanaghs' kitchen in some ways resembled that of *The Tailor and Ansty* in west Cork.[1] One was always assured of interesting conversation there, with snippets from the newspaper for entertainment, or an unusual school problem successfully solved. Describing the atmosphere that prevailed in his home, Peter recalls that since the shoemaking shop was part of the kitchen-living room, there were visitors coming and going constantly. If it were a wet day there might be several at the same time. Stories were exchanged and 'the mythology of Ireland constantly renewed'.[2]

Schooling was important in the Kavanagh household and James Kavanagh often accompanied his children along the mile of road to Kednaminsha National School which his children attended. Annie and Mary were already at school when Patrick started along with his sister Sissie in June, 1909. They were aged six and four respectively. Neither Sissie nor Patrick was promoted from Fifth Standard; each repeated a second year in Fifth, a practice not uncommon since Fifth and Sixth Standards were frequently taught together. Years later, Mary Kavanagh recalled a cupboard full of used schoolbooks in their kitchen, set aside carefully for the next family member who needed them. It was to this store that Patrick repeatedly returned during his post-school years to satisfy his craving for reading material. The enormous influence of these schoolbooks on Patrick's literary and spiritual awakening will be treated in the next chapter.

Patrick Hamill, a neighbour, recalls an unusual difficulty experienced while waiting to have his shoes mended in Kavanagh's. There could be a considerable delay in the work caused by the introduction of a school-book problem. Shoemaking was put aside while the 'reference library' of old school-books was consulted. If the problem was not satisfactorily resolved, one was fortunate if James Kavanagh did not leave the job altogether to consult Tom Quinn, the then schoolmaster of Inniskeen village school, in a effort to satisfy his intellectual curiosity.

Kednaminsha National School

Julia Cassidy was Principal teacher of the outlying Kednaminsha National School from 1877 until she became ill in 1917. She finally withdrew in 1918 and died the following August within a few weeks of receiving her pension. Kavanagh later remembered her when the school was burnt down in 1962, as 'the one and only cane-swinger' who taught 'fathers, sons and grandchildren' of the Kednaminsha area over a period of forty years. However much discredited by Kavanagh, she did in fact improve the school's official status and ensured a sound tradition of education in the area.

Miss Cassidy, came from a prominent family in Tierworker, in the historic parish of Moybologue, Co Meath. Her family were called the 'Prince' Cassidys, indicating a certain mark of hauteur if not genuine aristocracy in her pedigree. The Cassidys were farmers, possessed of a comfortable holding with rent accruing from some neighbouring farms as well. They owned the original school-house at Tiercork which may point to a tradition of education in the family. This school, long since derelict, was remembered as a reputable place of learning.[3]

Julia Cassidy studied first at home in Tiercork, or Tierworker as it is known today, and progressed as a monitor at the Model School in Bailieboro, a kind of 'finishing school' for more advanced pupils. Her younger sister, Alice, followed her into teaching and came

*Misses Alice and Julia Cassidy.
Julia Cassidy (right) was Patrick
Kavanagh's teacher.
Photo courtesy Finian Lynch.*

briefly with her sister to train as a monitor in Kednamisha school. Later she opted for a clerical position in the General Post Office in Dublin (1882-1923), and was there at the time of the historic Rising in 1916. None of the Cassidys married. All four of the family are buried, with their parents, in the family plot at Kilmainham Wood Cemetery.[4]

Julia arrived in the Inniskeen area as a young untrained teacher in 1877 and, by dint of continuous summer course-work and endless examinations, she worked her way to becoming an efficient and competent teacher. In 1904 she won the much-coveted Carlyle and Blake award which was a tribute to her standards of excellence in the school. A letter appended to the Inspector's Report on her work states that her 'merit mark' is 'Very Good' and that of the school is also 'Very Good'. Patrick Kavanagh was still at school when Miss Cassidy was nearing retirement. Because of her consistent standards of teaching, the Commissioners were prepared to retain 'efficient women teachers until they are 65 years of age'. They proposed, therefore, to 'continue her salary for an additional year until 16th June 1916' when the question of her continuance for a further period would be considered.[5]

There is little doubt that Miss Cassidy was fully devoted to her teaching and to the betterment of those in her charge. Her background indicates that she was strict, respectable, religious-minded and somewhat aloof. Kavanagh recalled her 'walking to her school' with 'a bundle of yellow canes with crooks on them under her arm, and she looked like a girl that could use them for all they were worth'.[6]

> She was a big woman with a heavy, coarse face, and across her round, massive shoulders she wore a small red shawl. In winter she wore heavy hob-nailed boots of my father's making. She liked my father because he wouldn't object no matter how hard she used the cane on any of his children.

Kavanagh's memory, however negative, tends to emphasise the fact that Miss Cassidy maintained a discipline similar to the parental control desired by the Kavanaghs at home. 'Spare the rod and spoil the child' was the slogan by which they lived at home and at school.

Brigid Agnew, nicknamed 'Miss Moore' in *The Green Fool*, was Miss Cassidy's devoted assistant from 1902 until 1913. She came from Courtbane in the next parish. She was twenty-two years old when she was appointed to teach the junior classes in Kednaminsha, teaching each of the Kavanagh children in turn. Brigid Agnew belonged to a family of teachers and greatly admired her Principal whose teaching methods she attempted to emulate. It was Miss Agnew who taught singing in all the classes and introduced Patrick Kavanagh to his favourite song, 'Hail Queen of Heaven', made all the sweeter since it signaled the end of the school day. These two women were now added to the already strong predominence of women in the young poet's life. His mother and three older sisters already surrounded him with attention. Supported by James Kavanagh, who had a strong spiritual influence on his son, they instructed him in his faith, prepared him for the sacraments and undoubtedly taught him to pray.

Patrick's attendance at school declined as he grew older. He did not get along well with Miss Cassidy, who dealt uneasily with the boy's strange answers and unusual store of knowledge. One incident recalled by a classmate, Mrs Katie Campbell (nee McGeough),[7] illustrates the unconventional way in which Kavanagh's mind worked, even as a youth. Once a week, Miss Cassidy brought her senior pupils together to read from 'an unseen reader'. The book she had chosen was 'The Voyage of Maeldun', an old Irish heroic wonder-tale. Each pupil would stand beside her and read from the book while the others listened carefully, awaiting their turn to read. She had gone to some pains to explain the meaning of 'posthumous', a word which occurred in the text. Maeldun was a posthumous child.

One morning, some weeks later, Miss Cassidy had news for her pupils. A local woman, whose husband had recently died, had this morning given birth to a baby! 'Can anyone tell me', she asked expectantly, 'what is this child called?' There was silence in the classroom. Then Patrick's hand shot up. Full of excitement he blurted out: 'Please Miss, a Maeldun!' Miss Cassidy's face registered dismay. She had hoped for a more conventional answer, a vindication of her good teaching. The class laughed, delighted that he, 'the know-it-all', had 'missed'. There was little appreciation for his imaginative response, his excitement at the arrival of a new Maeldun in the locality! Katie Campbell however never forgot his answer and still recalled it at eighty-seven years of age. Nor could she quite understand Miss Cassidy's disapproval, nor her classmates' cruel delight at their fellow pupil's discomfiture.

Years later he vindicated himself admirably, when in his introduction to his brother Peter's *Irish Mythology* (1959), he speaks with assurance of 'the marvellous adventures of Maeldun' which projected him 'beyond mortality' since it belonged to a mythology that seemed to 'spring out of Eden time'. No doubt he still remembered the school incident, and now roundly criticised the 'louts', advertisers and modern educators, who merely 'learned to read' but had failed to foster the imagination. 'Popular education more than anything else killed this ancient culture.'[8] Was he, by any chance, avenging himself on 'the louts' who long ago had mocked his imaginative answer at school?

Patrick, as we have noted, was not promoted into Sixth Class. His interest in school was waning. He had gone 'as far as Miss Cassidy could put him' and from the neighbours' assessment, 'that was good enough for any man'.[9] On a number of occasions, he was found 'mitching', or reading books and papers under the railway bridge adjacent to school.[10] Boredom, loss of interest, involvement in farmwork,[11] or Miss Cassidy's declining health, whatever the reason, it was decided that Patrick's formal education was over. Kavanagh rationalised it on the grounds of economy: 'What good is grammar to a man who has to work with a spade and shovel?'[12] But one senses that he lived to regret his decision.

Despite her impatience with him, Miss Cassidy spoke once to Patrick, as she neared retirement, in a manner which he never forgot. She spoke prophetically, to one who had so often infuriated her with his unorthodox answers:

> 'Oh, Patrick,' she said with all the pathos and sympathy of a sick woman, 'if *you* could get to high school you'd leave them all far behind.'[13]

Miss Cassidy, who has taught four generations of Inniskeen pupils, sensed in the end that she had allowed a talented pupil slip through her fingers.

Continuing Education in the Home

It was James Kavanagh who first provided his son with continuing education. Seated beside him at the shoemaker's bench, Patrick had full access to his father's learning and wisdom. In *The Green Fool* he states that his father 'had among the people a reputation for learning almost as great as the school-master'.[14] Indeed the people would not easily forget his blood connection with the banished ex-schoolmaster of Kednaminsha, Patrick Kevany.[15] There was almost a certain respectability for James Kavanagh in being the illegitimate son of a teacher. Kevany would certainly have had an educational impact on his son, had

The Kavanagh home at Mucker. Photo Una Agnew

he not been dismissed from the area before his birth. James
would carry the torch of learning for his father and in turn encourage his son's literary pursuits. Patrick was aware of his father's desire for him to succeed. He felt his presence beside him
as he wrote *The Green Fool*: 'As I write these words I know he is
beside me, encouraging me to go on .... to be a great writer.'[16]

James Kavanagh was unique among the farmers of the
neighbourhood in that he bought and read the newspaper. His
daily habit of buying the newspaper in the village was taken up
by Patrick when he left school, thus originating a lifelong appetite for newspapers. *The Freeman's Journal* (1725-1924) was the
first newspaper available to James Kavanagh. Later came the
Irish Daily Independent (1892-1904), followed by the *Irish Independent* (1905-) launched by William Martin Murphy at a halfpenny a
copy. The *Weekly Independent* and the *Dundalk Democrat* were
other important additions to the weekly reading of the
Kavanagh household. James read them aloud for his wife and
together they kept past copies for neighbours who might wish to
consult some item of local interest. The British magazines *Titbits*
and *Answers* were purchased in Dundalk and were special
favourites of James Kavanagh. Patrick continued to buy them
until he stumbled by accident on *The Irish Statesman*, George
Russell (AE)'s paper which was the beginning of a relationship

which would permanently influence Kavanagh's poetic development.

The *John O'London's Weekly* was another newspaper occasionally purchased by the Kavanaghs, but these English papers were gradually replaced by *Ireland's Own, Old Moore's Almanac* and *The Messenger of the Sacred Heart*, which Patrick relished especially because of a long religious poem published by Brian O'Higgins with a dedication to each month.[17] Patrick regretted the limits of his father's reading; that he never really got beyond the stage of *Titbits* and *Answers* as well as the 'doctor book' which he kept for emergencies.[18] Patrick, however, was gaining an important education. He was being introduced to items of world news and to contemporary literary figures. His horizons were being expanded.

From sitting together at the cobbler's bench and discussing local and world situations, a close spiritual bond formed between father and son. They communicated well with one another. Patrick admired the depth of his father's faith, a depth carved by suffering and love. 'From my father I have inherited the spirit' wrote Kavanagh in *The Green Fool*, confiding later in a letter to Celia, a Presentation nun stationed in the Isle of Wight, that any talent or genius he had was owing to his virtue – he was a saint.[19] Nevertheless, his father was anxious about his son's vulnerability. 'My father loved me and I loved him, but he did not like my day-dreaming way of living.'[20] His father watched over him jealously as a boy, fearful that he would get involved with the wrong company, fearful too perhaps that the 'wild' romantic traits of his legendary father would re-emerge in his grandson. James was undoubtedly strict on Patrick and vainly attempted to eradicate his day-dreaming, lazy habits.

James Kavanagh's early life could have been none too happy, a fact towards which Patrick was sensitive. Born into a home whose lands had been confiscated and who had barely survived eviction, he had learned to put dreams aside and grapple with hard realities. His own romantic temperament was fed by stories of far-off places told by journeymen shoemakers who on occasion stopped to share work at the cobbler's bench. Occasionally he allowed himself the luxury of playing the melodeon or singing a verse of his favourite song, *A Starry Night*, one of Patrick's most treasured memories. Hardworking and practical in his outlook, he was fortunate to have married Bridget Quinn, a woman who excelled in husbandry. Together they provided the knowledge, the skill and industry to build up a farm, for Patrick, out of patch of land.

His Mother, Brigid Kavanagh

Bridget Kavanagh's affection for her son, and her canny belief that there was something 'great' in him, was the encouragement Patrick needed to continue writing. She trusted his gentleness and secretly took pride in his bookish ways, while at the same time scolding him for wasting time with 'the curse-o-God books'. Two aspects of her nature seemed at war with one another, the woman who herself yearned for leisure to walk 'free in the oriental streets of thought' *(In Memory of My Mother)*, or the hunger for land that spurred her to spread 'her mind over the fields and the years'[21] and see her son a settled farmer. She was impatient with him for day-dreaming in the fields instead of labouring them into profit.

After his father's death, a small room upstairs in the Kavanagh home became available to Patrick. Though unheated and unlit except by candle-light, he found there an old Howe sewing-machine to use as a writing-table. Seated at this table he wrote his first poems, using the stub of a purple pencil and his father's old account book. Here he would read and write after his tasks on the farm were completed. When friends or customers would call for him, his mother would excuse him by saying 'he'll be out in a minute'. It is in such a setting that one can understand his complaint at being disturbed, when 'the first gay flight of (his) lyric/ Got caught in a peasant's prayer'. *(Stony Grey Soil)* Just as a final line of some 'immortal poem' dangled itself within reach, he found himself wrenched back to reality with 'Will you come down Patrick and put a patch on this man's boot!'[22]

hough his mother did not betray his secret occupation, vertheless the people scoffed and nicknamed him 'The Bard'. He was known to neglect his shoemaking and farming and became more and more engrossed in writing and study. The first son of James and Brigid Kavanagh was special. 'Being a spoiled boy and an only son during my early years',[23] he was often the centre of attention in the family, getting the best food available.[24] His mother, indulged him, making sure that he had a shilling for cigarettes. There was a bond between mother and son that was largely unspoken – a foretaste of a sympathetic understanding God. 'Surely my God is feminine' originated undoubtedly in the home. This relationship may have caused him persistently to dream of the 'Lost Eden,' his 'garden of the golden apples', a state of complete fusion with the 'lost Mother'. He wonders about this romantic yearning to create and possess 'a world of his own'. It is attachment to the Mother, he believes, and the longing to return to the womb which ultimately fosters the creation of a personal world.[25]

Patrick Kavanagh's sensory memory was developing in such a way that he *was* creating a world of his own and at the same time becoming a natural contemplative. He listened carefully, observed everything around him. Like his autobiographical character Tarry Flynn, he schooled his senses into extraordinary receptivity:

He concentrated on observing, on contemplating, to clean his soul. He enumerated the different things he saw: Kerley's four cows looking over a hedge near a distant house waiting to be milked. A flock of wild geese in the meadow beside Cassidy's bog. He heard the rattle of tin cans being picked up from the stones outside a door – somebody going to the well for water. But what bird was that making a noise like the ratchet of a new free-wheel? He stared through the bushes where the blue forget-me-nots and violets were creeping. No bird was there.[26]

There is something familiar yet idyllic in his earliest memories of Christmas morning in the Kavanagh home. Work and leisure, mothering and fathering, the earthy and the spiritual: all inter-mingle. Together they combine to make a rare flower, 'a white rose' of transcendent significance:

My father played the melodeon,
My mother milked the cows,
And I had a prayer like a white rose pinned
On the Virgin Mary's blouse. *(A Christmas Childhood)*

This domestic scene evokes something of the aura surrounding the Holy Family of Nazareth. Here, it is the 'holy family' of Mucker!

The Kavanagh Farm

Against this simple, faith-filled background Patrick Kavanagh's poetic sensibilities developed. His parents, living in constant struggle to make ends meet and rear a large family (nine eventu-ally), dreamed of acquiring their own land. Mrs Kavanagh lived to see the fulfilment of that dream. To have acquired land in 1926, to have a holding of one's own, was a triumph, a pledge of immortality, something of the joy and passion described by John B. Keane in his play 'The Field'. From owning merely a garden, they had progressed to becoming one of the small farmers of the locality. 'You have a whole lifetime's work before you in Mac Partland's farm,' was Johnny Cassidy's prophetic statement. His prophecy was fulfilled but not in the way he expected!

These few fields would play an even greater role in Patrick's life than the Kavanagh parents had envisaged. As a poet-farmer, he would learn enough about the land, ploughing, harrowing, sowing, spraying, digging potatoes, threshing and harvesting, to make the land yield its harvest. 'It grew good crops for me, more by good luck than good guiding...' Patrick had a dual task. He struggled 'with the crude ungainly crust of earth and spirit' to immortalise Irish rural life in poetry and prose.[27] 'The Great Hunger' was to become 'one of the twentieth-century's better long poems'.[28]

The small Kavanagh holding taught the emerging poet the mixed blessing of making a field one's 'bride' and the strange irony of a culture that produced fertile fields and impotent men.[29] Bachelorhood was inevitable in the small over-divided land of south Monaghan. Without imagination, life on the land was intolerable. Patrick Kavanagh would survive only by restoring for himself something of the transcendent beauty of sowing and reaping, and bringing home the harvest. These symbols became fertile in his hands. He learned to commune with nature and capture God's 'message in the humblest weeds'. In this way he rendered his landscape immortal.

Early Sacramental Formation

The Catholic Church, in which he was born and raised, had an undoubted influence on Patrick Kavanagh's life. The *Liber Baptizatorum* held at Inniskeen testifies, in entry No. 1245, that 'Patritius Josephus Cavanagh *(sic)* filius Jacobi Cavanagh et Brigidi Quinn' was born on October 22nd 1904, and baptised on October 23rd by Father James O'Daly, curate of the parish from 1903 to 1907.[30] St Mary's parish church, Inniskeen, which is now refurbished as a Heritage Centre in the poet's honour, was the location of Patrick's baptism. His sponsors were John Caffrey *(sic)* and Mary McCaffrey, neighbours and distant relatives of the Kavanagh family. Errors regarding the exact date of Kavanagh's birth abound. The year 1905 had for years been accepted as the year of his birth.[31] It is inscribed on the canal bank seat erected to his memory and is given as his birth-date in *The Oxford Companion to English Literature* (1987).[32] To confuse matters further, the family records, traditionally accepted as accurate give his birth-date as October 21st. James Kavanagh writes:

> Patrick Joseph Kavanagh, born 21st Oct, 1904 at 45 minutes past 8 on Sunday night in fine weather. Sponsors: John Mc Caffrey and Mary Mc Caffrey.[33]

The Family Record Book in this instance contains one of its few errors. James, head of the household, was generally accurate in details pertaining to the births of his ten children. He took pride in recording the exact time and dates of their births, their names and godparents. Nevertheless, October 21st, 1904, was not

Sunday as he states, but Friday, as can be verified in the universal Research Calendar. A further anomaly exists in the fact that the date of birth registered at Carrickmacross in the civil register, is October 23rd.[34] This date did in fact fall on Sunday. James Kavanagh never wavered in his belief that his son was the traditional child of the sabbath, 'bright and merry and good and gay'. With *three* birth-dates at his disposal, Patrick Kavanagh was well equipped to confuse those who wished to read his stars. Once baptised, Patrick followed the norm of religious and sacramental formation at home and at school. The sacraments of penance, eucharist and confirmation followed in quick succession.

Katie Mc Geogh,[35] a classmate of Patrick's, remembered the day and date on which they were both confirmed. Along with her classmates, she had received a confirmation medal from Fr Treanor who was then curate in Inniskeen.[36] June 16th, 1913, was the date inscribed on the medal, a day which announced 'the descending Paraclete', a literary and spiritual landmark for the future poet. Another reason why June 1913 is correct surrounds his eligibility for becoming god-father. In order to become sponsor to his sister Celia, who was baptised in September 1913, it was necessary, according to the Reilly Catechism, in the event of one not having reached the required age of fourteen years, to have at least received the sacrament of confirmation. Though not yet ten years of age, Patrick was considered eligible to be his sister's god-father. He later was sponsor to Peter, twelve years his junior, in 1916, a duty which he undertook with serious responsibility. One of the influences which cannot be discounted in his religious formation was the distinguished figure of Fr Maguire, the parish priest of Inniskeen.

Canon Bernard Maguire: Parish Priest of Inniskeen (1915-1948)
When one notices Kavanagh's thorough grasp of religion, in its various visionary, sacramental, liturgical and ethical dimensions, one searches for possible sources of influence. Apart from his family who were staunch believers, there was also the

colourful and influential figure of Father Bernard Maguire,
parish priest of Inniskeen from
1915 to 1948. He succeeded Fr
Mc Elroy, the old parish priest
who heard Patrick's first confession and assigned him 'the
penance' of learning to serve
his Mass. It was Fr Maguire
who was to be the beneficiary
of this penance. Of the priest, J.
E. McKenna has this to say:

The Rev Bernard Maguire
was appointed parish priest
by the Most Revd Dr Mc-
Kenna. He is a native of

*Fr Maguire, Parish Priest of
Inniskeen 1916-1948. 'Salamanca
Barney.' Photo courtesy his neice
Mrs Jenny Uí Chléirigh.*

Currin Parish, and an alumnus of the Diocesan Seminary and
St Patrick's College, Maynooth, in both of which he read a
distinguished course.[37]

Fr Maguire had a certain style about him as a priest. A distin-
guished scholar of classics, he had been Rector at the Irish
College, Salamanca, in Spain. This *Colegio de los Nobles Irlandeses*,
was founded in 1592 under the patronage of Philip II, King of
Spain. Its purpose was to educate Irish students for the priesthood, when seminary formation at home was non-existent due
to religious persecution. Among its students were Archbishop
Florence Conroy and Luke Wadding SJ. The Irish College in
Salamanca continued until 1954 when it was transferred by
General Franco to the University of Salamanca. A plaque on one
of its walls today reminds us that Fr Bernard Maguire once
walked its halls as professor and rector.

Born on February 28th, 1869, Bernard Maguire attended the
National School at Annaveagh and proceeded to St Macartan's
College, Monaghan. He studied for the priesthood in Maynooth
and was ordained at the cathedral in Monaghan on November
13th, 1892. He taught as Professor of Classics at St Macartan's

(1896-1898) and was subsequently appointed rector at Salamanca in 1898. He aspired to a professorship at St Patrick's
College Maynooth and applied for the Chair of Classics there in
the early 1900s.[38]   Had he been successful in this concursus,
Patrick Kavanagh might never have heard him preach, nor
would his novel *Tarry Flynn* (1947) have been enhanced by the
colourful presence of the parish priest Father Daly, modelled, no
doubt, on Father Maguire:

> When he turned round to preach, the congregation sat up
> and admired his fine-shaped head, his proud bearing and his
> flashing green eyes behind the rimless glasses on which the
> sun was playing.
>
> He had a silvery voice, so that even nonsense from him
> sounded wise. He took out a silk handkerchief from the fold
> of his chasuble and wiped his glasses. Then he made a dram-
> atic gesture with the fluttering handkerchief before blowing
> his nose like a motor horn.[39]

The people of Inniskeen revered their parish priest. He was
clever and well-educated and took a keen interest in his locality.
The elderly in the parish still remember him as 'a grand man' or,
in the words of Mrs Flynn, 'the educatedest man in the diocese'.[40] Only the more daring, who perhaps resented the awe he
inspired, risked the disrespect of nicknaming him 'Salamanca
Barney'. He wore rimless spectacles, and in his heyday drove a
white-roofed deluxe Renault car, and spoke authoritatively on
most topics. He had what the country people called a 'haughty'
bearing which gave an aristocratic flavour to the drabness of
rural life during the 'hungry thirties'. In church, one could hear
a pin drop during his sermons which were always colourful, interesting and educative. He encouraged his parishioners to 'do
all things well, even if it were only wringing out a dishcloth'.[41]

Canon Maguire brought glamour into poor people's lives.
He could, to quote one of his youngest listeners, 'describe foreign
places better than coloured television. If you had any imagination at all, you could actually *see* what he was describing'.[42] At
his best, he could keep the people 'for two hours at Mass and

they wouldn't even find it long'. 'He could talk about little bits of the gospel as if they could really happen.'[43] Was this where Kavanagh learned his sense of sacred story evident in 'Lough Derg' and in the wonderment of pilgrims who asked: 'Was that St Paul/ Riding his ass down a lane in Donegal?' For these simple people 'Christ was lately dead' and 'the apostle's Creed /Was a fireside poem'.

Without any real formal education, Kavanagh acquired a lively sense of the gospel narrative. Could it have been in any way due to the influence of this unusual parish priest whose extempore translations from the Latin Mass-book on Sundays is still remembered? Aware of a need for the vernacular at Mass, Father Maguire had provided this of his own accord. In this he was at least fifty years ahead of his time.

In order to supplement his income, the parish priest owned a small twelve-acre farm, kept a few cows, and with the help of his devoted servant, Tom Fitzpatrick, sowed crops and kept a good garden. Kavanagh was impressed by the priest's affinity with the people, due, apparently, to his own farming background at his home in Annaveagh, near Scotshouse, Co Monaghan.

> Ah, but the priest was one of the people too –
> A farmer's son – and surely he knew
> The needs of a brother and sister. (*The Great Hunger*)

This oneness with the people is well captured in the portrait of Fr Mat, though it is difficult to identify it completely with 'Salamanca Barney', the priest who was once a university professor:

> He was part of the place,
> Natural as a round stone in a grass field:
> (*Father Mat*)[44]

True to his portrayal as Father Daly, 'he took delight in knowing ordinary things', a quality which unconsciously set him in a mischievous competition with the inveterate dreamer Tarry Flynn who was specialist in the commonplace.

Kavanagh was fascinated by the mixture of dread and delight that prevailed when the priest 'spoke off the altar' concerning some local scandal, usually of a sexual nature! Fr Maguire's colourful expressions were memorable.[45] In describing the misdemeanours of the local football team he is alleged to have said: 'They'd be exceptional savages if found on the banks of the Congo.' As the ploughing season approached, he brought a breath of erudition into 'little tillage fields', suggesting that twenty-six inches wide was the correct width of a potato-drill, while two drills together formed the width of a Roman chariot! Such remarks were destined to set rural imaginations alight. In the case of illness in the home, or even among the animals, local people would say, 'You needn't pass Father Maguire', meaning that his diagnosis and prescriptions were among the best available.

Not surprisingly, Kavanagh and Maguire were often at loggerheads. Patrick was swift to see the comic irony in the priest's warning of the dangers of becoming a pseudo-intellectual taking on to 'know things that men have spent years in colleges to learn'.[46] Drawing on the full force of his classical background, the priest advised the poet to stick to his last! (*Ne sutor ultra crepidam*)! Maguire's erudition was not lost on Kavanagh. Happily he ignored his advice.

What was it then that attracted the poet to the character of the priest? Kavanagh recognised a vulnerability in Maguire. He saw perhaps something akin to the wasted potential of Paddy Maguire, tragic figure of the 'The Great Hunger'. He observed the priest closely, noticed his contemplation of ordinary things: his astonishment 'at a stick carried down a stream / Or the undying difference in the corner of a field'. Awe and wonder are qualities depicted by Kavanagh in the old priest's character, qualities especially sympathetic to the poet. But was there something else in the lonely priest with which he identified? He too dreamed of 'brighter possibilities'. He felt for the man of learning resigned to live among simple people, with unrealised dreams, dreams 'that Christ had closed the windows on'. He was reminded of his own dilemma as poet, solitary without soul-friend, or mentor, walking the hungry hills of Shancoduff with dreams of becoming a writer.

In an article entitled 'Sunday in the Country',[47] Kavanagh finally acknowledged his debt to his now aging parish priest:

> The parish priest of this parish of which I write is Canon Maguire. For the past thirty years he has ministered there. Previously he had been a professor in Salamanca. He is a fine preacher and has a nice wit. He has that capacity for finding the simple centre in complex or abstract subjects. That bringing of the chaos of generalities down to earth with a bang (of which Shaw and Chesterton were such masters) so that we – if we are not particularly wise – are inclined to smile, not realising that this is the droll turn of commonsense. Canon Maguire is also a very fine linguist.

To place Father Maguire in the company of Shaw and Chesterton was over-complimentary on Kavanagh's part. Maguire had, however, provided the poet with literary material worthy of comedy, satire, tragedy and lines of a high lyrical quality. 'Fr Mat' had been important in his early life. In the words of 'Why Sorrow', a long unfinished poem, Kavanagh acknowledged that '[His] words begat / old music in the silences'. Unknown to himself, Maguire had influenced the poet's faith and fed his mystical imagination. Whatever we might think about this 'haughty' man's contribution to parish life, ultimately it was Kavanagh who knew best the spiritual legacy left him by the priest.

Fr Pat McConnon – The Silenced Priest (185?-1925)

Another less orthodox priest, but of unquestionable significance in the life of the poet, was Fr Pat McConnon. Fr Pat was an eccentric, a kind of priest-faith-healer, who spent about fourteen years of his priesthood in the Inniskeen area.

It is difficult to establish Fr Pat McConnon's exact biography. He was born in Corduff in the 1850s, of a poor, simple, farming background. The late Bishop Mulligan of Clogher was in possession of papers which intimated that 'he was ordained at Pentecost, in 1872, probably in Maynooth'. James Murnane, a local historian from Ballybay, suggests, from his knowledge of Bishop Donnelly's papers, that Fr Pat is likely to have been ordained in the Irish College in Paris. His relatives, Philip and Minnie Mc Ardle of Upper Creggan parish in Co Louth, recall that their grand-uncle was supposed to be 'the seventh son of a seventh son', a fact which traditionally established him in the role of healer.

His first clerical appointment was as curate to Clontibret (1872-1880). But already, Fr Pat was in difficulty with the bishop, since he would disappear from the diocese for months on end. He was said to

Fr Pat McCannon.
Photo courtesy Mrs Minnie Gorman,
his grand-niece. Repaired by Máire
Muldowney SSL.

have travelled as far as Sydney in Australia without the customary diocesan leave.[48] He was suspended for some time and later regularised in 1888. His name appears in Aghabog in 1895, Ballybay (1900-1904) and Scotshouse (1905-1911). Eventually, he was appointed to Inniskeen in 1911 where he remained until his death in 1925. He is absent from official clerical lists after 1921, though he was suspended from 1919 onwards. *The Dundalk Democrat* records his burial on September 4th, 1925, affectionately calling him 'A much-loved soggarth' who dedicated 'his sacred ministry' to the people of Farney.

Kavanagh's description of the 'young priest', Fr Martin, in *By Night Unstarred*,[49] matches that of Fr Pat in many respects. He too had been 'suspended for something serious and his mind was not perfect'. But he was known to 'have power', a fact that fascinated Kavanagh. His eccentric behaviour is well documented in *The Green Fool* with facts which still live on in local memory. The designers of ladies' low-necked blouses he called 'a pack of flaming faggots', language considered too strong for church congregations. His healing power was sought far and wide: 'when you have a child sick you'll come for the penny doctor'.

The penny doctor was himself.[50] It was not surprising that in 1924, Patrick, distressed at the serious illness of his father and his brother Peter, went to Fr Pat for assistance. Celia Kavanagh remembered the incident in detail. It is one of the few portrayals of Patrick Kavanagh in his late teens.

When she returned from school she found Patrick distraught. Having put his father and mother on the train for Monaghan hospital, he went to see Fr Pat who was reputed to be holy and possessed of extraordinary healing power. As a result of this visit, both Patrick and Celia spent the afternoon upstairs on their knees saying over and over the prayers recommended by Fr Pat: 'Jesus, deliver us from evil' and 'O Mary conceived without sin, pray for us who have recourse to thee'. When more than an hour had elapsed, Celia, who was only ten years old, wiggled from knee to knee for relief, but Patrick insisted on renewed effort and dedication and so they continued praying. When Mrs Kavanagh, who had accompanied her husband to the hospital, returned, she was shocked to find them still at prayer and directed them at once to the needs of the farm and animals which had gone untended in the heat of their fervour.[51]

Here we see Patrick, a sensitive, distraught youth, taking refuge in prayer and in the power of a faith-healing priest. He was intent on atoning for his own sins, in the belief that his father and brother would be cured as a result. Given his fear of confession, his scruples regarding sexual sins, he found in Fr Pat someone in whom he could comfortably confide.[52] His religion at this time seems guilt-ridden and fear-inspired. Thirteen years later when writing *The Green Fool*, he still remembered Fr Pat with a mixture or humour and respect. He saw him as a priest with spiritual power, called upon when worldly remedies failed.

When he was silenced, Fr Pat's popularity increased, as if he was respected even more because of his marginalised stature. Though he no longer celebrated Mass publicly or was officially recompensed for his ministry, he continued to be supported privately. People trusted all the more in his special healing powers. Those who collected the parish priest's dues, put aside grain and provisions donated for Fr Pat. Pregnant women, cancer victims, parents with sick children, flocked to him for 'the cure'.[53]

On one occasion, recalled by Kavanagh, he was called upon to banish a ghost from a haunted house.[54] As a writer now he is older and more sophisticated, yet he retains a healthly respect for the supernatural. He views the occasion with a mixture of humour and a healthy scepticism: 'shadow on the wall, nothing on the floor'. When Father Pat had succeeded in banishing the ghost, he acknowledges in humorous admiration that from that moment, 'Fr Pat's stock soared on spiritual Wall Street'. Though the miracle-worker was revered by many, for others he was a pitiful figure, driving about in his pony and trap, armed with bundles of *Messengers* and miraculous medals. For others still, the unusual figure with the black umbrella … was a saint!

This eccentric faith-healer attracted Kavanagh's attention, perhaps because in a way he epitomised the artist, gifted with spiritual power, yet always under suspicion of being 'a con man'. He presented an oldworld figure, more akin to Carleton's era of patterns and cures, later frowned upon by the new age of Maynooth-based religion. He could heal, not by knowledge like Fr Maguire, but by faith. Unlike the scholarly Fr Maguire whose 'proud bearing' and 'fine-shaped head' occasionally struck terror in their hearts, Fr Pat was an outcast and, therefore, in the poet's opinion, bound to be holy.

He impressed Kavanagh more than he wished to admit, especially as a youth. Later, the marginalised figure of the faith-healer delighted the non-conformist in Kavanagh. Legends told about Fr Pat charmed him, especially one which concerned a diocesan meeting with the Bishop to which Fr Pat was summoned. As the regular clergy filed into the meeting, Fr Pat was swept aside and not offered a place to hang his coat. Looking up, he noted a ray of sunlight entering the hall. He casually reached up and hung his coat on the sunbeam where, to the consternation of all, it remained suspended! This kind of wonder-tale, common in folk tradition, underscores the kind of spiritual hunger that craved magic. Local people revered their priest-hero. Kavanagh identified with this alleged maker of miracles who, though a healer, was also an outcast. It was perhaps with Fr Pat in mind that the poet wrote in *Kavanagh's Weekly* (1952): 'The Church which cannot harness God's lunatics loses its best instruments'.[55]

Friends and Neighbours

There were those in the neighbourhood, outside the family circle, who had a formative influence on Kavanagh's life. The Caffrey family, related through his grandmother Nancy Callan, was descended from an old Inniskeen schoolmaster called 'Oul' Caffrey'. His well-stocked mind was filled with anecdotes and stories of the past. Celia Kavanagh writes: 'I was too young to be allowed to listen to the conversation between Johnny Caffrey and Patrick, but I gathered afterwards that it was mainly literary.'[56] They recited ballads and poems together. Whatever remnants of an oral tradition still lurked in the south Monaghan of Kavanagh's childhood, the young poet eagerly assimilated it.

The journeymen shoemakers, who took to the roads in search of work, brought tales of wonder and imagination to the Kavanagh household. Garret Plunket was the most lovable of these. 'Like strange men out of a magic land I remember them coming to my father's place, their cobblers' tools tied up in an ancient apron and a road weariness in their heart.'[57] Garret took Patrick on 'limb-stretching strolls across the hills' pointing out as he went 'all the places around for miles and their history'.[58] Kavanagh as a youth seemed to have a special predilection for older wisdom figures. He hungered for the tradition which they embodied and for the older world that they knew.

John Taaffe (Michael)

'Michael', though not an old man, was, he admits, his first friend and mentor on leaving school. He was the man, he said, 'who helped me to make my soul'.[59] Michael's real name was John Taaffe, from Drumnagrella, a pupil of Kednaminsha from the early 1890s until 1898. He was also taught by Miss Cassidy.

Although he did not remain in school beyond third class, he was obviously a man of natural intelligence and wisdom. Michael taught Patrick songs and poems as they thinned turnips and travelled by horse and cart along the road together. 'The Boston Burglar' was his favourite song, which he was anxious to teach well, for as he said, 'it was well composed'.

It was Michael who initiated Kavanagh into the 'mysteries of life'. From him he learned about sex, drinking, gambling and horses. The reverence with which he discussed these things imprinted itself on the young poet for life. Patrick paid tribute to him in glowing terms: 'There was sweetness and light in this teaching about sex. He was not cruel or vulgar.' Taaffe was something of a father-figure and soul-friend to the poet. His final tribute to him in touching:

> … he was my friend. He told me hard facts in soft words. He was kind. At his funeral the priest preached a fine panegyric over him. He was a near-saint, the priest said. I was glad. I had been soul-apprenticed to a saint.

People like John Taaffe were significant in the awakening of Kavanagh's spirit at this time. Taaffe loved and understood the land and its round of farming tasks. He also loved the poems he learned at school. This 'semi-literate ploughman' who could recite at will 'Charlemagne and the Bridge of Moonbeams' as he walked the furrows, played a small role in forming the poet's soul:

> Beauteous it is in the summer night and calm along the Rhine,
> And like molten silver shines the light that sleeps on wave and vine.[60]

His recitation was interspersed with directions to the horse: 'Woa, there, Charlie…woa'!

Instances like these imprinted on Kavanagh's developing mind the notion that literacy and farming can happily coexist. The earthy and the poetic were not mismatched. It was not uncommon that well-loved poems were transmitted from father to son, while tilling the earth or cutting turf in the bog.[61] Farming people had a keen awareness of the notion that learning was a skill easily carried. Kavanagh was not a natural farmer, he was more at home in the world of books. But he gradually grew to love and hate at the same time that sudden wrench back to reality, from poetic flights of fancy to the exigencies of farmyard tasks.

The Quarry-Man 'Bob'

Patrick also acknowledges the early influence of 'the quarry-man Bob', who passed his house daily on his way to work.[62] 'Bob' has never been satisfactorily identified locally. It is thought perhaps that it was Larry Carr (1915-1990), a clever young man, reared by his grandfather Thomas Carr, the local thatcher. This was the household referred to in 'Kerr's Ass'. Carr was interested in books and in literature to an unusual degree and would seek Kavanagh out so that he might listen to him and remember his phrases. He emigrated to Australia and from there to Auckland, New Zealand, where he died in 1990. The young man Bob, whatever his identity, gave impetus to the poetic and mystical awakening of the poet. He was intrigued by the sight of a youth going to work 'reading a book – an Irish grammar'. Kavanagh paid him the highest tribute of all:

> Bob was a flame. He touched the damp wood of my mind till sparks began to dance.[63]

Patrick was amazed at the range of unusual themes and subjects discussed by Bob: topics as varied as 'Canon Law, syphilis, and irregular verbs'. Bob was appreciated by Kavanagh because he was a thinker with a poetic turn of mind, who fed his fellow-workers in the quarry, 'the academy of stone', on elevated thoughts about God and religion. His grasp of religious truths went beyond orthodoxy. Religion, he believed, was broad in its scope, stretching even beyond the priest's thinking. To break out of a traditional mind-set was liberating for the young poet. Bob provided the 'million-forked tongue of truth' that encouraged independent thought.

Whoever Bob was, he boosted Paddy Kavanagh's confidence by declaring him 'the cleverest man he had ever met'. With these

words, he bestowed on this young self-educated farmer a kind
of unofficial honorary degree, for Bob was a well-read man. Bob
possessed 'a stock of interesting books' which Patrick must have
envied.[64] Such unofficial scholarship was not uncommon in the
quarries, bogs and at the crossroads where eagerness for knowledge and learning persisted despite the presence of those
'ridicule-making fellows' who regrettably inhibited some 'very
metaphysical debates'. Kavanagh struggled, as he always did,
between lovers of spiritual things and 'louts' whose only gospel
was the land and its produce.

But why did Patrick need to hide his poetic sensibility when
Bob, a simple quarryman, could be openly liberal with his? Was
it because Bob was an 'outsider', or suitably reticent, not 'a
prophet in his own country' like Kavanagh? A certain paranoia
or 'appetite for martyrdom', which Anthony Cronin was to detect in later years, may already have begun to manifest itself.[65]
Or was his sensitivity such that he had needed to protect himself? Many of his friends speak of an innate gentleness in him,
something easily disturbed by hardship or pain. For some reason, he found it necessary to develop a *persona* of vulgarity and
outer coarseness which gradually became his customary outer
mode. Only his friends, and especially his women friends, knew
his more vulnerable aspects. The deliberate hiding of his true
poetic nature was the beginning of an important development in
Kavanagh's personality.

In contrast with Bob, Kavanagh suffered at the hands of the
savage side of peasant life, which could deny reverie and up-
hold harsh realism. A neighbour chided him one day for day-
dreaming while there were cattle to be fed. This neighbour had
offended his sensibilities by his harsh tone of voice, his attitude
which was 'savage' and 'godless'. Kavanagh was beginning to
learn that '... realism untouched by the imagination is a sordid
petty thing'.[66] Describing the effect of such violence, he says: 'by
the heels he pulled me down from the stars and made me a
worm-cutter'. Kavanagh, peremptorily grounded, was gradually
awakening to an awareness of his own mystical and imaginative
bent. Was it possible to serve reality and mystical insight at the

same time? For Kavanagh, the marriage between the banal and the beautiful, the earthy and the spiritual, would involve a life-long struggle.

Fairy-Lore

Local fairy-lore stretched Kavanagh's growing imagination still further. Patrick was fond of visiting his neighbour and family connection, Barney Rooney, whom he called 'Old George'.[67] The old man, a 'teller of fairy-tales', filled his mind with folk memories:

> He believed in all the old things – ghosts, fairies, horses, scythes, sickles, and flails... 'Aw, Paddy,' he said, 'this part of Ireland is a gentle spot ... It isn't right to be trampin' the fields at night fall except on good business. The Wee Fellas be about'.[68]

Rooney's turn of phrase and sense of awe at the fairy-world around him, imprinted itself on Patrick's imagination. Fairy and Christian beliefs intermingled indiscriminately in his mind. As he watched George quietly puffing his pipe, 'I could see the fairies peering out like angels in a tom-boy mood'. The world of spirit was making its impact from two, generally held opposing directions, the world of paganism and the world of Christianity. When George looked at a whirlwind, he saw a movement of fairies through the countryside. Lone bushes, he believed, were sacred to the shee, and should not be disturbed. Though he could have benefited from firewood gathered from the bushes on his land, he allowed his lone bushes to grow untouched, a practice still common in rural Ireland today.[69]

Patrick Kavanagh regretted the passing of an ancient oral culture in south Monaghan. He knew he had been born on the edge of an old era, one rich in the language and poetry of south-east Ulster. The new era of political independence, compulsory education, the printed word, radio, mechanised farming, had not yet fully eradicated the old. He awkwardly straddled both eras, belonging to neither. Thus began the marginalised feeling of one culturally 'born between two stools'.[70] It was from this position of disadvantage that he, through his writing, moved the frontiers of Hiberno-English 'barehanded' into a new era.

Mythical giants such as Cuchulainn, Fionn MacCumhail and the Fianna peopled the poet's landscape, emanating from the nearby Fews. Many local fields boasted boulders, standing stones, allegedly thrown from Slieve Gullion or Urchar Hill by a local giant or his foreign rival. The Táin story rippled over the Cooley mountains with heroic intimations that spoke of courage and romance. Kavanagh's eye appraised his own mythologically rich landscape: the plain of Louth that runs out to the sea at Annagassan, scene of the great battle between Maeve and Cuchulainn. Baile's Strand, the mythical playground of Cuchulainn, locally called Seatown, was visible on a fine day from the hills near his home.

Echoes of Antiquity: Hints of Romance

Nor was Kavanagh's immediate environment in Inniskeen without its hints of history and romance. A round tower, set in an ancient graveyard, lent an aura of antiquity to the village. The McMahon vault, built to the memory of these great chiefs of Farney, provided a monument to the heroism of the past. James E. Mc Kenna, commenting on the antiquities of Inniskeen, has this to say:

> In the MacMahon vault, towards the east of the cemetery, a small stone is inscribed: 'I.H.S.-This Chapel was-built bye Ardell M-AC Coll MacMa-Hon for himsel-fe and Fame-lly in the year – Anno Dom, 1672'.[71]

McKenna traces this Ardell McMahon back to his grandfather, Ever McCooley, the chieftain of Farney who died in 1617. The celebrated 'Bard of Armagh' was alleged to be one of the Mc Mahon clan, a priest and leader of the people who often, at times of religious persecution, disguised himself as a wandering bard and musician. Stories of these local heroes fed Kavanagh's agile imagination, and nourished his mystical hunger:

> McMahon and his sixteen sons once rode into the town of Louth on sixteen white horses. They had a residence – or so

the story went – up the lane upon which I lived, and I often searched among the rocks hoping I might find some memory of their lives ... and there remained in the legends of their lives something not merely noble but mystical.[72]

Oral culture was still strong in south Monaghan in the early 1920s. There was little reading material available and everyone loved a story. The world of myth and folklore was for Kavanagh 'a world of sensibility' which stirred the imagination at its roots.[73] The greatest poverty of all when men gathered at a crossroads, or a threshing, was to be without a story or a yarn. The exchange of labour system which operated among farmers meant that they helped each other out whenever a boon of men was needed. Kavanagh, the outsider, could legitimately be one of the workers on occasions such as these:

O it was a delight
To be paying bills of laughter
And chaffy gossip in kind
With work thrown in to ballast
The fantasy-soaring mind. (*Tarry Flynn*)

Similarly, while spraying the potatoes, he relished the talk engaged in while working, over-rating it perhaps as 'a theme of kings'.

Leisurely unhurried living was essential to Kavanagh's mystical awakening. He insists that he did not go out in pursuit of beauty; he allowed himself to become passive to its presence around him, not forcing communication but letting the fields contemplate him. 'Ah, the fields looked at me more than I at them, and at this moment they are still staring at me'.[74]

He acknowledged that, as he grew up, he was being affected by his environment. 'Not everybody,' he suggests, 'can have the fields and lanes stare at him as they stare at a man driving a cow to a fair.' There was something contemplative in this 'wise passiveness' which gave him kinship with Wordsworth and with the simple philosophy of being 'open to Being'.[75] He savoured his contemplative moments of day-dreaming in the fields.

Conclusion

There is nothing extraordinary in Patrick Kavanagh's upbringing. Thousands can identify with the world and culture he knew. His hunger for learning, for story, for folklore and myth was nourished firstly in the home, and by those who came from far and near to the shoemaker's house. His principal educators were his parents who provided him with the spiritual and earthy garments of the soul. Fr Maguire added an exotic dash of learning, theology and style to the environment. His words, we have seen, 'begat old music in the silences'. The eccentric figure of Fr Pat, the silenced local priest, brought the world of William Carleton with its ghosts, cures and miracles, nearer to the poet's world.

Kavanagh learned from neighbours, whom others might dismiss as unlettered and ignorant. Later, when he walked the fields of Shancoduff, he ruminated upon stories, local incidents, historical data, until he had amassed a treasure-trove of potential literary material, and stashed it away in his memory. Small insignificent events became moments to be fondled and placed at his own memory's shrine. His neighbours, the Caffreys, John Taaffe, Old George, 'Bob', Johnny Cassidy – all provided the raw material for his writing. Just as his mother by her unconditional love, believed intuitively in her son, so too his father's spirit remained with him always as a soul-friend, reminding him that he would be present in 'every old man' he met.

Every old man I see

In October-coloured weather

Seems to say to me:

'I was once your father.' *(Memory of my Father)*

In the frailty and dreaming of old age, he learned a wisdom that was not uncongenial to his spirit.

The volume of personal autobiographical material available to the Kavanagh scholar in his novels, *The Green Fool* and *Tarry Flynn,* as well as in publications such as *The Irish Farmer's Journal* and *The RTE Guide*, make it is possible to examine potential awakening influences. One of the single greatest influences of all were the schoolbooks he studied both inside and out of school. His teachers and literary mentors provided sufficient stimuli to allow his soul and imagination blossom still further.

CHAPTER 3

Awakening II

I walked entranced through a land of morn...
(J. C. Mangan)

I

SCHOOLBOOK ROOTS

'If roots I had they were in the schoolbooks,' Kavanagh claims.[1] He recalls the very colour and odour of these books, one bright yellow another blue. The pleasurable smell from his new canvas schoolbag, with its treasure-trove of new books, remained fresh in his nostrils well into adulthood. Each well-loved poem evoked not only a particular schoolbook but a place, a literary landmark in the field of his imagination. These places were his intimate havens: 'the shaded corner of a field called Lurgankeel'[2] or the privet hedge near 'the field of turnips'. Certain schoolbooks reawakened for him the exact position of his desk at school, 'near the fire, near the map of Scotland'. Individual poems: Bret Harte's 'Dickens in Camp' and sections of Tennyson's 'Locksley Hall' reminded him of 'a virginal time' when he was surrounded by 'the protective fog of family life' with all his dreams 'sealed in the bud'. His youth was the happy time of his 'lost youth' spent in the literary company of Longfellow:

Often I think of that beautiful town
That is seated by the sea...

This poem set him an early example of a poet in love with place. It touched a personal chord within.

The Royal Readers
Among the school-books which fed Kavanagh's imagination

and awakened him to the gift of poetry were The Royal Readers, and especially the famous 'Sixth Book' used by previous generations of school pupils, possibly by James Kavanagh himself. But if the Royal Readers influenced him, they were not among the treasured books he carried in his satchel to school. He procured the 'Sixth Book' only after he had left school. Typical of Kavanagh, he 'borrowed' or 'stole' it from a neighbour's house.[3] It is more likely, with the advent of compulsory education in 1892 and the growing emphasis on Catholic education in Irish schools, that the Royal Readers, first published by Nelson in 1872, were replaced by several new sets of readers published in Ireland by Gills, Fallons, Browne and Nolan and The Educational Company. Sanction for these new readers was sought from the Commissioners of Education who were anxious to promote literacy in the English language among primary school pupils at that time. Statistics quoted in the Board of Education Reports for 1903 show that illiteracy in Monaghan County decreased from fifty-one per cent in 1841 to less than fourteen per cent in 1901.[4] Patrick Kavanagh belonged to this new generation of literates.

The Finlay Readers

One of the educators of that time who saw the need for a reader with a more Irish outlook was the Jesuit, Thomas A. Finlay. Along with Horace Plunkett and 'AE', Finlay was to play a role in the co-operative farming movement of the time as well as the Irish Literary Revival. Finlay was a teacher, first in Limerick and later in Belvedere College, Dublin. He knew the formative influence of material read, re-read and memorised at school. Dr Magennis, Inspector of school, who later became Professor of English at UCD and at Carysfort Training College, assisted Finlay in this work and occasionally wrote short introductions to his readers.

His *School and College Series* was popular from 1898 onwards. A 1908 reader bears the mark '265th thousand' which indicates the enormous circulation of these readers. They were re-issued

as *The New School and College Literary Series* in the early 1900s.
While revising the series, Finlay dropped the poet Southey to in-
clude Moore's 'O Blame not the Bard', and included Gerald
Griffin's 'Orange and Green' in place of an excerpt from
Longfellow's 'Evangeline'. Finlay became more and more interested in the Irish Literary Revival and introduced Irish poets
such as Goldsmith and Mangan into his anthologies.

Katie Campbell, Kavanagh's classmate, had in her possession until her death, the sixth class reader distributed to her class
by Miss Cassidy.[5] It was entitled *Advanced Book* of the later
Finlay editions. This reader contains many of Kavanagh's favourite poems: Longfellow's 'My Lost Youth', an excerpt from
Tennyson's 'Locksley Hall',[6] as well as portions of Scott's 'Lady
of the Lake' and Pope's 'Essay on Criticism'. All are quoted by
Kavanagh in the course of his writing, which leaves little doubt
that the Finlay readers were among those he used at school. And
if further proof were needed, the distinctive indigo 'blue' remembered by Kavanagh was indeed the regular binding of this
series.[7]

Kavanagh's passion for schoolbook poetry is well documented.
The Senior Book, his fifth class reader, contained three pieces
quoted, two in *Tarry Flynn* and one in an article entitled
'Schoolbook Poetry' in the *R.T.É. Guide*, June 10th 1966. 'The
Night' by Adelaide Procter was retained by Finlay from his earliest edition in 1898, as well as a piece by O. W. Holmes, 'Under
Violets',[8] and 'The Midnight Mail' by Samuel K. Cowan. Kavanagh remembered these pieces with precision; their sentiments
were his. These were authors frequently included in schoolbooks because of their simple style and improving tone. Eliza
Cook, whose phrenology and mental temperament were the
envy of the romantic Tarry Flynn, was represented in all junior
schoolbooks, as well as in the junior Royal Readers up until the
1950s.[9]

One could say that it was through the Royal Readers, especially the 'Sixth Book', that Kavanagh continued his on-going
education. Here he met the ballads of Campbell, as well as 'The

Burial of Sir John Moore' by Charles Wolfe, selections from Shakespeare, Goldsmith, Byron and one of Mangan's translations from the German: 'Charlemagne and the Bridge of Moonbeams' which his friend, John Taaffe, liked to recite aloud while ploughing in the fields. These poems had been memorised by successive generations of pupils as English gradually became the dominant language of the schools. Teachers continued to teach some of their favourite poems from the Royal Readers, even when these readers were discontinued. Poetry, we have seen, was transmitted outside school, in the bogs, in the fields, while churning, or cutting seed for the new potato crop.[10]

Patrick Kavanagh had cherished memories which he kept locked in 'the roundtower' of his heart. These early memories were vivid and lasting. He retained stories, poems, ballads, learned at home, at school or from neighbours. In later life he pondered philosophically on the contrast between his ability to remember and to forget. He was heard to say impatiently on one occasion: 'Don't you know it's much easier to remember than to forget,'[11] a remark fraught with notable psychological implications. Memory was for him, perhaps, a positive exercise to forget negative experiences. It was Longfellow's 'The Children's Hour' that gave him the lines he needed to comfort his soul:

> I have you fast in my fortress
> And will not let you depart
> But put you down into the dungeon
> In the roundtower of my heart.[12]

Kednaminsha School

His first conscious poetic awakening occurred at school. The tiny two-teacher school at Kednaminsha, a mile from the Kavanagh home, provided the setting for this event. Miss Cassidy, as we have seen, taught the senior classes, while Miss Agnew, her assistant, taught the junior pupils. Reading, writing and arithmetic were taught in turn to all seven classes. One class read aloud while another practised writing or chanted 'tables' by heart. The door between the two classrooms remained open,

to allow the single open turf fire heat both rooms. It also allowed
easy access from class to class. The teachers' bicycles were kept
indoors under supervision, lest they be found mysteriously
punctured at the end of the day!

It was on one such occasion that Patrick heard a girl reading
a poem by James Clarence Mangan.[13] It was customary then not
only to read a poem aloud but to declaim it. The pupil was
taught to stand, take a bow and, in a loud clear voice, give the
title and author before beginning the reading. Kavanagh has a
vivid memory of this incident:

> From the classroom on our left a girl's voice came through to
> us. She was reading a poem:
>
>> I walked entranced
>> Through a land of morn
>> The sun with wondrous excess of light
>> Shone down and glanced
>> Oe'r fields of corn
>> And lustrous gardens aleft and right.[14]

As he heard these lines, something stirred within him. It is most
likely that he was in the senior section of the school, aged about
eleven, supposedly engaged in writing an essay. Miss Cassidy's
attention was absorbed in teaching fifth class.[15] The room was
relatively quiet. This gave him the possibility of listening unob-
served. The girl's rendering of Mangan's words was striking: 'I
walked entranced / through a land of morn…' Patrick would remember it all his life:

> Listening to Mangan's poem, I was rapt to that golden time
> in which poets are born. I felt as though I were in the pres-
> ence of a magician, and I was; there was witchery in some of
> Mangan's poetry, it wasn't normal verse. Mangan's poem as
> read by that girl awoke in me for the first time those feelings
> that are beyond the reach of reason.

On leaving school, Patrick still relied on his schoolbooks for inspiration. He continued to read and learn extracts by heart. 'All
the bits and pieces that furnish Imagination's house come up by
magic' at the mere mention of one of these excerpts. At will he is

back in a land created by the grandeur of Tennyson's 'Locksley Hall,' or caught in the pathos of the hanging of 'Eugene Aram' for the murder of a shoemaker. His autobiographical *Tarry Flynn* finds 'something that made a man happy in the midst of desolation' in humming a schoolbook poem by Adelaide Procter:

Oh the summer night had a smile of light

As she sits on her sapphire throne.[16] *(Night)*

Through schoolbook authors Kavanagh found solace for his romantic temperament and made his own bonds of friendship with his Monaghan landscape. Poets in love taught him how to speak of his own unrequited love and helped him find comfort in the 'scent of the woodbine and the richer smell of potato stalks'.[17]

Thomas Campbell's 'Lord Ullin's Daughter' and 'The Burial of Sir John Moore', were among Kavanagh's favourite party pieces. Their drama, mystery and pathos all spoke to his soul:

Not a drum was heard, not a funeral note,

As his corpse to the ramparts we carried.[18]

Mangan continued to inspire him. He continued to be Kavanagh's kindred spirit. The lovelorn Tarry Flynn repeatedly finds consolation in the well-remembered lines from 'And Then No More':

I saw her once one little while and then no more,

Twas Paradise on earth awhile and then no more.[19]

His extravagant, impecunious love for Mary Reilly found an outlet in Samuel Ferguson's translation of an old Irish love-song:

Oh I'd wed you without herds, without money or rich array

And I'd wed you on a dewy morning at day dawn grey.[20]

Tennyson introduced him to the poetry of life around him. His 'Brook' was soon familiar territory; 'he knew it from its source among the coot and hern till it poured itself into the brimming river'.[21] The American poet Bret Harte whisked him off into a wondrous and unfamiliar territory. He especially loved his lines from 'Dickens in Camp':

Above the pines the moon was slowly drifting,

The river sang below,

The dim Sierras far beyond uplifting
Their minarets of snow.[22]

Kavanagh's selection of schoolbook verse was like a private art-collection; it followed the logic of his heart. He loved what was lyrical, mystical, lonely and lovelorn. Poetry was for him a necessary therapy for a soul-hunger that nothing else could assuage. Its rhythm and music was a solace to the hidden pain of adolescence and early adulthood.

Early Musical Formation

Hymns, ballads and songs were also influential in his spiritual formation. Brigid Agnew, or 'Miss Moore' of *The Green Fool*, brought enthusiasm to her teaching of music in Kednaminsha. As a monitor in neighbouring Shelagh School, she had learned to teach, play the harmonium and sing in the chapel choir. On her appointment to Kednaminsha she cycled the five-mile journey to school, and in winter stayed at 'Paris Row,' the grandiose local nickname given to the newly-

Brigid Agnew. 'Miss Moore'.
Photo courtesy Briege McCaughan,
daughter of Brigid Agnew.

built County Council houses where she and Miss Cassidy lodged. She started each class with the song 'Perseverance', sung in unison by all pupils while marching around the classroom in military fashion.[23] Miss Agnew was fortunate to have the use of an harmonium in school. No record exists of its having been furnished by the Commissioners of Education; it is more likely to have been donated by the Kennys of Rocksavage or from parish funds. The singing of this British public-school-type song, adapted from the Royal Readers Book II, was likely to be affirmed by the Commissioners of Education, unaware at that time of its sexist language! The object of the song was to instil motivation for learning into a largely unmotivated school population. Lustily they sang:

Strike the nail aright boys
Hit it on the head
Strike with all your might boys
While the iron's red.

When you've work to do boys
Do it with a will
Those who reach the top boys
First must climb the hill.

Standing at the foot boys
Gazing at the sky
How can you get up boys
If you never try?

Though you stumble oft boys
Never be downcast
Try and try again boys
You'll succeed at last.[24]

Patrick Kavanagh, who had a musical ear and a tuneful voice at this time, joined in with the rest. In his own unique way he was already determined to 'climb the hill' of life and 'succeed at last', but in a way no one expected.

Thomas Moore provided the pupils with both poetry and song. *Moore's Melodies* was Miss Agnew's favourite songbook,[25] which is undoubtedly why Kavanagh christened her 'Miss Moore'! He recalls the steady diet of Moore she provided: 'We had Tom Moore for the singing lesson each day.'[26] The school repertoire included 'Oft in the Stilly night', 'Let Erin Remember' and 'The Harp that Once through Tara's Halls'. The Kavanaghs were musical. Patrick's ability to play the melodeon never reached his father's level of competence, but he had a taste for music and tried his hand at the tin whistle. Singing for Kavanagh involved the soul, it was an activity reserved for special company and circumstances:

... I have never been able to read Moore without putting an air – generally the tune the old cow died on – to his words. I was ashamed once when someone heard me singing 'Let Erin Remember' – it was like being caught praying.

Anthony Cronin attests to Kavanagh's 'enormous love for the Irish sub-culture represented by schoolbook poems and ballads:

He ... would sing: 'The Burial of Sir John Moore', 'Lord Ullin's Daughter' and Richard Dalton William's 'From a Munster Vale they Brought Her'. He had a perfect ear and was delighted to sing in the right company and on the right occasion. When he had the operation for cancer it damaged his vocal chords somehow and his voice lost its resonance, but his ear of course remained impeccable and he simply adapted his highly individual style to the new possibilities.[27]

On the day Brigid Agnew left Kednaminsha, in 1913, she asked the pupils to sing Moore's 'When Through Life Unblest we Rove'. The tears in her eyes noticed by one of her better singers, Katie McGeough, were evidence that she was lonely leaving Kednaminsha. Among her prized possessions at the time of her death was her personal copy of *Moore's Melodies*. Enthusiasm for Moore had sustained her to the end.[28]

Years later, Tom Moore provided inspiration for Kavanagh. Moore sets the scene for one of Fr Maguire's (Fr Daly) memorable denunciations of the local 'blackguards' who were 'sullying the fair name of this parish'.[29]

'There was a great poet one time,' Fr Daly began, he began slowly and in a minor key, 'and his name was Tom Moore. He wrote a song called "Rich and Rare". "Rich and rare were the gems she wore..." The priest spoke solemnly, enunciating every word separately...

> Rich and rare were the gems she wore
> And a bright gold ring on her wand she bore;
> But O her beauty was far beyond
> Her sparkling gem and snow-white wand.

> Lady, dost thou not fear to stray
> So lone and lovely on this bleak way?
> Are Erin's sons so good or so cold
> As not to be tempted by woman or gold?
>
> Sir Knight, I fear not the least alarm,
> No son of Erin would offer me harm.
> For though they love women and golden store,
> Sir Knight, they love honour and virtue more.[30]

Moore's idealisation of woman was appropriate for Kavanagh's literary purposes. Indeed it may have come close to his own idealised notions of the female. Moore's knight-like sentiments clothed in virtue and idealism matched a certain Victorian attitude towards male-female relationships current at this time. The chivalrous, sentimental poetry of Moore and Byron provided a necessary romantic outlet. Marriagelessness was prevalent in this country of 'The Great Hunger', a rural community where poverty and over-divided farms produced widespread bachelorhood and enforced celibacy.

'A Wreath for Thomas Moore's Statue' was written, not so much about Moore, as about the role of the poet in society. The wreathing of Moore's statue in College Green in 1944 evoked criticism from Kavanagh:

> They put a wreath upon the dead
> For the dead will wear the cap of any racket,
> The corpse will not put his elbows through his jacket
> Or contradict the words some liar has said.

By now, Kavanagh could be both bitter and cynical. Nevertheless he could be melodious even in satire. More striking still is his superb lyrical and musical sense at the end of this poem where the *living* poet's work is its own vindication:

> But hope! the poet comes again to build
> A new city high above lust and logic,
> The trucks of language overflow and magic
> At every turn of the living road is spilled.

Kavanagh's 'trucks of language' overflow with a robust music capable of transforming banal city corners into 'turn(s)' of 'living road', bright with traces of infinity. Kavanagh's power with words is exquisite. His use of the rural 'turn' rather than the urban 'corner', sets the scene for 'a brightening', a moment of revelation. 'Logic' and 'lust' create the slightly jolted metre, proper to a street-cart, which rhythmically carries forward the sense, only to 'overflow' and 'spill' 'magic' 'on the living road'.

At his best Kavanagh's poetry is tuneful. His effective alternating of short and long vowel-sounds creates a light-hearted, exciting melody in

> Girls in red blouses,
> Steps up to houses,
> Sunlight round gables,
> Gossip's young fables,
> The life of a street. *(Is)*

In the same poem he basks in the liquid consonants of regenerative water:

> Mention water again
> Always virginal,
> Always original,
> It washes away Original Sin

There are portions of 'The Great Hunger' which attest to unmistakable musical and rhythmic competence:

> Sitting on a wooden gate,
> Sitting on a wooden gate,
> Sitting on a wooden gate
> He didn't care a damn.
> Said whatever came into his head,
> Said whatever came into his head,
> Said whatever came into his head,
> And inconsequently sang…

The swinging movement evoked by the main stresses in each line give moments of tragi-comic relief to the sombre atmosphere of the 'The Great Hunger' and provides a chorus-like interlude within the narrative of the poem.[31]

But 'Raglan Road' was to be Kavanagh's greatest musical enterprise. He set his lyric to music with the help of a well-known

Irish tune, 'The Dawning of the Day'. This tune, comprising a single octave span, was taught to every aspiring tin-whistle or bagpipe player in Ireland. Renewed as 'Raglan Road', and coupled with the voice of Luke Kelly,[32] it took on a new existence, and was to serve the romantic needs of ordinary Irish people in pubs and at weddings, just as fittingly as Yeats had entertained the drawingroom gentry with 'Down by the Sally Garden'. Miss Agnew had not realised that she had a popular song-writer in her class at Kednaminsha!

Geography class also provided Kavanagh with the stuff of daydreams. Though good at all subjects, Patrick excelled at geography. When examined at the wall-map by Miss Cassidy, his performance was flawless. Closely allied to geography was the interest he shared with his father in current affairs. When the 1914-18 war broke out he knew the names of generals on both sides and impressed the School Inspector by his knowledge.[33] The contours of wall-maps spoke to him of exotic places which he visited in his imagination. In 'The Great Hunger', Patrick Maguire resorted to similar reverie in a vain attempt to escape monotony:

A man might imagine then
Himself in Brazil and these birds the birds of paradise
And the Amazon and the romance traced on the map lived again.

Among his school readers there was one, a Sterling Reader, published by Brown and Nolan in the 1900s, which contained a vivid illustration in brightest colours of 'The Birds of Paradise'. A detail such as this, in an otherwise drab milieu, was sufficient to set the imagination alight. This book also contained Cowper's 'Alexander Selkirk's Soliloquy' which undoubtedly inspired 'Inniskeen Road'. His 'mile of kingdom' on a country road is the setting Kavanagh chooses to be 'monarch of all (he) survey(s)'. 'I am king,' he concludes whimsically, 'Of banks and stones and every blooming thing'.

It is on public record that Patrick Kavanagh was not promoted beyond fifth class.[34] Nevertheless he had garnered enough learning to introduce him to the world of writing. Romantic poems and the call of distant places had eased the longings of youth and given him an entrance to a transcendent world. Memory became the nourisher of the imagination and an endless source of meditation. His mystical journey, begun at school, continued in the fields. To ensure that he would never be without the comfort of literature, he kept loose leaves from schoolbooks placed at strategic points on his farm, 'between the rafters and the galvanised roof of the horse stable',[35] or out-of-doors in the hedgerows 'in the forked branches of the stunted ash-trees' or 'at the root of the boortree'.[36]

> I stocked every fence with a book or paper of some kind. As I walked around the hedges, bill-hook on my shoulder, I might feel an inclination to read a poem or short story...[37]

Hidden away in the fields of Shancoduff, out of sight of his mother, he read and ruminated at will. She wanted him, above all, to become a comfortable farmer but, to him, the fields were treasure of a different order. In the solitude of the fields Patrick pursued his passion for poetry. Stirred inwardly by the repetition of memorised fragments, he lived a hidden life of rural contemplation. Monk-like he went to the fields pondering in his heart some life-giving text.

Other influences, too, contributed to Kavanagh's literary awakening. Among them was a man called Brennan, and the local Bard of Callenberg; these opened doors onto Kavanagh's literary career.

II

LITERARY MODELS

The world of books

Though deprived of open access to literature, Kavanagh did not live entirely without literary discourse. He tells how one of his neighbours, called Brennan, possessed a fine house and owned 'a large stock of inherited books'. Among these books were the works of Pope and Byron and Shelley's 'The Cenci'. Their owner and he were kindred spirits. Gradually the gap was widening between the world of books and the business of farming. Literature became the food of his soul while farming was his cloak of respectability among the neighbours. When Patrick visited this house he was often dismayed by the interruption of 'hob-nailed boots (coming) up the cobbled yard' during his literary tête-à-têtes – 'a bull to the china-shop of the angels'. His 'holy ground' was shattered and his angelic discourse desecrated. He was forced to revert to 'vulgar talk' which 'would turn on the loud wheel of present day'. Such talk, he says, 'went against the grain of my soul'.[38] A man in the process of becoming a poet had to quickly simulate vulgarity. No one must guess at the presence of a fine-grained soul.

The Bard of Callenberg

One of the local people who cannot be completely discounted in the poetic formation of Kavanagh, if only because he 'left doors open as he passed', was the local Bard of Callenberg.[39] During Kavanagh's youth the Bard recorded local events in verse and published them in the *Dundalk Democrat*. His real name was John McEnaney, born in the townland of Gortin and, while still young, moved with his family to Callenberg, a townland which gave the bard his name. He married Mary Moley from Shelagh where his daughter Annie (1904-) still lives. Being physically disabled, he travelled around in a donkey and cart protecting his personal interests by prolific verse, often caustic in tone and directed against any injustices he encountered. On one occasion, having loaded his cart with provisions at McGee's shop, he returned to find it empty. The shopkeeper had reclaimed his goods:

> ... in less than an hour
> Male (sic) pollard and flour
> Was whipped off my cart
> By Consaity Mc Gee.[40]

The local shopkeeper was sorely stung by the verse even though it was generally known that the Bard had no intention of paying for the goods. The incident, however, was fixed indelibly in folk memory and is quoted even today. Kavanagh would have secretly admired the Bard's ingenuity and sensed already the power of verse.[41]

Following at first in the tradition of The Bard McEnaney, Kavanagh wrote of local events: football matches, dances, parish outings. These were his first verbal challenges and a means of exercising language. He turned later to pious verse because of a competition published in the Holy Poets' corner of the *Weekly Independent* (1928-29) and met with favourable mention.[42] Soon Kavanagh's early verse was being recited at threshings or weddings. The Kavanagh family, however, were nervous of Patrick's following in The Bard's footsteps. For his own part, although he was happy to have known the last of the bards, he had aspirations beyond The Bard of Callenberg. Once when his sisters were taunted, 'Your brother's a bard', they complained to Patrick about this slur on the family name! Patrick was swift to reply, 'Shakespeare was called The Bard of Avon', so being a bard was no disgrace![43] Gradually he began to discard doggerel and pious verse for a broader canvas. William Carleton helped provide him with a guideline.

William Carleton

Kavanagh could most easily identify with the Clogher writer, William Carleton. Carleton had visited this locality, and found lodgings for a time with his uncle, the parish priest of nearby Killanny. He had collected stories on his travels which he published as *Traits and Stories of the Irish Peasantry*.[44] Kavanagh delighted in this book which he 'borrowed' from a neighbour, and read numerous times. The story entitled 'The Wild Goose Lodge' was a local saga and had been told in low tones by the fireside long before it appeared in print. Kavanagh saw that Carleton wrote about local events and incorporated local characters into his stories. He considered him as one of the few Irish writers who was aware of the rich vein of colourful life present in the Irish peasantry.

Kavanagh's identification with Carleton began to inspire his own writing. What Carleton did for the Clogher Valley during the early nineteenth century, Kavanagh would attempt to do for south Monaghan in the first half of the twentieth century. Together, though separated by decades, they would investigate country characters, explore the notion of pilgrimage to Lough Derg and to holy wells. Kavanagh knew that Carleton had also come from a poor background, had attended a hedge-school, learned the same catechism as himself, listened to local stories and yarns. He too had seen the literary potential in colourful rural characters, quarrelled with the church and yet retained his own spiritual integrity. Kavanagh knew he could learn a lot from this first writer in English who faithfully portrayed Irish rural life.

But Kavanagh's real 'candle of vision' was to come through his discovery of *The Irish Statesman*. There he read AE's poems and heard 'mention of a man called Joyce'. This was a memorable moment of awakening.

A Candle of Vision – 'AE'

AE or George Russell (1867-1939) was a poet, a mystic, an artist and a social activist. He had many qualities that fitted him to be the first mentor, patron and visionary inspiration of Kavanagh as a young writer. Born in Lurgan in Co Armagh, he came to live in Dublin where he worked as a clerk in Pym's in Georges Street. He always retained the humility of a clerk, a quality which endeared him to Kavanagh who took an immediate liking to him. Because of his mystical

AE – George Russell 1867-1939 Photo courtesy National Library of Ireland

poetry and other-worldly aspects, few realised that AE was an intensely practical person, working first as editor of *The Irish*

Homestead and later for its successor, *The Irish Statesman*. Through the instrumentality of these journals he promoted, as far distant as the United States, the benefits of co-operative farming and rural economics. In Kavanagh's eyes he was some-one who happily combined an interest in both poetry and farming.

AE's monthly newspapers had as their sole aim the support of 'the efforts of the great body of Irish farmers'.[45] He sought to do this 'by every means which a newspaper can command'. His task was crucial, given the widespread poverty that existed in the wake of the Great Famine of the nineteenth century. Along with Sir Horace Plunkett and Thomas Finlay SJ, editor of many of Kavanagh's schoolbooks, he set out to convince farmers of the benefits of co-operation, community development and scientific farming. Together they founded the Irish Agriculture Organisation Society (IAOS). Farmers, before isolated, could now be instructed in new methods of agriculture, banking and rural economy. They could also enjoy the leisure of poems, short stories and literary articles, printed in 'At the Fireside' section of the paper. The blend of farming news with literary items typifies the variety of objectives which AE hoped to serve in the same journal.

Understandably, many farmers were interested solely in the markets and in the price of hayseed and other farming news. Not so Kavanagh. In *The Green Fool*, he recounts how *The Irish Statesman* fell accidentally into his hands. He had gone to Dundalk with the intention of purchasing *Titbits*, a paper much loved by his father, when his eye fell on the *Irish Statesman*. *Titbits* was at that time in the process of being withdrawn, in favour of the more nationalistic *Ireland's Own*, so Patrick changed his allegiance. It was providential; an occasion which would change his life and be a further step on the road to poetic awakening. This is how he describes the moment:[46]

'Any stir on the paper?' a fellow asked me.
'Plenty,' I replied, 'Gertrude Stein is after writing a new book.'
'Quit the coddin'! How's the markets goin'?'

The 'stir' of great literature was beckoning him. It was through this encounter with *The Irish Statesman* that Patrick Kavanagh first heard of AE, James Joyce, Gertrude Stein, T.S. Eliot, Padraic Colum, Frank O'Connor, Sean O'Faolain. The Irish Literary Revival was in full swing. A new stimulus entered Kavanagh's life, though he did not fully realise its source. Dedicated to the monthly literary treat provided by *The Irish Statesman*, he would cycle several miles to Dundalk to procure it and avidly devour its contents. Later, he would select poems and articles from it as additions to his 'library' of cuttings. There were new poems now to replace the schoolbook poetry of the past. These he ruminated upon while working in the fields and more and more reluctantly tending his farm.

New Horizons

It was one of AE's poems which appeared in the *Irish Statesman* in 1929, that awakened him to a new sense of his own destiny as a poet. This was a new milestone in Kavanagh's awakening. He read and re-read the lines, intuitively sensing that something here had struck a new chord in him:

Paris and Babel
London and Tyre
Reborn from darkness
Shall sparkle like fire...[47]

He did not fully understand the lines but felt them open up a new inner horizon. He sensed in them 'a meaning and a message that had come from hills of the imagination far beyond the flat fields of common sense'. Furthermore, he experienced a strong sensation, the presence of something mystical, something virginal. 'It was an Eden time and Eve not yet violated. Men were not subject to death. I was happy.'

Patrick was mesmerised by his first contact with AE's poetry. Here at last was someone who knew the world as sacred as he did. He read and re-read the lines and was so mesmerised he could scarcely find his way back to Inniskeen. On that day Kavanagh says, 'I was wandering among the hills of a timeless world'. He realised that he too could express his vision in poetry; he too could contribute to the world of letters through this publication. Tentatively, he sent a poem to the editor. AE himself wrote back. Kavanagh was unable to believe his luck and was surprised that AE was offering to pay him. He thought it was a great thing not to have to pay for its publication himself.[48]

Spiritual Legacy

It is obvious from AE's poetry and paintings that he was a spiritual man. His interest in spirituality was neither Protestant nor Catholic, although he had been brought up in the Protestant evangelical tradition in Co Armagh. His interest had been mostly in the rich tradition of prayer and hymn-singing provided by his upbringing. This nourished his mystical predisposition.[49]

He was interested in a universal religion that belonged to all creeds, to the sacred dimension of life itself. Fr Finlay spoke of his friend and colleague AE in a way that may explain Kavanagh's affinity for the man:

He is of the world unworldly – the world's stain has never touched him. Without religion, yet profoundly religious: the peace of God which passeth understanding lies all about him ... he finds gods in the earth and air – rather I would say he finds God; and his life has unconsciously cast incense on the Altars of the Unknown God.[50]

AE had read widely in the holy books of all traditions, east and west, and had discovered a synthesis derived from all of them which satisfied his personal religious needs. He did not impose his private beliefs on anyone; his only 'gospel' being that of co-operative farming. His humility was his most compelling quality.

A talented artist and poet, yet he sacrificed these talents in the service of his work for the Irish farming community. He travelled Ireland by bicycle, holding meetings, founding creameries and having his writings on rural economy translated into a number of languages.[51] All who met him could not but be struck by his kindliness, his respect, and the depth of wisdom that emanated from his sage-like, white-bearded appearance. Under the leadership of Horace Plunkett, AE continued his work for the Co-operative Movement as a poorly-paid journalist, contributing much of his service free, so that he might sell his paper cheaply and reach as many Irish homes as possible. It was through his newspaper that he found a voice for many of Ireland's emerging young writers.

AE became deeply involved in the Irish Literary Revival and was a friend of W. B. Yeats for many years. They visited one another and together became interested in dreams, in theosophy and oriental mysticism. AE's home on Rathgar Avenue was a literary rendezvous. He gave himself unreservedly to the encouragement of young poets and writers – Higgins, O'Connor, O'Faolain, O'Sullivan. 'There was hardly a young writer in Ireland who did not owe to AE his initial encouragement in literature'.[52]

Kavanagh's early association with AE, as well as the success at having some of his poems accepted for publication in the *Irish Statesman*, gave him the impetus he needed to get launched as a writer. AE's own poems provided an initial guideline. Soon Kavanagh's poem 'The Intangible' appears in print bearing an undeniable resemblance to the work of his mentor AE.

> Rapt to starriness – not quite
> I go through fields and fens of night,
> The nameless, the void
> Where ghostly poplars whisper to
> A silent countryside.
> (Two and two are not four
> On every shore).

The final couplet included by Alan Warner, omitted in later editions of the poem, shows Kavanagh's early belief in the non-calculable and is, in Warner's opinion, distinctly reminiscent of AE's influence.[53] Indeed, the mystical seascapes painted by AE show ethereal nymphs and goddesses playing on idyllic shores. His canvases reflect intimations of a world beyond the sensory world. Lines from Kavanagh's 'Ploughman', published in the *Irish Statesman* in February 1930, impressed AE to the extent that he felt this young Co Monaghan farmer was not to be under-estimated as a poet:

I find a star-lovely art

In a dark sod.

'Any man who can write that line,' he said, 'is a genius, even if other lines are dismissible'.[54]

Kavanagh, at this time, was anxious to find a direction for his literary life. Eager to touch the centre of literary inspiration, he set out for Dublin on foot during the late autumn of 1930. He badly wanted to meet AE in person, and any of the literary names whom he had he had discovered through the *Irish Statesman*. AE was at home in Rathgar Avenue for this brief visit during which he became Kavanagh's first real literary professor. Kavanagh, footsore from his travels, left AE's house that evening laden with books which, though heavy in weight, were eagerly perused on the long journey back to Inniskeen. Dependent no longer solely on schoolbook anthologies which had served him well, he could now read and re-read authors which until now had been unavailable to him. It was AE who gave him the first real books he owned which he could now study at leisure. He discovered Melville and the symbolic world of *Moby Dick* which for Kavanagh was a spiritual landscape. From *Moby Dick* and later from *Ulysses*, he learnt the possibilities within literature of exploring a physical space that is placeless, bound not by geographical confines but limitless as the human soul.[55] With little formal education, Kavanagh had chosen the best of literary models.

Though the *Irish Statesman* was soon to become defunct as a publication, it had helped Kavanagh on his literary journey. AE had cleared a path for the young writer. Kavanagh identified with the wisdom and spiritual depth of AE. He had perhaps found in him a literary wisdom figure who confirmed his belief in a world of spirit beyond the world of commonsense. Kavanagh was indeed aware of a beauty hidden at the heart of life which was always on the verge of breaking through. For AE, Kavanagh was likely to have represented the ideal of Irish farming life itself – the authentic peasant he had so often idealised. In AE's own poem 'Ploughman', he is prophetically making way for a new and authentic rural Irish voice, 'the hero of the plough'.

> Clear the brown path, to meet his coulter's gleam
> Lo! on he comes behind his smoking team
> With toil's bright dewdrops on his sunburnt brow
> The lord of earth, the hero of the plough.

Where Kavanagh and he most concurred was in the belief that appearances do not capture the whole truth. Kavanagh's senses continually probed beneath the surface of life. He saw the lissome figure of a woman hidden in the scavenging of a tinker's wife on a dunghill, and Christ in the 'uncouth ballad seller/ With tail-matted hair'. (*Street-Corner Christ*)

Likewise, AE believed that every man 'deep beneath his rustic habit finds himself a king'.[56] Both had spiritual insight capable of penetrating to the heart of things. But Kavanagh, it must be said, was gifted with powers of expression that out-dazzled his contemporaries. Paul Vincent Carroll believed that AE would have wanted to guide his protege towards Indian thought, seeing the potential mystic in him. But Kavanagh was too deeply immersed in the faith of his childhood. He even took responsibility on occasion for keeping the springs of his religion clean and unsullied, and drinking only where its depths were purest. Years later, in one of his sweeping critiques of Irish poetry in *Kavanagh's Weekly*, he spoke, with regret presumably, of his religious divergence from his first 'candle of vision'.

> AE, a remarkable man, wrote some good poems, and it was a pity that he should have buried his authentic genius in the vasty deeps of the Upanishads.[57]

Kavanagh gradually discovered his own voice and his own mysticism which remained foundationally Christian. He soon outgrew and surpassed his first poetic mentor. But he did not forget his debt to AE. In a radio broadcast for BBC in 1946, he paid tribute to the goodness and authentic patriotism of the man who first published his work. Kavanagh admired the virtue and goodness of a man who he said did more to produce a 'union of hearts' in this country than 'any Wolfe Tonery'.[58]

AE was the first to see that Kavanagh had his own authentic vision. This encouragement was vital to the fuller awakening which would occur when, freed from the daily round of farming tasks, he would explore his vision still further. AE's legacy of books meant that he now had models to study at will. His method of reading shows how he designed his own 'university' courses in literature!

Kavanagh's Method of Reading

To appreciate the literary and spiritual preparation that was taking place in the young poet, it is important to notice the method of reading which Patrick Kavanagh practised as a young man. Apart from newspapers which he is said to have 'devoured', he tended to read small amounts rather than at length. He describes the ritual he has devised for entering into the world of a poem. First, he repaired to his favourite den, the attic-room above the kitchen with its slanting ceiling. Winter and summer, seated beside the old Howe sewing-machine table, thick with the candle-grease of years, he studied and wrote. This corner was his Parnassus'.[59] The moment is described in *The Green Fool:*

> I would open a secret drawer and take out a bundle of newspaper and magazine cuttings. These cuttings were my real library: every one of these cuttings contained a poem that was important for me: there was one among them could visualise the moment's mood ... I seldom read a book through; when I had found and read the significant word or phrase, I would close the book, feeling that to read further would only do harm. I had again been baptised by fire and the Holy Spirit.[60]

Reading slowly and meditatively provided healing and nourishment for the young poet. Sometimes it was 'a school reader, brown with the droppings of thatch' described in 'The Great Hunger', which sustained him or a few lines of *Madame Bovary* which he kept within reach in his Parnassus-den. His character Tarry Flynn deployed the same reading technique:

His method of getting a thrill out of this book and of all exciting books was by not reading them through, but by opening
them at random and giving a quick look inside. Then he
would shut the book again lest the magic should escape.[61]

By deliberately limiting the amount he read, he discovered 'that
the single poem by itself possessed far more power than when
included in a volume'.[62] This art of reading which he practised,
albeit unknowingly, was that of *lectio divina*, the daily medita-
tive exercise engaged in by monks of the monastic tradition.[63]
Each day the monk took a passage of scripture, his 'sacred page',
read it slowly, paying attention to each word and its various
shades of meaning, and as the Holy Spirit illumined the page
with insight, the monk was counselled to stay where he found
nourishment, to ruminate, repeat it continuously until he had
learned it by heart. Passages thus learned belonged to the memory of the heart and lead the monk to prayer. Patrick Kavanagh
unwittingly used the monastic reading-method which was a
preparation for contemplative prayer. He became inspired by
this well-practised ritual and often admitted to feeling the
power of the Holy Spirit at work in him. He continued the practice into later life:

My system is curious. I keep reading the same book over and
over, perhaps for six months, every day, and then switch to
another which may last me the same time. Altogether I have
not read more than six or seven books during the past number of years.[64]

From frequent rumination of texts he was gradually developing,
wittingly or unwittingly, his contemplative and mystical facul-
ties. For the monk the goal of *lectio* is *oratio* or *contemplatio*, and
so it was for Kavanagh. His method of reading inspired texts
was a kind of prayer. Indeed he frequently likened poetry to
prayer and monitored the gradual awakening of his poetic soul,
from its birth in a 'Mucker fog' to his 'rebirth' as a poet 'on the
Banks of the Grand Canal'.

III

AWAKENING: A LITERARY THEME IN KAVANAGH

For Patrick Kavanagh, the experience of awakening poetically and spiritually were virtually synonymous. Though unsophisticated in formal psychology, Kavanagh nevertheless attempted to confront a lack of self-awareness in himself and in his environment. He knew it was possible to 'awaken' out of the slumber of 'unconsciousness' and experience a higher level of existence. The struggle to awaken into consciousness took a long time and became one of the central themes of his writing.

'It was a long journey … from … Monaghan … to the banks of the Grand Canal in nineteen-fifty-five, the year of my hegira.'[65] For Kavanagh, this was an inner journey as well as an outer one. He journeyed out of what he calls his 'the chrysalis stage' into full awakening as a poet and as a person in 1955. The blinkers of unawareness, he believes, had only then fallen from his eyes. Before, he had seen partially as through a fog, now he had finally 'awakened spiritually'.[66] In describing his self-emergence Kavanagh uses a language full of spiritual overtones, a language not unlike that used by Underhill in her treatment of mysticism. His awakening from embeddedness in 'the fog of family life' reaches a state of illumination which he marks as his 'hegira'.

Even while asleep in the womb of family life, a process of awakening was already taking place. A family well predisposed towards faith, education, schoolbook poetry, legends and folklore, were feeding 'the chrysalis' and preparing its eventual emergence. School, church and neighbourhood, as we have seen, also contributed to this spiritual preparation. Yet he insists he was still 'asleep', 'all my dreams were sealed in the bud'.[67] The 'sleep' or 'fog' that surrounded the first twenty years of his life was, in the main, positive. This was his Eden time, his 'garden of the golden apples', a period when he was 'happy all the time', his first Paradise.

Awakening was taking place in a relatively secure ambience, nourished mythologically by a 'view (that reached) back to the days of St Patrick and the druids'.[68] Despite its confines, it allowed him to thrive on the spiritual food he needed. In an environment materially poor, yet rich in folk-wisdom and oral tradition, the imagination was stretched. Here (in south-east Ulster) he says, 'the soul must expand or die'.[69] Though Kavanagh would later become aware of the detrimental dimension of his past, nevertheless it provided him with an initial world that was 'pure positive', a state of mind he would always seek to recapture. He recalls a typical idyllic scene from his youth where he already heard the signals of his awakening:

> (I was) walking through a field called Lurgankeel … it is an October evening and all around me is the protecting fog of family life. How shall I live when the fog is blown away and I am left alone naked?[70]

The thought of launching out alone as a writer filled him with dread.

The Stalk of Memory

Constant rumination on the past allowed the poet reach new levels of awareness. 'On the stalk of memory,' he says, 'imagination blossoms.' Kavanagh is often more eloquent in retrospect when he recalls a moment from the past. The poem 'Kerr's Ass' harkens back to an early phase of his life, a vivid childhood event, a defining moment of awakening. The scene is poetically built up with meticulous attention to detail. The first ten lines prepare the setting which is to become revelatory, prophetic.

> We borrowed the loan of Kerr's big ass
> To go to Dundalk with butter,
> Brought him home the evening before the market
> An exile that night in Mucker.
>
> We heeled up the cart before the door,
> We took the harness inside –
> The straw-stuffed straddle, the broken breeching
> With bits of bull-wire tied;
>
> The winkers that had no choke-band,
> The collar and the reins...

In Ealing Broadway, London Town
I name their several names…
(Kerr's Ass)

The poet, an exile himself in London, dreams himself back into 'the protecting fog of family life' where he is not yet awakened to his destiny. The family then moved in unison; he is part of the 'we' that was immersed in 'pre-reflective lived experience' which poets like Heaney and Kavanagh hold to be the very stuff of poetry.[71] Here life is unthinking, serene in the sureness and certainty of traditional know-how. The well-worn harness with its 'bits of bull-wire tied', speaks of generations of use and taken-for-granted skills. The poet's retentive memory caressingly names each detail with the wonder of a child and the nostalgia of a romantic. Until, overcome with poetic passion, he delivers what he has carried faithfully in the 'roundtower of his heart', a memory of his early poetic awakening. This birth has incubated deep within his soul.

… A world comes to life –
Morning, the silent bog,
And the God of imagination waking
In a Mucker fog.

The birth of a poet, a new day packed with expectation, a rural townland on the brink of immortalisation, a brand new literary idiom, a single individual rising Icarus-like out of the soil … out of the crowd … Kavanagh realises that the possibilities within this moment are endless. It has the signs of a spiritual event.

Trapped in the 'fog'
But the pernicious dimension of the 'fog' that enveloped him also slowly became apparent. In many ways the mind-set induced by this 'fog' stifled personal thought and cramped originality. The 'true flame' which is at the heart of poetry was being dampened by a kind of unconscious torpor or lethargy that characterised peasant rural life at this time. Herd mentality and tribal ethos were rampant. In a Kierkegaardian way he was aware of the mindless anonymity caused by unthinking people

/ho lack authentic selfhood. He also saw the peasant in a negative light: one who exists in 'a state of permanent darkness'… 'who never thinks, who has no mind to be damaged'.[72] The unthinking peasant or artisan, he felt, typified an inferior quality of life of which he too was a victim. In his early years he felt he belonged to 'that mass of mankind which lives below a certain level of consciousness'. To emerge from this 'sub-soil of existence', Kavanagh realised, was tantamount to being born anew and uttering again the first terrified primal scream. For those who 'live in the dark cave of the unconscious' it would be painful to emerge into a state of 'awakenness.' These unfortunates 'scream when they see the light'.[73]

Although he believed that he was once part of the fog and only very gradually emerged from it, he was awake to his condition sooner than he realised. By 1947, his autobiographical Tarry Flynn was in a state of awakenness. He is aware of a transcendent light playing on the earth: 'Tarry had seen beyond the fog, the Eternal light shining on the stones'.[74] When Kavanagh embarked on his major work, 'The Great Hunger', in the early 1940s, it is already evident that he had awakened to the futility of being fog-bound, mentally enslaved by the land, by his mother's gospel of hard work, and by oppressive church teaching. The chrysalis was stirring into life. His prophetic eyes were slowly opening. The experience was frightening:

> If any man of them in that country were to open his eyes, if the fog in which they lived lifted, they would be unable to endure the futility of it all.

Kavanagh's lone, original vision was awaiting expression. His reading of T. S. Eliot had had its influence. Through *The Irish Statesman* he had become aware of 'The Waste Land' and had hoped to borrow a copy when he visited the National Library in Dublin in 1930. 'Human kind / Cannot bear very much reality,' says Eliot in 'Burnt Norton'; likewise the people of Kavanagh's 'waste land' were unable to confront the 'great hunger' that gnawed at their vitals. Kavanagh, alone would name the demon:

the hungry fiend (that)

Screams the apocalypse of clay

In every corner of this land.

He would face the futility of it all, not with 'the courage of the blind' which he believed was the way of pseudo-Christian courage, but as one awake, open-eyed, aware of the full reality. Layer by layer, the protective fog was stripped away until, like Kierkegaard, he became 'that individual', 'alone, alone in the whole world, alone before God'.[75] Ultimately he knew:

You have not got a chance with fraud

And might as well be true to God. *(Prelude)*

Kavanagh would be 'naked and alone' as he had once forecast while 'walking through a field called Lurgankeel'. Nakedness and aloneness was the price he must pay for his unique vision and rare sensibility. His only reward was that he became himself an original authentic voice, unswayed by the popular idioms and images of the Literary Revival in vogue at that time:

I almost achieved being born eight years earlier, that was in 1947 when I realised for the first time the absurdity and the lie called 'the Irish Literary movement'.[76]

One by one he confronted and discarded peripheral disguises. The Dublin literary set were anxious to affix to this 'rare bird' a label. Here was the authentic peasant poet, the perfect specimen of rural Ireland. He refused easy labels, preferring to plough a lone furrow, intent on being his own inalienable self. His spiritual genesis occurred when, stripped of everything, reduced to failure and the ignominy of a lost law-suit, he was, as a final blow, struck down by a life-threatening illness. He was facing death. He described the anguish and mental suffering of this period as 'unspeakable'. This was 1954, the year he developed lung cancer which brought with it 'a horrible desolation of spirit' coupled with a 'feeling of degradation'. He believed that his involvement that year in a painful lawsuit against *The Leader* was responsible for his debility. Spiritually speaking, he was undergoing the most intense purification of his life. But this agony thankfully signalled the stirring of regeneration. Being born 'spiritually', he told the students of UCD in 1956, was 'like coming out of darkness into light' – a terrible pain.[77]

Spiritual Rebirth

It was while recuperating from a successful surgery that he experienced the first fruits of his spiritual rebirth. The new voice that speaks in the Canal Bank poems is sure, original, 'eloquently new and abandoned'. A spiritual event of this magnitude calls for some religious ritual celebration, a commemoration akin to baptism, a new life or a death to the past:

Commemorate me where there is water,

Canal water preferably…

(Lines Written on a Seat on the Grand Canal)

He asks not for a tomb, but for the new garment of mystical initiation:

For this soul needs to be honoured with a new dress woven

From green and blue things and arguments that cannot be proven.

His spiritual genesis had originated when a girl's voice broke into his consciousness with lines from Mangan's poem:

I walked entranced

Through a land of morn …

'That girl' he said, 'awoke in me for the first time those feelings that are beyond the reach of reason.' In 'Canal Bank Walk' he had returned to that place glimpsed as a boy, and recovered a new-found belief in 'arguments that cannot be proven'. He called this his 'hegira,' his spiritual rebirth; a new beginning, though it was indeed the culmination of a long and arduous spiritual journey.

The end of all our exploring

Will be to arrive where we started

And know the place for the first time.[78]

Kavanagh's rebirth, as we shall see in more detail in Chapter Seven, had much more in common with Christian resurrection than it had with the Muslim experience of 'hegira'.

Conclusion

Although it is important to take Kavanagh at his word when he declares that 'a man's environment has nothing to do with his soul',[79] the effects of his first milieu were important. They made an indelible imprint on the poet's early development and spiritual formation. 'The world that matters is the world we have created,' he insists.[80] He did indeed create his Monaghan hills poetically, but they in turn made him 'the kind of man' he was. *(Monaghan Hills)*.

'The land keeps a man silent for a generation or two and then the crust gives way. A poet is born or a prophet'.[81] Kavanagh was never quite sure which he was. In his case there was little difference between them. He became the eloquent and often blunt spokesman for a world that was timeless and placeless. Although he was inculturated by his whitethorn hedges, he became mentally independent of his environment.

Indeed, Kavanagh's first environment was packed with hidden stimuli which contributed in no small way to the awakening of his poetic and mystical sensibilities. Scenically, the little hills and small triangular fields prepared him for moments of revelation when he climbed Rocksavage ring-fort and contemplated 'Slieve Gullion, the sacred mountain … a place of mystery'. Sage-like figures inhabited his landscape, primitive minds untouched by formal education stirred his imagination and brought him into contact with a rich vein of native lore. Oral tradition achieved this even more powerfully than the written word, since Kavanagh was capable of communing deeply with all living bearers of tradition.

Fr Finlay SJ was well-versed in the Jesuit pedagogy that promised a spiritually healthy manhood based on sound early training. He undoubtedly influenced the student-poet through his schoolbook anthologies which were designed to mould the sensibilities of readers and shape hearts and spirits as well as youthful minds. Many of the educators of that era understood the nation's struggle for recovery in the post-Famine years. Irish schools were attempting to combat illiteracy and demoralisation. Finlay was one of those who laboured towards the goal of a new and better Ireland. Kavanagh, unknowingly, came under his influence.

Booklessness, school anthologies apart, was not a handicap for Kavanagh, who could ruminate a text like a monk and suck out all its marrow, drawing vital nourishment from the material at his disposal. His schoolbooks were sufficiently rich and varied to furnish him with an excellent foundation for his literary and spiritual journey. When a text appealed to him he completely appropriated it, often copying it by hand and committing it to memory.

Miss Cassidy's proficiency as a teacher imposed the discipline he needed. She was after all an award-winning teacher, which inspired confidence in parents and children alike. The two women teachers of Kednaminsha National School had their own aesthetic standards. Kavanagh recalls: 'when there was no more fire in the grate in our school the fireplace was filled with lilac in due season'. Such a splash of colour and the 'madly gay scent' of the blooms in the classroom brought a breath of poetry into the young boy's life. Writing in the *Irish Farmers Journal* in May 1959, he cannot but recall Walt Whitman's poem 'When Lilacs Last in the Dooryard Bloom'd', 1865-66:

When lilacs last in the dooryard bloom'd
And the Great star early droop'd in the western sky in the night ...

Similarly, the erudite Canon Maguire with his punctilious attention to words and to the translation of Mass texts was an added enrichment for an aspiring wordsmith.[82]

During his formative years Kavanagh was intent on filling his poetic 'trucks of language' as he pleased. Even after he left school he purused his sisters' and brother's schoolbooks and made his own selections. His personal likes were subjective. He sampled Hood, Campbell, Tennyson, Byron and Harte, repeating their lines as though they were his own. He allowed Mangan bewitch him, Moore fill his ears with music, Proctor console him with romantic thoughts, and Longfellow fashion a 'roundtower' in his heart, a sanctuary where he stored his romantic longings.

During his long preparation as a poet, 1918-1930, he drew solace from this hidden repertoire. His fondness for the ballads that appeared in *Ireland's Own* and *Old Moore's Almanac* remained with him all his life. Moved at the news of the poet's death while on temporary leave in Canada, John Jordan wrote:

> ... when I realise that all the gaiety has been eclipsed, that never again will I hear him sing a ballad by Richard D'Alton Williams or 'Lord Ullin's Daughter', never again quote with alarming accuracy Pope or Johnson or Goldsmith or Edward Martyn trying to get George Moore to go to Mass, my eyes wetten and I feel I can write no more.[83]

Jordan was aware that Kavanagh's education was unique and probably more extensive than was generally believed. Self-selected, it aimed at nourishing the heart and soul. He was not burdened by inert mental luggage likely to bloat his ego and inhibit him spiritually. His sensibility had been fine-tuned to his own liking.

Coincidentally, it was Finlay's colleague and friend, AE, who was the 'candle of vision' in Kavanagh's emerging life as a poet. Here he was to meet a kindred spirit, one who understood the strange light he saw on the hills and who believed in a reality which lay beyond appearances. It was fitting that AE, the established mystic, should introduce Kavanagh to the literary world. He encouraged him to write. Kavanagh needed this encouragement to leave farming, and head for 'the City of the Kings'. *(Temptation in Harvest)* Exile in Dublin was to be a necessary purification of his poetic and mystical consciousness. Distance and separation from his native Inniskeen would induce new levels of awareness in an already sensitised spirit. Indeed suffering and purification, as we shall see, were no strangers to Kavanagh.

At great personal cost to himself, he would continue to awaken until the moment of his spiritual rebirth, his nirvana ... enlightenment ... hegira ... resurrection ... on the banks of the Grand Canal. Clearsightedness and wide-awakeness cost him a lifetime's suffering and loneliness.[84] His hegira was, as the Muslim word denotes, both a departure and a return to where he had always been. But Kavanagh was really speaking of Christian res-urrection, a re-baptism into the one he had always been, 'a child of God' doing 'the will of God', wallow(ing) in the habitual. He would date this baptism as a poet from the summer of 1955. In the words of Eliot's 'Little Gidding', he had now reached a sim-plification and transformation of soul:

A condition of complete simplicity

(Costing not less than everything)

Purification, patiently and impatiently borne, we shall see, be-came central to Kavanagh's life as a writer and as a person.

CHAPTER 4

Purification I

The sharp knife of Jansen
Cuts all the green branches...
(Lough Derg)

Through a chink too wide there comes in no wonder.
(Advent)

I

CONTINENTAL CATHOLICISM

Patrick Kavanagh, born and bred in a Catholic environment, was instinctively religious-minded. He regretted the passing of an older Celtic faith which was slowly disintegrating during his boyhood. 'The ghost of a culture,' he felt 'haunted the snub-nosed hills'.[1]

> The arrival of continental Catholicism finally disposed of the druidic culture ... So the wakes passed out, and we all began to wear long faces.[2]

Wistfully he hankered back to an older Celtic belief in the blessedness of the earth. He extolled the beauty of 'whitethorn blossoms' and 'the smell from ditches that were not Christian'. *(Why Sorrow?)* As a youth he found affinity with the blackbird who, like himself, was 'a pagan poet', a celtic sun-worshipper who lost his god 'at set of sun'. *(To a Blackbird)* Early Celtic Christianity had prayerfully ritualised each daily task, from the kindling of the fire in the morning to 'smooring' it at night.[3] There were birth blessings, milking prayers, a prayer at the new moon, and protection blessings. Romanised Catholicism, however, was church-centred with emphasis on ecclesial laws and rubrics. It sought to wean people away from the superstitious, chaotic, colourful world of Carleton's nineteenth century *Trait and Stories*, and bring them into the newly reformed post-Synod-of-Thurles church.

To Archbishop Paul Cullen (1850-1878) was entrusted the task of reforming the Irish Church in the wake of the Great Famine, and so in August 1850, he convoked a Synod at Thurles at which the bishop of every diocese was ordered to attend. As a result of this Synod, new laws were promulgated. The priests were henceforth ordered to wear 'black or dark clothes', keep their distance from the people, and discourage participation in local patterns and pilgrimages to holy wells.[4] These were seen to be filled, as they oftentimes were, with superstition and even idolatry. Instead of reforming these practices, they were summarily replaced. In their place, there emerged 'a rash of "continental devotions"', Missions, Novenas, Sodalities and Confraternities which changed the face of Irish Catholicism during the second half of the nineteenth century.

Kavanagh felt personally betrayed by 'romanised catholicism'. He remonstrated that St Patrick had created a healthy precedent by incorporating 'the colours and mystical depths' of paganism into his new teaching of Christianity. Not so Cardinal Cullen, who sought to eradicate the old by implanting the new. The outcome for Kavanagh was that religion had now become church-centred, over-serious, over-legalised and had deliberately broken with the local patterns and pilgrimages of the past. His conclusion that 'we all began to wear long faces' pointed to a Jansenistic influence that was all-pervasive.[5] The official church undertook the promotion of a strong theology of suffering to make bearable 'the poverty-stricken society' which prevailed in Ireland in the wake of the famine.[6]

Pastoral Practice in Ireland: 'The Sharp knife of Jansen'

There was much that Kavanagh deplored in the religious ethos of his time. The Ireland of the early 1900s, he felt, had lost touch with its past. Gone were colourful festivals with their healthy blend of religion and celebration. Fasting and prayer was followed, on such occasions, by dancing and merry-making. His own local 'Bohar Bhee' was the old pilgrim's way to Lady Well on the outskirts of Dundalk. This ancient road, he felt, 'twisted by quiet fields away from the clever villages that laughed at ancient holiness'. The new romanised pastoral practice promulgated after the Synod of Thurles seemed, by comparison, solemn, rubric-conscious, guilt-ridden, and permeated with Jansenistic teaching. More pernicious still, it was considered more respectable than its Celtic antecedent.

Kavanagh was correct in his assessment of the change that had occurred. Its damage had been far-reaching. To make matters worse, periodic letters were issued from Maynooth by the joint body of archbishops and bishops on matters pertaining to faith and morals to consolidate the work done by the Synod. One of these letters, the famous denunciation-of-dance-halls letter, came as 'a word of entreaty, advice and instruction... on a very grave subject'. The diary of *The Irish Catholic Directory* for 1926 records the statement in full. It is entitled: 'Statement of the Archbishops and Bishops of Ireland issued at their Meeting, held in Maynooth, on October 6, 1925.' This letter, still alive in the memory of our oldest citizens, was to be read 'until otherwise arranged ... at the principal Mass on the first Sunday of each Quarter of the Ecclesiastical year'. Thus, the people were constantly reminded of 'the dangers of the flesh' and the 'occasions of sin' which they must avoid. Kavanagh, a young man of twenty-two, heard the letter read, probably at eleven-thirty Mass in Inniskeen. The tone of the letter was ominous:

> We have a word of entreaty, advice and instruction to speak to our flocks on a very grave subject. There is danger of losing the name which the chivalrous honour of Irish boys and the Christian reserve of Irish maidens has won for Ireland.[7]

The great name of Ireland, it seems, was being sullied, our national strength dissipated, 'the Christian reserve of Irish maidens' abandoned and 'the chivalrous honour of Irish boys' placed in jeopardy. And there was 'no worse fomenter of this great evil than the dancing hall'. Purity and faith were the two great virtues being assailed, purity being in greatest danger:

The danger comes from pictures and papers and drink. It comes more from the keeping of improper company than from any other cause ...We know too well the fruit of these halls all over the country ... They have brought many a good innocent girl into sin, shame and scandal and set her unwary feet on the road that leads to perdition ... Action has to be taken while the character of the people as a whole is still sound to stop the dangerous laxity that has been creeping into town and country.[8]

Imported dances from London and Paris were also denounced. Irish dances were promoted on the grounds that 'Irish dances do not make degenerates'. 'All-night Dances' (nine until two) were seen to be the worst occasions of sin and were allowed 'only in special circumstances and under the most careful control'. Dances until midnight were the alternative, but even these were suspended during the season of Lent, implying that, though tolerated, dancing was an impediment to real holiness. Knox, writing on Jansenism in his book *Enthusiasm*, explains that 'disapproval of dancing ... or of the theatre was a mark of Jansenism long after Jansenism had ceased to be a genuine religious inspiration'.[9] Indeed, theatre-going was forbidden to priests until after the Second Vatican Council (1965).

The episcopal letter denouncing dances and their attendant dangers was read in every parish throughout the country to the consternation of the dance-going population. In some places where common sense prevailed, the letter, after a few initial readings, was conveniently forgotten. Nevertheless, 'company-keeping' was seen to be a transgression serious enough to be mentioned at monthly confession. Fr Gilmartin, the local curate at Inniskeen (1917-1935), was renowned for his efforts at keeping the letter of the law in this matter. He was to be seen on the road after the dances armed with a blackthorn stick, chasing couples away from 'dangerous occasions of sin'.

But church letters continued. A full-scale Pastoral Address was issued in 1927 by the Plenary Synod held at Maynooth in August 1927. The clergy were asked to redouble their efforts to safeguard the moral fibre of society. It was shortly after this time that 'dancing at the crossroads' was finally banished and a new phase of commercial dance hall building began.

An anti-life mentality

Deck-dancing had been in vogue in rural Ireland long before dance-halls became fashionable. Patrick Kavanagh and his friends, Tarry Lennon (alias Eusebius Cassidy) and Frank Cassidy, would congregate near the deck at Annavackey on summer Sunday evenings in the early 1930s. Annavackey, about two miles from Inniskeen, belonged to a different diocese. It was in the parish of Upper Creggan, in Louth in the diocese of Armagh, just outside the limits of what was once the Pale. Regulations regarding the times and duration of dances varied from diocese to diocese, so that the local people, straddling two sets of diocesan regulations, would check in *The Dundalk Democrat* for the less stringent rules. To Kavanagh's mind, Annavackey provided the most liberal choice at that time.

This crossroads was unremarkable except that it formed the intersection between the Inniskeen and Dundalk roads. It was a popular location for gatherings engaged at 'pitch and toss'. Kavanagh enjoyed the view it afforded of Slieve Gullion and south-Armagh, the country of south-east Ulster poets like MacCubhthaigh, MacCuarta and Ó Doirnín. From his customary perch on the roadside bank he held Glassdrummond chapel in his direct line of vision. During the early 1930s he recalls standing there contemplating the magical setting, enjoying its gaiety and simplicity. His joy was short-lived when a young priest 'fresh from Maynooth' descended on the scene with orders to disperse. In a scathing article entitled 'Sex and Christianity', Kavanagh recalls this occasion and deplores the erroneousness of its 'anti-life' gospel.[10]

> ... In this exciting country, the melodeons were playing and life itself was dancing, when up the road on his bicycle came a little black priest who could not have been long out of college. This little man got up on the fence and ordered us to

disperse, which we did. I was ashamed of these young boys and girls, who knew so little about their own religion not to realise that this little man was acting from impulses that were pernicious.

Thus ended the cross-roads dance in that part of the country. Thus was ushered in the era of the commercial dance hall with its disease-laden atmosphere.[11]

The suppression of deck-dancing at Annavackey left a vacuum in people's lives. It had been organised and financed by the people themselves.[12] It was an outdoor, Sunday afternoon activity, regulated by the elements and by natural daylight. The criticism against deck-dancing was that it encouraged courting, drinking and fist-fighting, incidents well documented by Carleton. The clergy considered that deck-dancing was responsible for many disorderly crossroads scenes such as the one described in *Tarry Flynn* when 'a young girl … was set upon by a crowd of black-guards … and the clothes torn off her back'. It is obvious from the *Tarry Flynn* narrative that this incident is more imaginary, wishful thinking even, than actual.

The removal of the decks set the scene for a new era of commercial dance halls.[13] The clergy, originally convinced that dancing was 'a dangerous occasion of sin', were now, in many cases, ready to control it along with its revenue for parish funds. They became involved in a strict supervision of the dance hall area. Kavanagh was aware that they were not equipped for this job. Moreover, by removing the decks, the people were denied the task of organising their own amusement. He concludes by stating angrily: 'if there is disease in the body of Irish society, the young priests sent out by Maynooth are not free from the blame'.[14] Jansenism, he perceived, was sapping the vitality of the people. Ironically it was controversy between the promoters of 'Mullagh' dance hall at one end of the parish of Inniskeen and the 'Parochial Hall' at the other which initially inspired Kavanagh to write his novel *Tarry Flynn*.

'Somewhere in the nineteenth century … an anti-life heresy entered religion,' was Kavanagh's assessment in the *Kavanagh's*

Weekly, 24 May, 1951. Jansenism, Kavanagh believed, was 'the root cause of much of the puritanical brand of pastoral theology with which young emigre professors from the Sorbonne infected Maynooth in its foundations'. He was to some degree correct in his assertions. A deeply pessimistic view of human nature, along with a belief in the virtual impossibility of being saved by God's grace, was at the heart of Jansenism. Its proponents preached a religion of rigorism and legalism, relying more on principles of law than of an understanding of God's mercy and love.[15] Reviewing Joseph O' Connor's novel *Hostage to Fortune* (1952) in *Kavanagh's Weekly*, Kavanagh agrees with the author that Jansenism propounded a 'gloomy doctrine' that 'man's natural appetites are breaches in his defences against the assaults of Satan on the citadel of his immortal soul'.[16] Morality was seen not as the soul's protection but as a boulder set to crush life:

> In the gap there's a bush weighted with boulders like morality,
>
> The fools of life bleed if they climb over. *(The Great Hunger)*

Ironically, the priest described by O'Connor was preaching an anti-life doctrine to a congregation too starved to be interested in concupiscence. Likewise, the customary renewal of baptismal vows at the end of the Inniskeen Mission presented Kavanagh with an equally ludicrous anomaly. Tarry Flynn saw this collection of confirmed bachelors as 'old blackguards … being flattered by bawdy suggestions' and 'as intense a crowd of barren virgins as had ever gathered together at the same time in that church'.[17] All vowed 'to renounce the World, the Flesh and the Devil'. Whatever about the devil, the sad truth was that they had access to very little temptation in matters of the world and the flesh. Their 'self-abnegation' and earnest promise 'to control their passions' the author saw as 'pathetic'.

The church, he believed, had somehow failed to respond to the real needs of the people. He strongly advocates that Irish priests 'return to "real Catholicism"', and root their religion 'in life'. He also recommends that they 'accept sin as a commonplace' … and 'look at it clearly without fear'.[18] The Irish Catholicism being preached, he believed, lacked depth. It was 'too sentimental and pious to have real roots'. Consequently immigrants working in England fell away quickly from the practice of their religion. He concluded that 'what is needed is depth of spirituality and real backbone'. Religion had driven a wedge between life and spirituality. Its creed was an almost complete negation of incarnation. In Jordan's words, it was 'an extended blasphemy against Creation'.[19]

Kavanagh was correct in stating that the 'anti-life' gospel currently preached was bordering on the heretical. The new age in the Irish church seemed to expect its followers to be immune from concupiscence. The beauty of the flesh became the reserve of an ancient pagan Irish religion which had been banished by an erroneous interpretation of Christianity:

'I renounce the World,' a young woman cried

Her breasts stood high in the pagan sun.

'I renounce...' an old monk followed. Then a fat lawyer.

They rejected one by one

The music of Time's choir. (Lough Derg)

The 'music of Time's choir' was Kavanagh's real interest. His 'Lough Derg' and his unfinished 'Why sorrow?' were intent on exploring the unresolved tension between flesh and spirit, between life and anti-life, between a joyous and sorrowful religion. How can love of created beauty, including the attraction of the flesh, be consonant with the love of God? Does the church which purports to be a wise Mother, sometimes not offer its children stones instead of bread? He struggled with the rigorous teaching of this new brand of religion which required that the erotic dimension of life be eliminated until expressed within the bonds of marriage:

The sharp knife of Jansen

Cuts all the green branches,

Not sunlight comes in

But the hot-iron sin

Branding the shame

Of a beast in the Name

Of Christ on the breast

Of a child of the West.(Lough Derg)

Kavanagh perceived the condemnation of all matters sexual, along with an exaggerated emphasis on self-denial, as destructive of religion. Life itself was endangered by the over zealous 'knife of Jansen'. He wondered if the literal interpretation of church teaching could co-exist with the continuance of human life itself. He was perhaps nearer the truth than he realised, since St Augustine's categoric humiliation of the flesh had resulted in a strongly pessimistic view of sexuality. The implicit slur on marriage incurred by such thinking resulted not only in spectres of frustrated desire stalking the landscape of 'The Great Hunger', but the unnatural predominance of singleness even among city-girls during the 1950s:

> Not a kick, not a kick in the heart
> Of the land
> But only a slow desperation –
> Girls hurrying to their sodality meetings,
> Girls hurrying to the theatre,
> Girls with girls,
> Walking to their chastity graves.
> (The Ghost Land)[20]

Jordan is one of the few critics who gives Kavanagh credit for his astute theological reflection. He believes that Kavanagh is one of the few Catholic writers who attempts 'to understand ... and treat with compassion' the current 'perversion of the Catholic teaching on sex and marriage'. The scene in Tarry Flynn of a church filled with bachelors and 'barren virgins' corresponds with the low marriage-rate in rural Ireland from the early 1900s onwards. The Central Statistics Office shows that from a population of 74,611 in Co Monaghan in 1901, only 0.4 per cent were married while 99.5 per cent were single or widowed.[21] The underlying sociological reasons for this state of affairs were being ignored by the church. Inniskeen's state of marriagelessness was typical of rural Irish society at this time. Land holdings were miserably small and could not afford further subdivisions. Kavanagh's words were quite true when he has his Old Priest say:

> In my parish for twenty years
> There isn't a marriage to sneer at.
> (*The Wake of the Books*)

The parish Mission provided the only place where sex was discussed, so that parishioners flocked to hear sermons where sex and company-keeping were denounced. With mischievous innuendo, Kavanagh suggests that only at such times was the 'limp body of society' momentarily 'lifted up'. Yet once the mission was over, people returned of necessity to their unimaginative, death-like existence where, in the words of 'The Great Hunger', 'life is more lousy than savage'. The awfulness of the spectre is captured in Kavanagh's unforgettable lines:

> Like the after-birth of a cow stretched on a branch in the wind
> Life dried in the veins of these women and men:
> the grey and grief and unlove,
> the bones in the back of their hands,
> And the chapel pressing its low ceiling over them.

Church and State were colluding in the 'anti-life heresy' that stalked the land. 'A wake is what is in progress in this country,' writes Kavanagh bitterly,[22] where 'the undertaker in his long black cloak moves around on padded feet ... and his job is to be nice to everybody'. Ideas which might be life-promoting are unwelcome to the undertaker; 'they are bad for trade'. The undertaker in his long black coat was de Valera!

Oppressive Catholicism, though much maligned by Kavanagh, seemed to find a kind of temperamental affinity in his psyche. He feared it, perhaps because an innate fear of sex within himself made him susceptible to its pernicious influence. In spite of his denunciation of the jansenistic, puritanical mind-set which permeated society at this time, Kavanagh had also to come to terms with a certain ambivalence within himself towards that very deprivation which he sought to denounce.

II

THE POET'S AMBIVALENCE TOWARDS DEPRIVATION

From early adulthood, Kavanagh portrays himself as a lonely, disconsolate youth, a half-hearted farmer of a few watery fields. His attitude towards the dark, sun-deprived hills of Mucker and Shancoduff was ambivalent. He entertained a love-hate relationship with his 'stony grey soil', which persisted throughout his life. Placenames, like Shancoduff (*dubh*, black), indicated that the land faced northwards and never enjoyed full sunlight.[23]

My black hills have never seen the sun rising,

Eternally they look north towards Armagh. (*Shancoduff*)

North-facing land was scant in vegetation; it was 'sour' and 'lime deficient'. It was difficult to till because of the little hills which were 'sharp, crooked and triangular'.[24] In more positive moments, these were the poet's 'black slanting Ulster hills', his 'Alps', his 'hundred little heads/ on none of which foot-room for genius'. Kavanagh's 'black hills' reflected a certain darkness in his own temperament as well as something of the austere, ascetical turn of mind he inherited from his father. He learned to assimilate restriction as part of his cramped surroundings in drumlin country. He was rewarded occasionally with glimpses of the sun through a gap, and a sunnier landscape on the farther horizon of south Armagh, 'when dawn whitens Glassdrummond chapel'. Darkness heightened the contrast with occasional glimpses of brightness.

Sensuous by nature, he loved summer and suntraps, and the heady sight and scent of colourful wild flowers in the bog. These, we can be assured, fed 'the gaping need of (his) senses'. Because of the double pull within his nature towards austerity on the one hand and sensuousness on the other, he experienced all the more keenly the miserliness of a land which jealously hoarded its sun-spots:

My hills hoard the bright shillings of March

While the sun searches in every pocket. (*Shancoduff*)

This latter line was originally written as:

Till the sun searches *the last pocket*. [25]

This variation of the text indicates that the poet was schooled in self-denial by the very fickleness of the elements. Adverse seasonal conditions, 'sleety winds' and 'perishing calves', undoubtedly tested the poet-farmer's endurance. By contrast, the small sunlit pockets, snow-filled perhaps, were the 'bright shillings of March' which mystically 'lift(ed) to importance (his) sixteen-acre farm'. *(Literary Adventures)* Analogously, and with a hint of the comic spirit characteristic of Kavanagh, a little 'money in his pocket', the occasional shilling hoarded for him by his mother, completely transformed the downcast outlook of the notoriously impecunious Tarry Flynn.

> 'There's a shilling there on the dresser and you can take it,' she said at last, 'but try not to spend it. I like a man to have money in his pocket.' He went out singing. The shilling in his pocket made all the difference between a man who hated the parish and a lover of it.[26]

Deprivation, spiritual and temporal, played a significant role in Kavanagh's life. Though he resented his suffering, he confronted it, without seeking to escape its meaning. His lot was that of the dark mystical journey proposed by St John of the Cross. 'These darknesses and trials, spiritual and temporal' purify the soul who journeys towards illumination and ultimate union with God.[27] Darkness, unknowingly, communicated its own spiritual knowledge to Kavanagh. Much of his best writing was conceived in darkness though, from the start, he knew he had access to a mystical light which he could not yet name with confidence:

> A light that might be mystic or a fraud
> Played on far hills beyond all common sight. *(After May)*

Poverty that became Poverty of Spirit

Kavanagh's poverty, however, was not destitution. In these early years at Inniskeen, his family enjoyed the scant luxuries that 'the droppin' shilling' allowed.[28] This 'droppin' shilling' was the small but regular income partly derived from Mrs Kavanagh's weekly sale of eggs at Dundalk market. Cash also accrued from the sale and repair of boots, though credit was often asked for and granted. The Kavanaghs lived thriftily: 'waste not, want not' was their maxim. Indeed money was universally scarce in rural Ireland during the 30s and 40s.

Acceptance of poverty was part of the prevailing ethos within home and church. Gratitude for avoiding the Poor House was widespread in post-Famine Ireland. Gratitude was also in keeping with the simplicity of the gospel. The Beatitudes were known by heart by schoolgoers, learned by heart in the exact same formula by succeeding generations:[29]

Blessed are the poor in spirit, for theirs is the kingdom of Heaven.

Poetically transposed, Kavanagh accepted poverty as a key to exploring other kingdoms. There was enormous freedom in installing himself as king of 'Inniskeen Road'. His possessions might be simple and his companions few, but he was 'king of banks and stone and every blooming thing'. He repudiated 'soft ease' in order to practise 'earnest young loving' that uncovered beauty in humble circumstances. Comfort and good things of themselves did not produce poetry:

Good things on my table, and yet

Beyond reach of my arm the potion of charm. *(Soft Ease)*

Kavanagh declared early in life that he was prepared to suffer for his vision. He accepted 'the rags of hunger' so that he might feast in 'the other lands'. *(Ascetic)* Few would deny that he did, in fact, enjoy a clearsightedness by which he gained personal glimpses of God. In his Primrose sonnet, he 'saw Christ transfigured without fear' and, in the person of Tarry Flynn, had free access to 'fields that were part of no earthly estate'. Nevertheless few suffered as he did, the 'agonising pincer-jaws of Heaven' in whose dual claws he persistently writhed. Poetically, he was consoled by the fact that his 'kingdom was not of this world'.

'Blessed are the clean of heart, for they shall see God' is another Beatitude Kavanagh cherished. Innate 'cleanness' of heart and innocence of vision drew from him instances of illumination and purity of language unrivalled by almost any other Irish poet. Yet, he regretted his platonic loving and his over-idealisation of woman. He longed for more flesh-and-blood comfort:

... but I am tired
Of loving through the medium of a sonnet
I want by Man, not God to be inspired.
This year O maiden of the dream-vague face
You'll come to me, a thing of Time and Space.
(In the Same Mood)

Deprivation was endured with necessary resignation, yet at his best he laced it with incisive humour, seeing his dilemma as being heaven-sent:

To be a poet and not know the trade,
To be a lover and repel all women;
Twin ironies by which great saints are made,
The agonising pincer-jaws of Heaven. *(Sanctity)*

One could mistake Kavanagh's well-reasoned philosophy of spiritual emptiness as that of a professional guide. But this wisdom was self-taught. In his fourth lecture in the series entitled 'Studies in the Technique of Poetry' (UCD 1956), he explains to the students that the apparent emptiness of experience can be its fullness especially when emptiness is seen as a spiritual reality. He says that as soon as one accepts the 'nothing' of one's fate, it becomes a richness. He warns against writers trying to conceal emptiness by inventing experience. They are mistaken. Digging out the 'ore' of our nothingness, he holds, is the true wisdom of which all are capable.[30]

Suffering, we can see from these musings, was to become a creative and almost necessary ingredient in his life. The spiritual riches of poverty was an acceptable Christian belief. The 'lilies of the field' in their simple resplendence were symbols of a magnificence born of poverty and naked dependence on God. Writing in the *Irish Farmer's Journal* in 1959, he acknowledges that these lilies afford us the most thrilling statement as a guide to human behaviour.[31] He was undoubtedly remembering 'the lilies of the field' of the gospel (Lk 12:27).

Likewise, the poet's restricting 'little hills' were his poverty and riches in one. Conscious of being enriched and deprived at the same time, he responds to his 'black hills' with deep affection laced with a wry sense of humour:

'Who owns them hungry hills
That the water-hen and snipe must have forsaken?
A Poet? Then by heavens he must be poor'
I hear and is my heart not badly shaken? *(Shancoduff)*

The clever, affluent 'cattle-drovers' from Crossmaglen might laugh at his 'hungry hills' from their shelter 'in Fetherna Bush'. As poet, Kavanagh can laugh at his poverty but at the same time consider himself rich.

In Dublin too, he was seen as a figure of poverty, often close to destitution, walking the streets, 'dishevelled with shoes untied'. He was often forced to borrow a shilling for food, though he pretended he needed a coin for the gas-metre.[32] Despite his periodic loud conversation and noisy cantankerous demeanour, he was also intensely private and 'walked apart' communing with his soul. He was filled with the acute pain of being different, of being the fool, the in-nocent, the stigmatised, the ill-treated. Ironically it was these negative experiences that also made his soul.

Patrick Kavanagh, 1951
Photo courtesy National Library of Ireland.

He knew that posterity had no use
For anything but the soul,
The lines that speak the passionate heart,
The spirit that lives alone.
O he was a lone one,
Fol do the di do
Yet he lived happily
I tell you. *(If ever you go to Dublin town)*

Chinks of Light

A man of acute sensitivity, he learned, early in life, that poetry could ease his burden of suffering. From youth, his imagination had quickened through enforced interiority and introspection caused by shyness, shame and ostracisation. Country people feared 'the bard' who might write about them in verse. Kavanagh felt his alienation keenly. Imprisoned in his interiority, his powerful sensibility and cramped view welcomed the tiniest aperture of light to give his vision expression. His best poetic moments were often those which he perceived through a chink of light:

> The light between the ricks of hay and straw
> Was a hole in Heaven's gable. (*A Christmas Childhood*)

Later, as a mature poet and with consummate skill and technique, he catches in his mystical lens, a moment of time framed 'in the tremendous silence/ of mid-July'. Intensified and rendered 'fantastic' by its restriction, Kavanagh's great mystical light 'looks through the eyes of bridges'. The moment is blessed in a way that defies words. 'No one will speak in prose' in this elevated setting. The poet defers with humility to the 'eye' which holds the images, and to the 'swan' who 'goes by head low', in reverential gesture appropriate to the moment. The focus of attention is diverted away from the poet, though the sonnet is intensely personal:

> … No one will speak in prose
> Who find his way to these Parnassian islands
> A swan goes by head low with many apologies,
> Fantastic light looks through the eyes of bridges –
> And look! a barge comes bringing from Athy
> And other far-flung towns mythologies.
> (*Lines Written on a Seat on the Grand Canal*)

In conclusion, he asks for nothing more than a seat for the passerby. This seat will afford further opportunity to contemplate these 'narrow slice(s) of divine instruction'. Moments such as these called forth from Kavanagh some of his best lyrical and mystical qualities.

Restricted vision was often his chosen posture, though when dealing with any hint of captivity, he cursed its hampering effects. In 'The Great Hunger' he sees Paddy Maguire 'locked in a stable with pigs and cows forever'. Yet, his whimsical Tarry Flynn, from the recesses of the stable, frequently chose to contemplate 'the light seen through the slit in the wall over the manger' rather than through the open door.[33] This choice suited Kavanagh's own predisposition for self-denial, which he felt sharpened his capacity for wonder and concentrated his energies. It prepared him for those inspired moments when he experienced himself baptised by the Holy Spirit.

Sunlight for Kavanagh bears a certain likeness to the sun-metaphor used by St John of the Cross to describe God's radiance at work in the purified soul.[34] Unimpeded by dust and grime the sun transforms the clean window-pane making it 'appear to be light'. This transformed condition is reminiscent of the Lough Derg pilgrim of whom Kavanagh says: 'Your innocence is pure glass that I see through'. Excerpts from the Spanish mystics may well have been incorporated into the learned and colourful sermons of Fr Maguire in Inniskeen. In a more exotic mood, Kavanagh's attention is not infrequently drawn to patterns of stained-glass sunlight in the chapels of Inniskeen, Drumcatton and Lough Derg, contrasting powerfully with 'the grey-faced' congregation of worshippers. He sorely needed his moments of 'stained sunlight'.[35]

> The sunlight through the coloured windows played on that congregation but could not smooth parchment faces and wrinkled necks to polished ivory. Skin was the colour of clay, and clay was in their hair and clothes.[36]

One of the poet's most radiant moments of illumination comes 'when the sun comes through a gap', while Paddy Maguire is engaged in spring-ploughing. It is a bitterly cold March day when the 'cold black wind is blowing from Dundalk'. This is the east wind – the dread of farmers. It is a normal farming day – ploughing a hill field under the watchful eye of curious neighbours who are envious of another's industry. Then the unexpected occurs: a ray of sunlight floods the scene through a gap in the drumlins, and people are transformed:

Yet sometimes when the sun comes through a gap
These men see God the Father in a tree:
The Holy Spirit is the rising sap,
And Christ will be the green leaves that will come
At Easter from the sealed and guarded tomb.
(The Great Hunger)

It is through a gap that the Trinity becomes visible. Eyes once narrowed in envy now see 'God the Father in a tree'. In moments such as these, divine radiance becomes visible. Gaps, slits, chinks, buttonholes, eyes of bridges, his own 'quarter-seeing eyes': these are Kavanagh's slim but magnificent vistas on miracle. His experience had something in common with that of St John of the Cross whose vision of God is glimpsed as through a tiny slit: 'You have revealed Yourself to me as through the fissures in a rock'.[37] Or like Catherine of Siena who images God as 'light filtering through a narrow street'.[38]

In 'Advent' the poet sets about remaking his soul, opting for simplicity over superfluity. The 'chink' is now seen as the cleanser, the purifier and renewer of vision: 'Through a chink too wide, there comes in no wonder'. He must surrender again to the purification of darkness, fasting and penance, territory familiar, though not generally self-imposed or even freely chosen:

But here in the Advent-darkened room
Where the dry black bread and sugarless tea
Of penance will charm back the luxury
Of a child's soul, we'll return to Doom
The knowledge we stole but could not use. *(Advent)*

Poverty, often cursed and unwillingly borne, now becomes preparatory for, and even conditional upon, the moment of illumination when

... Christ comes with a January flower.

Even when confronted with abject failure as a poet and a writer during the 1940s, he asks if he cannot turn this straitened circumstance to good use. He does not allow himself the luxury of wallowing in 'the rubble that was his achievement', but challenges the moment to produce 'something humble as a dandelion or a daisy / Something to wear as a buttonhole in Heaven'. Even in the throes of despair, Kavanagh can envisage a celestial future:

Can a man grow from the dead clod of failure
Some consoling flower
Something humble as a dandelion or a daisy,
Something to wear as a buttonhole in Heaven?
(From Failure Up)

During his life he became expert at discerning unusual buttonholes simply because of his great belief in gaps, slits and chinks. These, like the common buttonhole, could be simply a rent or an opening into opportunity. Dandelions and daisies, he knew, thrive even in the most unfavourable conditions and produce a God-given beauty. As a child Patrick had written in an essay for Miss Cassidy that the lover of nature can 'see the finger of God even in a nettle'.[39] If buttonholes are worn in heaven Patrick Kavanagh's will be simple and worn with pride.

The Sonnet: A Form of Literary Restriction

Kavanagh's affinity for restriction and limitation is further exemplified by his preference for the sonnet-form as a vehicle for poetry. He believed that it concentrated his mind and served poetic intensity. Its strict rules, he insisted, forced the mind to moral activity but was not itself forced.[40] It also provided a necessary discipline for that 'flash of Divine Intelligence' which Kavanagh saw as the inspiration of all great poetry. He studied the sonnet form from schoolbooks, possibly from the introduction to his sister Lucy's *Intermediate Poetry and Prose*, by Fr Corcoran, D. Litt. Father Finlay's 'Sixth Reader' also contained several essays: one entitled 'What is Poetry'? and another 'Various Kinds of Poetry'. Here the sonnet was discussed and examples given. Subsequently Kavanagh attempted to execute the theory himself and, like Shakespeare and Petrarch, used it to 'unlock his heart' and ease his own 'wound'.[41]

His first success was 'Inniskeen Road' where 'a mile of road' exquisitely compressed a complete Kavanagh 'kingdom' in its confines. Here, the details of a rural July evening where the whirr of passing bicycles, 'the half-talk code of mysteries' and 'the wink-and-elbow language of delight' are skillfully interwoven to reach their full and final significance in the run-on line:

… I am king

Of banks and stone and every blooming thing.

Fullness and variety are ideally compressed in the sonnet form. Succinctness and brevity suit Kavanagh's affinity for what is small, and yet of infinite significance. As a mature writer he can say with assurance: 'When the eternal moment appears on the screen of my imagination I do not want to let it go.' Such moments, though short in duration are 'as big as years'.[42] Contemplation stretches the moment toward infinity.

'Primrose', like 'Inniskeen Road', begins with the particular and moves towards the eternal; from a single flower to an extraordinary spiritual vision. Similarly when Kavanagh writes his 'Epic' in sonnet-form, the particular evolves into the universal. Inspired by the commonplace, he delineates the 'local row', with its 'pitchfork-armed claims' and dramatic interlude: 'Here is the march along these iron stones.' The poet, raised to full mystical stature, delivers himself of one of his most transfiguring poetic utterances:

I inclined to lose my faith in Ballyrush and Gortin

Till Homer's ghost came whispering to my mind. He said:

'I made the Iliad from such a local row…'

Influenced by schoolbook poetry, he not infrequently refers to 'poetic pregnancy', recalling undoubtedly Gray's elegy and 'some heart once pregnant with celestial fire'.[43] On a more caustic note he adds: 'It takes only a short time to give birth if you've anything to give birth to.' The sonnet was Kavanagh's favourite and most successful mode of confinement and delivery; its limits and discipline elicited from him some of his best moments of creativity. Temperamentally he liked to be cornered. It is not surprising that he played in goal for his local football team.[44] For some strange set of known and unknown reasons, Kavanagh was in love with restriction.

Suffering As Discipline

It is not difficult to see how Patrick Kavanagh, willingly or unwillingly, became schooled in the discipline of self-denial. From early youth he experienced the sense of being cramped and impoverished by the 'hungry hills' and view-impeding ditches of his native landscape. The Kavanagh dwelling was situated on the edge of bogland, with 'Cassidy's hanging hill' blocking its direct line of vision.

> The house that I was born in was a traditional Irish cabin, wedge-shaped, to trick the western winds. It was surrounded on three sides by a neighbour's field ...[45]

He was dependent on his neighbour's goodwill for unimpeded daylight through the single rear window at the back of the house. A misplaced haycock could considerably darken the house during the harvest season.[46] Everywhere Patrick looked he was confined, hemmed into a small space. His poem 'Stony Grey Soil' captures the physical and mental barriers that hampered his poetic emergence:

> You flung a ditch in my vision
> Of beauty love and truth
> O stony grey soil of Monaghan
> You burgled my bank of youth
>
> Lost the long hours of pleasure
> All the women that love young men.
> O can I still stroke the monster's back
> Or write with unpoisoned pen
>
> His name in these lonely verses
> Or mention the dark fields where
> The first gay flight of my lyric
> Got caught in a peasant's prayer

This is the cry of the trapped songbird, like the impaled nightingale of Oscar Wilde which sings most sweetly while being pierced by a rose-thorn.[47] Kavanagh, the trapped blackbird, sings most sweetly in adversity. The townland of Mucker, with its 'stony grey soil', its 'hungry hills', and impoverished people tested the poet severely. Here narrow-mindedness and lack of poetic interest were constant sources of purification. Unlike many of the textbook ascetics who were happy to be called upon to suffer for the kingdom of God, Kavanagh frequently deplored his circumstances and aspired to a more affluent way of life. He even had dreams of grandeur in the shape of 'a car, a big suburban house' … (Auditors In)

Purification, nonetheless, dogged his footsteps, sorely harrowing his poetic soul. His choice of the harrow as a poetic metaphor indicates his belief in the pain that is a necessary for fruition:

For destiny will not fulfill
Unless you let the harrow play. (To the Man after the Harrow)

The poet echoes the gospel words:

Unless a wheat grain falls on the ground and dies,
it remains only a single grain;
but if it dies, it yields a rich harvest. (Jn 12:24)

The place occupied by suffering in Kavanagh's life and work is worthy of careful attention, in order to assess its undeniable influence on his life and literary work. In 'The Great Hunger' Kavanagh seems to question the quest for happiness and settle for the inevitability of suffering:

Maybe life is not for joking or finding happiness in –
This tiny light in Oriental Darkness
Looking through chance windows of poetry or prayer.
(The Great Hunger)

Indeed Kavanagh's poetic technique is at its best when he is forced to find his own 'tiny light', 'chance window', or sunlit gap onto vistas of vision. Kavanagh had discovered a technique suited to his temperament. It was different altogether when he sensed that mental restriction was being imposed by the Catholic ethos of his time. Against such restriction he stoutly rebelled. He openly criticised the narrowminded view which obtained during the early decades of the twentieth century. An 'anti-life mentality' promulgated in parts of the Irish church darkened the atmosphere in which Kavanagh resolutely developed his unique poetic creed.

Kavanagh: Poet of Poverty

Few Irish poets had a better insight into the poverty of the people than Patrick Kavanagh. When he spoke of farmland that was 'like putty spread on stones' we are spirited back to his 'north-facing townland', where the cultivation of crops in poor soil was close to penury. He sees his poverty-stricken neighbours 'scraidins of farmers with their watery little hills that would physic a snipe'.[48] Add to this the interminable round of 'half-boiled pots and unmilked cows' – a life of drudgery with scant rewards, a typical analysis of rural Ireland in the nineteen thirties and forties before the advent of mechanised farming and rural electrification.

When reviewing his life in a television broadcast in 1962, to be published later as *Self Portrait*, Kavanagh stated that he saw little virtue in poverty. On the contrary, he strongly subscribed to a life of sufficient comfort and freedom from anxiety. Poverty, he believed, caused obsession with material things and not freedom from their grasp. The poor thatched cabin often romanticised in the Irish literary movement, was to Kavanagh's mind 'a lie'. He attempts with a certain arrogance to embrace with one sweep of his pen the whole spectrum of material, mental, spiritual and evangelical poverty:

> I have never seen poverty properly analysed. Poverty is a mental condition. You hear of men and women who have chosen poverty, but you cannot choose poverty. Poverty has nothing to do with eating your fill today; it is anxiety about what's going to happen next week. The cliche poverty that you get in the working-class novel or play is a formula.[49]

He goes on to decry the effects of poverty, rightly concluding that 'the real poverty was the lack of enlightenment to get out and get under the moon'. For Kavanagh, the fulfilment of his spiritual needs was as important as his daily bread, though he was quite partial to that too. The freedom to dream, to contemplate, was for him a basic need. His circumstances were rarely so straitened as to exclude poetry:

> My room is a dusty attic
> But its little window
> Lets in the stars. *(My Room)*

To have a lifestyle which allowed him time to be devoted to non-material values, was something he struggled for. This was closer to evangelical poverty than he realised.

Part of the contradiction in Kavanagh's personality was the notion he had that 'a rich woman might take a fancy to his poetry and keep him in the decency and comfort which are a necessity of the poet'. 'Getting hitched up to a rich woman … the only way a true poet can remain true and keep up an adequate supply of good whiskey', was a kind of fantasy he needed to entertain.[50] Or was this just talk? Did he need to create some kind of illusion about himself as a kind of Rasputin? Without realising it, he created his best work in poverty. Little, if any, creative work came from Kavanagh's pen during those times when he seemed to be living in comfort. No work of consequence came of his visits to the US, nor from the times spent in Brown's Hotel, London, as judge of the Guinness awards. After his marriage to Katherine Moloney, it is said he lived in comfort and was well cared for, yet here again his creative spark had disappeared.

Material poverty never fully robbed Kavanagh of the freedom to 'get out and get under the moon', yet he sorely felt its sting. Perhaps his greatest sense of poverty was that he had never got a proper post-primary education and that he educated himself during furtive breaks in farm-work on the 'Sixth Book' and other schoolbooks acquired from members of his family. There is hidden pathos in his remark on leaving school, that he missed his opportunity for further education: 'between twelve and fourteen – when the affairs of most men is at the full, I missed the tide'.[51] His loss at this time becomes more evident in an essay entitled 'On a Liberal Education' published in *X Magazine*, 1961:

Surely the purpose of a good education is to prevent one from squandering one's life in useless suffering.[52]

Part of his problem on coming to Dublin in 1939 was that he was unemployable through lack of formal education. Kavanagh expected to be given a job by some of the influential members of 'literary Dublin' or by some authorities of church or state. This was the 'literary Dublin', 'the City of the Kings', for which he had left his 'little hills' and 'hawthorn hedges'. Kavanagh had been naïve in his expectations and therefore more vulnerable. The poverty of his life in Dublin during the forties and early fifties was a cruel blow to his pride.

Dublin was, at that time, over-populated with poets and literary people seeking a living. When war broke out in 1939, there was no longer a possibility of going to war-torn Europe, even London. Kavanagh, along with his contemporaries, was to be further constrained by political boundaries. Robert Garratt, in his book entitled *Modern Irish Poetry*, describes Kavanagh's plight in the face of the over-crowded and 'gossipy viciousness' of the Dublin literati:

Most of the established writers resented a new talent, since it meant further competition in already crowded circumstances. Thus to protect themselves they greeted Kavanagh's arrival on the Dublin scene with characteristic reductive humour, seizing upon his raw-boned physique, his unpolished manner, his poverty and, most of all, his country background.[53]

He had earlier confided to his brother Peter from London (August, 1939), before the outbreak of war, that he could come back to Ireland and write if he had three pounds weekly.[54] It seemed a modest sum, but there was no Arts Council or literary grants to ensure even this. Peter summarised the story which stretched over the remainder of Patrick's life as one of storming every barricade of business, politics, religion, and being constantly rebuffed.[55]

In 1942 he went to Lough Derg and subsequently wrote his long poem of the same title. In it he included prayers, 'in the

shape of sonnets', ascribed to pilgrims, though at least one of
them bore a close resemblance to his own personal dilemma.
Was it really Kavanagh's own prayer?

O Sacred Heart of Jesus I ask of you
A job so I can settle down and marry;
I want to live a decent life.
And through the flames of St Patrick's Purgatory
I go offering every stone-bruise, all my hunger;
In the back-room of my penance I am weaving
An inside-shirt for charity. How much longer
Must a fifty-shilling a week job be day-dreaming?
The dole and empty minds and empty pockets,
Cup finals seen from the branches of a tree,
Old films that break the eye-balls in their sockets,
A toss-pit. This is life for such as me.
And I know a girl and I know a room to be let
And a job in a builder's yard to be given yet.[56]

It was true that he lacked a job, that he was at times a reluctant
film critic, that, through lack of funds, he watched football
matches in Croke Park from 'the branches of a tree', and that he
wanted to get married. In 'Lough Derg', he called himself a
'half-pilgrim', probably because of his failure to observe the pre-
scribed fast. He was well accustomed, in his daily life in Dublin,
to 'the dry bread and the sugarless tea of penance'. (*Advent*)
Lough Derg was to bring him face to face with the even deeper
poverties of his life. He realised that Lough Derg was, for generations, 'the penance of the poor'. He was one of them, perhaps
more that he realised since 'in the back-room of (his) poverty' he
was 'weaving an inside-shirt for charity'.

For a man of Kavanagh's sensibility, condemned to live close
to the poverty line, depending financially on his brother and on
small payments from newspapers, life must have been barely
tolerable. Living on charity from various sources, clerical and
lay, only added salt to his wounds. He was a proud man. His arrears in rent and electricity payments were a constant reminder
of impending destitution. Just as permanent eviction might

seem imminent arrears were cleared, willingly or unwillingly,
by one or other benefactor. Kavanagh blamed poverty for de-
priving him of marriage. At the end, his one regret in life was
that he had not 'reproduced himself'. When he made an audit of
his life in the 50s, his own self-description has the ring of truth:

> A lonely lecher whom the fates
> By a financial trick castrates. *(Auditors In)*

Anthony Cronin knew him for sixteen of his years in Dublin,
and could therefore describe accurately the circumstances in
which the poet lived and wrote. He was once invited to his flat
in Pembroke Road where he was shocked by the poet's living
conditions:

> We walked back through the summer evening to the flat in
> Pembroke Road where … he provided me with black tea and
> dry bread and I saw for the first time the battered sofa, the
> old newspapers, books and yellowing typescripts scattered
> over the floor, the tea-leaves in the bath, the mountain of ash
> that spilled out of the grate. I asked him rather stupidly, did
> he usually cook for himself, and he answered: 'I sometimes
> boil an egg in the teapot, if you call that cooking.'[57]

Poverty Transformed Through Love

We have seen how familiar Kavanagh was with the vagaries of
poverty, from Shancoduff in the 30s to the poverty of Dublin in
the 40s and 50s. He even admits to experiencing hunger-pains in
London in 1939. He frequently transcended poverty, as Paddy
Maguire did occasionally in 'The Great Hunger' when he discovers momentarily the illusionary but beautiful 'pearl necklace
round the neck of poverty'. Miraculously, Kavanagh became
master of 'pearl necklaces' whose brightnesses transfigured destitution. He found 'the gay imaginative God' in lowly places and
in simple gestures:

> Men build their heavens as they build their circles
> Of friends. God in the bits and pieces of Everyday –
> A kiss here and a laugh again and sometimes tears,
> A pearl necklace round the neck of poverty.
> *(The Great Hunger)*

Poverty could elicit from him a sense of gratitude for life akin to that of a St Francis of Assisi.

Nothing was too small or menial to be blessed by Kavanagh: 'A stone lying sideways in a ditch', 'the bright stick trapped', dandelions, weeds, 'the Rialto Bridge', 'banks and stones and every blooming thing'. And he can bless these things precisely because he is poor. He echoed the gospel message which stresses the care of Divine providence for little things: 'two sparrows, sold for a penny' and the magnificence of the common 'lilies of the field' who neither labour nor spin. Love was the transforming agent. It was love that transformed gravel paths into 'eternal lanes of joy'; love that in 'Lough Derg' hears the voices of the poor spoken as 'Homeric utterances'.

This intensity of love changed moments of dire poverty into moments of vivid illumination. Kavanagh, from his youth, had learned the secret of sublimation. By the time he writes his 'Prelude', he can speak with the authority of one who has struggled to transcend adversity. Poverty without love he knows to be penury. Transforming love, on the contrary, comes from a deep inner source. When he gratefully summons up past experience, Kavanagh engages in a magical work of poetic transfiguration:

> Gather the bits of road that were
> Not gravel to the traveller
> But eternal lanes of joy
> On which no man who walks can die.
>
> Collect the river and the stream
> That flashed upon a pensive theme,
> And a positive world make,
> A world man's world cannot shake.

The secret of Kavanagh's life was in his firm resolve never to abandon love 'though face to face with destitution'. Few will guess how difficult it was to remain steadfast to this promise.

His love resembles that of St Francis of Assisi, wanting to love poverty even when it hurt most. He refuses to allow 'destitution' sour his poetic impulse which is based on love.

Deprivation in Kavanagh was never mere stoicism; it moved willy nilly into the realm of spiritual poverty – the freedom and serenity of the 'birds of the air' who, while possessing nothing have everything. He reaches a climax of detachment and celebration of life in his poem 'October':

O leafy yellowness you create for me
A world that was and now is poised above time,
I do not need to puzzle out Eternity
As I walk this arboreal street on the edge of a town.

Bitterness crept in only when poetry and prayer deserted him. In its throes he resorted to writing satire and doggeral.

When the 'leafy-with-love' canal banks slowly effected their healing in his over-wrought mind and cancer-torn body, he experienced a full 'flowering of (his) catharsis'. He now celebrated with renewed poetic energy his healing God, in a full-throated song of praise:

Green, blue, yellow and red –
God is down in the swamps and marshes
Sensational as April and almost incredible
the flowering of our catharsis.
A humble scene in a backward place
Where no one important ever looked
The raving flowers looked up in the face
Of the One and the Endless, the mind that has baulked
The profoundest of mortals. *(The One)*

Yet Kavanagh can be full of contradictions. He has almost a fixation about wealth while claiming to denounce its decadence and excesses. He speaks enthusiastically about the journey 'from simplicity back to simplicity' yet, given the opportunity, he wanted the best living quarters, the best chair in the house, the best whiskey, the best cooking.[58] He is firmly convinced that he is thwarted by Providence which guides or misguides his life – blesses him with plenty or with hunger, with love or with ridicule, with chastity and with lust. Again and again he squirms within the 'agonising pincer-jaws of Heaven', yet wallows in this sanctifying dilemma. Suffering for Kavanagh may have been the crucifying reminder that he was vibrantly alive.

Though he rails against society, blaming church and state for his poverty, he inwardly takes responsibility for his gift of poetry and finds unexpected riches in destitution. As well as the enormous vitality he finds in weedy ditches, his pitifully small farm yielded an unusually rich harvest of irreplaceable lyrics, and poems of great visionary beauty. He lives the Christian gospel as a matter of course; he cannot help it. As a way of life, he practised what spiritual writers call 'the sacrament of the present moment', finding God everywhere but especially 'in the bits and pieces of everyday'. These characteristics likened him more to a medieval monk than to a twentieth-century poet. Poetically speaking he had integrity. As his anonymous critic in *The Leader* said: 'a lean, athletic figure sinuates itself through the tangled undergrowth' of his mind.[59] His critics admit that he is interiorly incorruptible. In spite of a noisy cantankerous exterior, he retained the inner spiritual dispositions to be schooled and purified in mystical love. One could say that a contemplative monk lurked within his ungainly form.

Conclusion

Kavanagh was purified by external societal factors as well as by internal temperamental ones. Jansenistic teaching on sexual matters, as well as oppressive church teaching on dating and recreations, galled him. They caused him to reject aspects of contemporary pastoral practice. At no time, however, did he renounce the basic doctrines of his faith. The Irish church was, since the latter half of the nineteenth century, undergoing a process of romanisation, a fact which grieved the poet since he considered that it was moving farther away from its ancient religious roots. Gone were the picturesque patterns and pilgrimages of the past. Instead, there was ushered in a wave of continental devotions. Missions and novenas were sources of amusement for the poet as well as occasions of playful satire. 'Voteens', he felt, worshipped a mechanical God who rewarded numerical performance. They seemed to ignore the healthy integration of religion and daily life. Kavanagh satirises this in the local devotees of the 'The Nine Fridays':

On the first Friday of every month ... (they) could be seen
strolling home from the village church, their sharp tongues
in keeping with their sharp noses. Tarry, when he reflected
on this devotion, was glad that he had gone through it, for
there was a story that anyone who had done so would never
die unrepentant. That gave a man a great chance to have a
good time. [60]

Temperamentally Kavanagh had an affinity for some of the
darker elements of his beloved landscape. He loved his 'Shancoduff', his wonder-inducing 'black slanting Ulster hill'. In order
to purify his poetic vision he schooled himself in darkness so as
to glimpse heaven through chinks of light. 'All art is life
squeezed through a repression' was one of his favourite aphor-
isms.[61] Kavanagh, it would seem, had many repressions but he
had just as many mystical moments.

Poverty dogged his footsteps yet his spirit could heroically
accommodate itself to self-denial. Ultimately, with what amount
of stoicism we will never know, he did not allow destitution rob
him of 'love's resolution'. He knew one Beatitude better than
most and embraced the blessedness of 'the poor in spirit' with
judicious reluctance and enthusiasm. His reward was in a real
sense both 'the kingdom of heaven' and the kingdom of earth.

CHAPTER 5

Purification II

And tell how trampled, derided, hated,
And worn by weakness, disease, and wrong,
He fled for shelter to God, who mated
His soul with song.
(James Clarence Mangan, *The Nameless One*)

Despite his ability to sublimate deprivation and poverty through poetry, Patrick Kavanagh also wrote frequently and spoke often as one who was victimised. This tendency was not entirely without foundation. One reason in particular why Kavanagh felt that life had been unfair to him has, until now, been given little attention. It concerned the fact that he was in some way wounded by the secrecy that surrounded his father's illegitimacy and the subsequent loss of paternal ancestry.

The Stigma of Illegitimacy

A true, largely unspoken story of tragedy and romance wrapped itself mysteriously around the Kavanagh household. This story surfaced occasionally, when an infuriated neighbour might retaliate against the pranking Kavanagh youngsters with a tirade against them as 'bastards and breed bastards'.[1] Patrick sensed the hidden pain in his father's reticence on the subject of his illegitimacy. Father and son, we have seen, were kindred spirits and thought alike on many subjects. Was it embarrassment that caused James Kavanagh to write down, rather than speak directly about his 'accident of birth'? Or did Patrick come by chance on letters or documents that revealed a hidden past that had to be explained?

My father wrote the history of his family for me on a sheet of foolscap. I have often wondered since if he had some instinct that I should some day give it the permanency of print. It was the romantic story of his father who had come out of the West to sow the wild, vigorous seed of Connaught among the little hills of south Ulster.[2]

The greatest anomaly was the fact that 'Kavanagh' was not the real name of this now famous Monaghan family; it was 'Kevany'! The 'accident' which befell James 'Kevany' at baptism was that he was christened James Cavanagh, instead of James Kevany, son of Patrick Kevany, the local schoolmaster. Once incorrectly registered, the mistake was permanent; all future records would follow the birth register.[3] The Kavanagh family must now carry this fiction for life.

But who was Patrick Kevany from whom the Kavanaghs descended? The story goes back to 1849, when Mr Tristram Kennedy, agent of the Bath Estate at Carrickmacross, built a new school on his estate at Kednaminsha and Rocksavage. He needed a teacher to implement the new combined agricultural and literary syllabus for primary-school students. Patrick Kevany, the twenty-three-year-old student-teacher from Castletown, Co Sligo,[4] was well qualified to fill the position. He applied for the job and was successful. As a student, Kevany had given satisfaction to his teachers in the Royal Albert Agricultural School.[5] He was one of its earliest students: No. 168 on the Register. Admitted on July 4th, 1848, he was among the thirty students there who followed courses in practical agricultural methods, as well as in the literary subjects necessary for the training of school-teachers. The yearly fee of five pounds was sponsored by Mr Thomas Howley Esq., of Beleek Castle near Ballina and formerly of Cooga Lodge, Easkey. The Howleys were important Catholic land-agents and also influential members of the local Education Board at Ballina.[6] Their protege completed his course on February 7th, 1850 but was destined not for Easkey but for Monaghan.

The register of pupils from the now defunct Agricultural College has preserved information concerning its students,

Register of pupils at the Royal Albert Agricultural School, with Patrick Kevany's entry at the bottom of the page. Photo courtesy UCD Archives.

which is vital to our research.[7] Here are found addresses, dates of admissions and withdrawals, the names of those responsible for paying fees, along with a brief critical comment on each student. As research-material, it provides a vital link between Patrick Kevany of Easkey, Co Sligo, and the new Principal of Kednaminsha and Rocksavage NS in Co Monaghan. The Educational records in the National Archives confirm that this was the teacher's second appointment. He had already been Principal of Owenbeg NS from 1846 to 1848. This competent, well-educated young man was to become the Kavanaghs' grandfather.

The remarks which follow Kevany's name on the Glasnevin register, give us a rare glimpse of this young man who was to become central to the Kavanagh story:

Patrick Kevany was appointed to one of Tristram Kennedy's Schools, Carrickmacross.[8] A well-conducted young man and pretty well qualified – but has an awkward address, and speaks too thickly to be a good teacher.

Despite his 'thick' speech and 'awkward address', curiously forecasting the self-styled 'thick-tongued mumble' of his future grandson, Kevany succeeded well as a teacher and agriculturist. His 'thick' speech probably indicated that his English was strongly overlaid with Gaelic. He impressed his school manager, Tristram Kennedy, so much that he sent three proteges from his estate on scholarships to be trained at Glasnevin Agricultural College during the years 1850 and 1851. These students were intended to upgrade agricultural standards on the Bath Estate in the wake of the Great Famine.

The Commissioners of Education showed their appreciation for the new graduate of agriculture at Kednaminsha. They raised his classification as a teacher from his original grade 3 to the higher and better paid grade 2. Kevany's teaching records for these first four years in Kednaminsha are impeccable. He prepared the ground around the school for crops, ordered books and school-furnishings as required and among them a school clock, which his future grandson often contemplated wistfully during school hours. 'The Old School Clock' by John Boyle O'Reilly was one of his favourite poems.

Reports on Kevany were excellent, considering the Commissioners' notorious reputation for encouraging inspectors to punish even minor irregularities, and thereby lower teachers' salaries. By 1854 he earned twenty pounds yearly which, compared with the eight pounds he had earned in Owenbeg in 1847, gave him financial security. He could afford to marry and settle down. At twenty-eight years of age he probably intended this, but fate was to determine otherwise.

Patrick Kevany and Nancy Callan: A Local Scandal
It was the custom for teachers who taught at a distance from home to find lodgings convenient to their work. Patrick Kevany found his in McEnteggart's house, close to the school.[9] It was here that he first made the acquaintance of the servant-girl, a young widow, Nancy Callan from Mucker. It is not clear how soon their relationship began. Nancy had already been married

although she was still only nineteen. Her husband had died within a year of their marriage and left her to rear her son, Pat McCue in the Callan home. She was still called by her maiden name, Nancy Callan, which was not unusual in rural Ireland at this time.

The Callans were poor, though they once owned at least one acre of land around their dwelling.[10] This had been confiscated because of inability to pay the rent. They barely succeeded in keeping a roof over their heads. Nancy was, by all accounts, a tall, blond, big-boned, good-looking woman, the *femme fatale*, of Inniskeen. Kevany became her lover and by the winter of 1854 she was pregnant. In April 1855, five years exactly since his appointment as Principal in Kednaminsha NS, it was obvious that Nancy Callan was carrying his child.

Many questions about their relationship remain unsolved. Why Kevany did not marry Nancy Callan, and escape the censure of the then landlord, Stuart Trench, remains a mystery. It seems clear from his pleas for forgiveness and request to be reinstated, along with his willingness to give his name to the child, that he had intended to marry the future mother of his child. On the other hand, there is no evidence that Nancy wished to marry, or that she would be allowed to do so by her family on whom she still depended for shelter. According to local sources, she was ostracised by her infuriated family who left her to make a home for herself in a nearby makeshift shed. As for Kevany, the prospect of living among the enraged Callans, without land or means of livelihood, seemed untenable. He would have to leave and find a means of supporting his common-law wife and future child.

The full tragedy of the story becomes evident from official records held in education files at the National Archives in Dublin. It was Stuart Trench, then manager of the Bath Estate schools, who compounded the injury still further by reporting his teacher to the Commissioners of Education.[11] The minutes of the Commissioners' Board for the year 1855 record the full diary of events concerning Patrick Kevany and his 'immoral' liaison with Nancy Callan.[12]

The Official Story
On 4 April 1855, the Commissioners received a letter from Stuart Trench stating that he had suspended a teacher for 'immorality', 'as he has been for some time living with a widow who is with child by him and not married to him'. Trench enclosed a letter from Kevany requesting forgiveness and promising amendment. Three weeks later came the dreaded ultimatum that Kevany would 'be immediately removed from the school'. The Commissioners had dismissed him from service from the first day of May, and stated that they would not again recognise him as a National School teacher. An order demanding the closure of Kednaminsha School was issued by the Commissioners on 16 April. This action would ensure Kevany's public disgrace. His salary was suspended forthwith, and a notice served that the school would be closed until further notice.

Kevany was forced to leave the area, though he continued to plead his case with the Commissioners. He wrote to them again on July 6, asking that he be fully reinstated 'should he on a future occasion be employed as teacher of a National School'. To strengthen his case he had enclosed testimonials from the curate of Inniskeen (1849-54), Revd P. O'Carroll, and from Mr Donaghy, a member of the Board of Guardians at Carrickmacross. A final letter from Patrick Kevany on 20 September asks for his Certificate of Classification, evidence of his past service as a teacher. He had earned a class two rating which was certain to promote his cause were he to apply for another job. Unfortunately, these letters have not been filed in the archives. It is therefore impossible to establish Kevany's whereabouts at this time. Had he returned to Easkey? Or had he found gainful employment somewhere else? Finally, on 13 October a letter was sent by the Commissioners stating categorically that 'having been dismissed from the Service Board he cannot again be recognised as a National Teacher'.

This diary of events touching the personal life of Patrick Kevany has its own poignancy. His life as a school-teacher was ruined, or so it seemed. Spring and summer of the year 1855 found Kevany pleading for clemency but to no avail. The birth of a son carrying his name brought only pain and disgrace for both parents. Could Kevany have redeemed the situation? How could he provide for a wife and two children (Nancy had a son already) with no land or prospect of teaching again? Out of this tragedy arises a ghost which will haunt the unborn progeny of Patrick Kevany for years to come. His fine literary and agricultural training now counted for nothing. He had forfeited his livelihood and good name. His five years work for education and for agriculture in the area would be forgotten. An illegitimate child would be his only claim to remembrance, 'a stain' described by his future grandson 'that will be revived in three generations to come'.[13] In raising it as I do now, I do so for two reasons. One, that Patrick Kavanagh's real background be finally known and his ancestry restored. Secondly, to assess, if possible, the effects of this hidden information on the poet's life and work.

The love-child, James Cavanagh, born to Nancy Callen (sic) and Patrick Cavanagh (sic) had at his baptism on August 25th 1855, unknowingly lost half his birthright. His father's name had disappeared from official records and been replaced by a false name. There are a number of theories as to how 'Kevany' became 'Cavanagh'. Some assume that it was a deliberate falsification to shield the teacher's good name. This is possible, in view of the prevailing attitudes towards illegitimacy and the strange belief that well-concealed information could be obliterated. But there are other reasons why, I believe, the name was accidentally changed. Firstly, it was not unprecedented for 'Kevany' to be confused with 'Kaveny'. Anglicisation of place-names and family-names was taking place on a large scale, a fact powerfully exemplified by Brian Friel's play *Translations*. A different spelling of 'Kevany' – Keaveny or Keveney, adopted by other branches of the Kevany clann – might have lessened the chances of corruption. But this Kevany family firmly adhered to its own spelling and do so to this day.[14] Secondly, there was a natural linguistic reason why in Inniskeen 'Kevany' was interpreted as 'Kavanagh'. In south Monaghan the first interconson-antal 'a' of surnames is often pronounced 'e'. For instance, in Inniskeen the name 'Cassidy' is commonly pronounced 'Kessidy' which could lead one to assume that 'Kevany' was really 'Kavanagh'.

The outcome of this 'mistake' was that the Kavanaghs' true line of descent had been lost. Kevany, according to McLysaght, is derived from Mac Géibheannaigh, of the Hy Many tribes of Connaught. The *Mac Géibheannaigh* tribe was reported to have been constant and brave in battle, but defeated at the battle of Magh Currain. Kavanagh, on the other hand, is derived from *Caomhánach*, originally a Co Wicklow name which denotes sweet-ness and mildness of temperament.

Kevany or Kavanagh, both names were regarded as 'foreign' in Co Monaghan. This fact is perhaps alluded to in *Tarry Flynn*, where 'the ferocious voice' of Joe Finnegan sought vengeance not only on Tarry Flynn, but on the whole Flynn family: 'Bleddy pack of foreigners … I'll break his bleddy neck.'[15] This incident in the largely autobiographical novel highlights the truth that Patrick knew in his heart that neighbours would never forget that the Kavanaghs were outsiders. They did not belong to the local Monaghan 'tribes' of Duffys, Finnegans, Meegans or Callans![16]

The falsification of a name, however understandable, leaves a gap in the lives of those concerned. The Kavanaghs would never know who they really were. James would grow up unsure as to how he should sign his name. On his marriage certificate he is 'James Kavanagh', whereas when he came to sign his mother's death-certificate, he signed himself 'James Kevany'. In Innis-keen, of course, his public name was 'James Kavanagh', some-times spelt 'Cavanagh'. His family would grow up ignorant of their grandfather's background and deprived of their family roots. They had lost name, paternal relatives and identity. Is it perhaps from a deep groaning within the poet's unconscious for the humiliation of his grandfather, that the ghosts of the past cry out?

> O stony grey soil of Monaghan
> The laugh from my love you thieved
> You took the gay child of my passion
> And gave me your clod-conceived
>
> You flung a ditch in my vision
> Of beauty, love and truth.
> O stony grey soil of Monaghan
> You burgled my bank of youth! *(Stony Grey Soil)*

The 'stony grey soil of Monaghan' had indeed 'burgled' the Kavanaghs' lives. How could one 'write with unpoisoned pen' or 'stroke the monster's back', and not feel victimised by past shame, injustice and public disgrace?

Had James Kavanagh told his son the story of his birth, Patrick would have been unlikely to forget it. With his poet's gift of understanding and sensitivity, he would have enshrined the romantic-tragedy in 'the round tower of his heart'. He would have minutely pondered its implications. Remembering may have been painful for James Kavanagh. It may have been easier to assemble the facts, write them down and then stash 'the manuscript' in what Patrick considered 'a safe place'. His father had done his duty. The 'delf jug' contained the secret. The manuscript was there as evidence. But fate ordained otherwise!

> Because I knew I had the manuscript to read any time, I only scanned it once. I put it in what I thought a safe place in the bottom of a large delf jug – a preposterous heirloom that was never in use. When my father was dead a month, I looked in the jug and it was empty: and whether it was the handmaid of Prudery or Cleanliness swept it away I do not know. I was filled with grief as I never now could have a copy.[17]

Did James know the full truth or, as is often with illegitimacy, were the facts still vague? James was protective of Patrick; he recognised in him the mixed blessing of 'an unprotected heart'. He feared for his sensitive, romantic nature. The story, partly known, partly hidden, was bound to leave its imprint on the poet's emerging spirit. Knowing the facts would have helped, the hidden was always more damaging. Already the writer's 'humorosity' was present when he suggested that his family-background had been 'swept away by the handmaid of Prudery or Cleanliness'. Kavanagh grieved for the lost manuscript. On the death of his father he grieved not only for a parent but for the vital information that had died with him.

Implications of these findings

It is only possible to guess at some of the implications of these new biographical findings for the poet. 'What's in a name?' one might ask. Very little, because undoubtedly Patrick Kavanagh made his own name, just as he fashioned, in Heaney's now famous words, a poetic diction for himself, 'barehanded out of a literary nowhere'.[18] Perhaps the reason he succeeded in the mammoth task of fashioning his own diction, was that he had already fashioned his personal identity alone and unaided out of an impaired genealogy. He knew only partially who he was.

Irish poets in the past placed great store in tracing their origins back to Irish kings and chieftains. If Kavanagh were to seek to follow in their footsteps he was likely to find himself at a loss. I believe that for years he carried his stigma as a hidden and personal wound. Because of this loss he had to probe for his identity deep within himself. He may have been driven to search for his spiritual roots, a sad but eventually happy alternative. From an early age he harkened back to that 'far mysterious place … the world from which I came'. He had arrived in this world, he believed, 'trailing clouds of glory'. His identity had to be one that transcended family, neighbourhood and nationality. It is from his spiritual identity that he spoke as a poet, breaking with the older and more constricting labels of kinship and tribe. In his *Self-Portrait* (1962), he dismisses the mere historical circumstances of his life in favour of the birth of his spirit. He believed that 'poetry has to do with the reality of the spirit' and that other labels were irrelevant.

We have already seen that Kavanagh found it necessary to build a persona of vulgarity around himself. The family story, partly known and partly lost, is bound to have had its effect. It may have been responsible for a shy defensiveness to grow up around Patrick as a youth. It may have caused him to fear sexuality since he knew his father had suffered from the scandal involved in being a by-child. The structure of introversion in a shy, imaginative youth contributed even further to the development of an outward persona of vulgarity. To shield his 'unprotected heart' he learned to masquerade as coarse and outspoken, which did not endear him to the people of Inniskeen or Dublin.

The tragedy relating to Kavanagh's background was likely to deepen his pre-disposition for loneliness and sense of 'not belonging.'[19] This feeling of being an outsider fostered in him a fascination for the poems of Mangan.[20] His identified strongly with Mangan's 'The Nameless One' which he knew by heart, learned most likely from his sister Lucy's schoolbooks. The words seem to capture his own sense of isolation and need for a 'song' which would 'roll forth … like a rushing river' and deliver his soul of pain. Poems were his therapy, his necessary 'catharsis':

Tell how this Nameless, condemned for years long
To herd with demons from hell beneath
Saw things that made him, with groans and tears long
For even death.

And tell how trampled, derided, hated,
And worn by weakness, disease, and wrong,
He fled for shelter to God, who mated
His soul with song.

In spite of his father's belief that he would one day become a great writer, it is clear that the afflictions of his youth caused Patrick to see himself from an early age in a position of low esteem. He felt he was an outcast, despised, alone like the 'old wooden gate' which was the subject of one of his earliest poems. He wrote about weeds, coltsfoot, dandelions – the outcasts, one might say, of the plant world. Yet he continually exalts them as though aware that their authenticity was their real beauty. People, he knew, found it hard to be themselves. Weeds were unselfconscious. 'Dandelions growing on headlands, showing/

Their unloved hearts to everyone'. Kavanagh was learning authenticity in the company of common weeds and flowers. They taught him to abandon himself to the joy of integral selfhood.

The 'weeds' symbol followed him from Inniskeen: from 'the weeds that grew / somewhere specially for you' to the canal-bank sonnets, lush with uncelebrated life. His 'leafy-with-love' banks were as prolific as 'the bogs and marshes' filled with 'anonymous performers'. Despite Kavanagh's at-homeness with weeds, symbolic of his low self esteem, he was aware nevertheless of a sense of being destined for something great. His theology of the commonplace was the fruit of a lifelong conviction that the lowliest life is blessed with inalienable dignity before God.

Ultimately, one might ask, what difference did Kavanagh's impaired background make? As we reflect on the hidden Kavanagh story, we are helped to better understand his defensiveness and initial fear of being different. The wound he carried might also explain his cantankerousness and impatience towards a society that cared little for the needless pain it inflicted on 'accidents of birth'. Does it perhaps, too, explain his idealised love of women, many of whom he loved from a distance but failed to marry? Does it explain why he heaped his love on weeds and grass, yet failed to come to terms with love of people? He married eventually, only months before his death, when he was already ill and more in need of a nurse than a wife.

Kavanagh's life might have been different had he been born a Kevany. He would have then been a Sligo poet instead of a lover of the whitethorn hedges of south Monaghan! The fine Kevany inheritance of flat fertile land sweeping down to the shore in Easkey might have been partly his instead of the hard-won watery drumlin fields, the 'stony grey soil of Monaghan'. He might have had to share Sligo with W. B. Yeats, undoubtedly making that locality the literary epicentre of Ireland!

But Kavanagh had been trapped by fate. He could use his solitary position to free himself from the 'fog' which smothered individual thought in a small rural community. He could forge an identity for himself, deeper than kinship can offer. He would choose 'the narrow pass' of the gospel as entry to his poetic kingdom. He could sing as the captive blackbird of whitehorn hedges and primrose banks. He could transcend darkness by celebrating its chinks of radiant light.

Patrick undoubtedly felt the loss of blood-relatives. Life on the land without relatives was isolating, as is evident from the cry of the autobiographical character 'Tarry Flynn' who bemoans the absence of 'one first cousin itself', who would support him against the unfair attacks of his aggressive neighbours 'the Finnegans'. 'But he had not a single relation to back him up'.[21] This was Kavanagh's personal plight. He did in fact continue to search for his relatives, making enquiries in Tullamore, where his grandfather had settled after his expulsion from Kednaminsha.[22] Patrick Kavanagh never fully pieced together the information contained in the manuscript once consigned to the bottom of the 'large delf jug'.

Most painful of all was the realisation that neighbours knew more about him than he did, since the scandal was whispered from one generation to the next. He would have picked up some information from those he trusted: from John Taaffe ('Michael'), Johnny Cassidy, Pat McCue his half-uncle, and his distant cousins, the Caffreys. From these he would have learned that Kevany supported his child until such time as James was trained as a shoemaker and able to support his mother, Nancy Callan.[23] The abandoned mother had reared her son with whatever help she received by post from the teacher and from her brother who worked locally as a farm labourer. Pat McCue, her son from an early marriage, left home to earn his living in Sunderland, England. He is likely to have helped support them. James it was who looked after his uncle and his mother until their deaths. He won the respect of his neighbours for the way he carried out his filial duties.

Peter, Patrick's brother, believes that James occasionally met his father by appointment in Dublin and so he would have been told of his relatives in Tullamore and in Co Sligo. In 1896 Patrick Kevany died in Tullamore aged 70. He is buried in an unmarked grave in Durrow, Tullamore. Two months later Nancy Callan died at Mucker, aged 64. The signature 'James Kevany' on his mother's death-certificate indicates her son's presence at her death. This correct spelling of his name was a recognition, at last, of his true identity. When his father died in Tullamore, his estate amounted to almost eight hundred pounds, then a large sum money. Did James receive money from this will? It is significant that the following year, James Kavanagh, who seemed to have neither land nor fortune, was in a position to marry Brigid Quinn, a farmer's daughter from Tullyrane. It was whispered among the neighbours that he had inherited money!

What Patrick Kavanagh did not know

It was easy for Patrick Kavanagh to know his Callan ancestors. Nancy, his grandmother, had remained unmarried and had brought up her son, his father James, to be industrious, intelligent, and caring of herself and her brother Michael. His half-uncle Pat McCue and family came home periodically from Sunderland in England. What Patrick Kavanagh did not know was that his intrepid grandfather had, within six months of his expulsion from Inniskeen, found his way back into education through the workhouse in Tullamore. He was employed there

Tullamore Workhouse, built 1841 and demolished in 1977. Patrick Kevany worked here, as a teacher 1856-61 and as Master of the workhouse from 1862 until his death in 1896. Photo courtesy Michael Byrne and The Historical Society, Tullamore, Co Offaly.

Harbour Street, Tullamore. Patrick Kevany lived in the fourth house on the left-hand side, with his wife Mary, daughters Mary Brigid and Catherine, and son Patrick. Photo courtesy Historical Society, Tullamore.

for a year before the Commissioners of Education detected the connection between their new employee and the 'Patrick Kevany', late of Kednaminsha. By then he was acting as an exemplary educator and agriculturalist so that the Board of Guardians of Tullamore, well known to the Trench family, found a way to pardon and reinstate him. In 1861 he was promoted to the prestigious position of Master of the Workhouse, a position which he held until his death in 1896. Seventeen years of employment in the workhouse had passed before Kevany married Mary Molloy, also in workhouse employment in Mountmellick. As well as his position of responsibility in the workhouse, he had rented a house and shop in Harbour Street where he and his wife conducted a drapery business and reared their family. They had four children, two boys and two girls. One boy (Owen) died before reaching maturity and the other, also Patrick Kevany, inherited the family business on the death of his mother. He sold his stock and moved to Dublin sometime during the 1940s, where he worked as a clerk and a minor journalist.[24] He had a flat at 52, Shelbourne Road, which he held until his death in 1950 aged sixty-eight. He might have been seen by his nephew, a quiet reserved clerical-looking man, making his way slowly along the street with the help of a walking-stick. He lived only a short distance from Patrick's flat at 62, Pembroke Road. Neither may have known of the other's existence, although this new information throws a strange light on Patrick's poem 'Memory of my Father', which significantly says little about his father's life in Monaghan and a lot more about old men in cities:

> Every old man I see
> Reminds me of my father.
> When he had fallen in love with death
> One time when sheaves were gathered.
>
> That man I saw in Gardiner Street
> Stumble on the kerb was one,
> He stared at me half-eyed,
> I have been his son.

The two Kevany daughters were more difficult to trace. Eventually it has emerged that they became Mercy nuns in Galway and that one of them, Sr Louis, had, by a strange twist of irony, spent years of her religious life working with the women of the Magdalen Laundry in Galway. Sr Francis nursed in the Galway Infirmary. Their graves can be found in front of Our Lady's Grotto which Sr Louis had arranged to be built. People

Srs Francis and Louis Kevany, Patrick's two aunts whom he never knew.

Sr Louis's grave, at the Magdalen Laundry, Galway.

who knew her were not surprised at the information that she was Patrick Kavanagh's aunt, since she was a character in her own right and left many anecdotes of her originality and eccentricity behind her.

The 'Magdalens' or 'Maggies' whom she looked after were were mostly unmarried mothers who had been abandoned by their families because of having become pregnant out of wedlock. Sr Louis, by all reports, was kindly towards them. They helped her weed the outdoor grotto in the convent grounds as an occasional relief from laundry work. The sins against Nancy Callan were unknowingly atoned for by the next generation of Kevanys. Sr Louis Kevany's grave is marked with the traditional black iron cross customary for a nun's grave and is located in the grounds of the Magdalen Laundry. Her grave is sheltered by the grotto she once lovingly tended.

Patrick Kavanagh knew only vaguely of his relatives in Tullamore. Fictitiously he speaks of Tarry Flynn's having an 'uncle Petey' who wrote infrequently and was 'Ringmaster' of 'a circus in Tullamore'. Kevany (Senior) might well have described his job of Master of the Workhouse as ringmaster of a circus. The Minute-Books of The Board of Guardians in Tullamore suggest that the task of Master was an unenviable one where he often had to cope with difficult characters.

But how much did Patrick really know? Were there letters perhaps in the Kavanagh home from Tullamore? Patrick's 'humourosity' as a writer was able to play with the facts, disguising the truth yet getting the story so nearly right. Or was he unsure? His father James was dead. There was no one to ask.

Whatever the disadvantages, stigmas or personal afflictions Kavanagh endured, he saw himself from an early age as 'different'. There was a 'kink' in him, a defect, he said, that made people treat him as a fool! He accepted this truth with the unexpected help of Dostoyevsky!

Patrick – The 'Gam' of the family
When I was born the people weren't expecting a poet ... The

people didn't want a poet but a fool, yes they could be doing
with one of these. And I grew up not exactly 'like another'. I
was installed the fool.[25]

The stigma of 'fool' or the position of being 'not like another',
was familiar to Kavanagh from youth.[26] His brother Peter,
twelve years his junior, recalls how Patrick was the designated
'Gam' of the family, a title which suggests stupidity and lack of
practical know-how. He was frequently laughed at within the
family and his love of writing ridiculed. Patrick always claimed
that this early abuse damaged him.[27]

James Kavanagh may also unknowingly have contributed to
Patrick's position of low self-esteem, through the severity of the
beatings he gave his son in his youth. Although father and son
were close, nevertheless the industrious James Kavanagh disap-
proved of his son's 'day-dreaming ways'. The greatest threat in
post-Famine Ireland was the prospect of ending one's days 'in
the workhouse'. Like many of his contemporaries, James was
determined that famine would never again visit the Kavanagh
household. 'Spare the rod and spoil the child' was a common
maxim in the rearing of children. James Kavanagh did not spare
the rod on Patrick:

Like Solomon he was a firm believer in the virtue-giving
qualities of the rod, except that he used the strap, and many's
the flogging I got from him, most of which I deserved…[28]

On the death of his father, he mentions these beatings again but
this time with even more effort at rationalising them. 'They had
helped to make me pliant and resilient in a world where proud
things get broken'.[29] However well he tried to rationalise these
painful incidents, their memory still lingers. In *Sacred Keeper*,
Peter tells us that, later in life, Patrick took 'a more caustic view'
of their friendship, objecting to those beatings as psychologically
damaging and unworthy of a father'.[30]

Though Patrick's mother saved him occasionally from the
harshness of his father's beatings, she too experienced frustration at his impracticality. Under the thinly disguised character of
Mrs Flynn, he saw that she was frequently puzzled as to the true

nature of her son's character who could never, she thought, see his own advantage. Had he looked after his 'little farm', 'instead of the oul' books and the writing', she believed he could be 'richer than the Reillys' who were to Mrs Flynn, the epitome of style![31]

Meanwhile, a battle waged within him as to the relevance of poetry. Significant voices seemed to demand, for his own good, a more practical contribution to life. Interiorly he remained true to his muse while externally he made efforts to be what they wanted. Poetry became at once his salvation and 'his crucifixion.'[32] He was a fool to follow it, but follow it he must! He felt misunderstood, knowing that his mother must surely believe that she had an idiot for a son:

> When I was growing up and for many years after
> I was led to believe that poems were thin
> Irrelevant, well out of the draught of laughter
> With headquarters the size of the head of a pin.
> I do not wonder that his mother moaned
> To see her beloved son an idiot boy. *(Poetry)*

To add to his familial discomfort, Patrick soon became the object of his neighbours' scorn also. 'Many of my neighbours treated me with cruelty and derision,' he remembered. The taunt 'your brother's a bard!' only aggravated the problem. When Patrick's first verses appeared in the *Weekly Independent*, he became ostracised even further. The stigma of being 'not like another', or having 'a kink' clung to Patrick. When neighbours saw him stop the plough midway in a furrow and write something on a cigarette packet, they thought he was mad. When he sat in his horse and cart reading a book while allowing the horse to lead him home, they believed he was steadily 'on the road to Ardee', the local lunatic asylum! Kavanagh knew he was a fool but he had to decide if he were an *authentic*, fool:

> I was the butt of many an assembly ... At wake, fair or dance for many years I was the fellow whom the jokers took a hand at when conversational funds fell low. I very nearly began to think myself an authentic fool.[33]

His sense of humour was a help, but there were limits to what he could tolerate. He shielded himself from ridicule by directing his thoughts to a world within.

The Tradition of 'Holy Fool'

In the Russian spiritual tradition, the cult of 'holy fool' gave rise to a particular style of holiness. The 'holy fool' lived out in practice the words of St Paul, 'If any one among you thinks that he is wise in this age, let him become a fool that he may become wise' (1 Cor 3:18) To be a fool 'for the sake of Christ' was to take on an unenviable burden. It involved embracing suffering, injustice, oppression and hardship at the hands of oppressors.[34] Despite his unlikely demeanour, the fool then became the real protector of the people. This role involved the acceptance of a guise of folly, even madness, which drew on him constant humiliation.

Louis Bouyer suggests that these 'fools for Christ', the *yurodivy*[35] of the Russian tradition, had an exaggerated attraction for those who saw them merely through the literary presentations of Tolstoy's Grisha and Dostoyevsky's Myshkin.[36] But this was a genuine religious cult which promoted the idea of 'oddity' as a means of sanctity. This Russian ascetical tradition is also paralleled in the ancient Celtic practice of *peregrinatio* – the holy voyage for the love of God. These saints left the security of homeland in primitive sea-faring vessels, abandoning themselves 'foolishly to the sea' in search of 'the lost country'. Reliance on God's providence was essential. In the Russian tradition the 'holy fool' became a voluntary outlaw living in dire poverty, free to perceive society's weaknesses and expose them.

Kavanagh was not unaware of an Irish charism for holy folly known to him through folklore, and especially through the writings of William Carleton. Tramps and beggarmen who roamed the roads were often inspired by the idea of abandoning themselves to the world and becoming fools for Christ's sake, living on charity and relying on Divine Providence. Robin Flower described these holy Irish madmen as 'troubled wits … sharing their couches with the creatures of the wild'. They spoke 'a medley of obscure folly and inspired wisdom'. Though their minds were dimmed in rationality, 'another part was illuminated by the divine light'. This combination of irrationality and illumination found expression in the exquisite poetry for which they were renowned.[37] Kavanagh, in particular, revelled in the 'dimming' of reason, knowing instead 'the speech of mountains'. He castigated knowledge that robbed him of primeval innocence:

> Before you came I knew the speech
> Of mountains, I could pray
> With stone and water.
> O foul leech
> That sucks truth's blood away! (*To Knowledge*)

Mad Sweeney, or 'Sweeney Astray' was an ancient Irish poet at odds with the institutional church, condemned by a curse and trapped in the shape of a bird.[38] He was forced to wander the length and breadth of Ireland, drunk with beauty, with loneliness and the presence of God. Sweeney provides an early model in the Celtic spiritual tradition of the Russian counterpart of 'holy fool'. Was Patrick Kavanagh a kind of 'Mad Sweeney' or a more up-to-date 'fool for Christ', 'a Matt Talbot of Monaghan'? (*The Great Hunger*)

Dostoyevsky's 'Idiot'

It is not surprising then that the spiritual childlikeness of Prince Myshkin attracted Kavanagh to Dostoyevsky's *Idiot*.[39] He had read it and re-read it. It was one of his favourite books. He identified with Myshkin who was frank, innocent and trusting, taking a foolish delight in self-abasement and frequently becoming the butt of others' criticism and scorn. Myshkin follows an impossible ideal of Christianity, refusing to believe evil of others and forgiving even their worst insults. The prince, rejected by his family, had a great need to be loved which rendered him exceptionally vulnerable. Kavanagh's own repeated love-strickenness found a kindred spirit in the prince who had fallen hopelessly in love with the haughty Aglaya. The prince wanted limitless time to contemplate his forlorn state and utter aloneness:

> At moments he dreamed of the mountains, and one familiar

spot in the mountains in particular, a place he always liked to remember and had been fond of visiting when he was there, from where he could look down on the village, on the faint gleaming streak of the waterfall below, the white clouds and the ruins of an ancient castle. Oh how he wished he could be there now and think of one thing only – oh, all his life of that one thing only – it would have kept him occupied for a thousand years! And let them – let them all forget him entirely here.[40]

Reflecting on Dostoyevsky's *Idiot* made Kavanagh think of his own lot.

Being made a fool of is good for the soul. It produces a sensitivity of one kind or other; it makes a man into something unusual, a saint or a poet or an imbecile.

Like the 'holy fool', Kavanagh would leave the reader guessing which he is: saint, poet or imbecile? Or does he see himself as a combination of all three: abandoned and spiritually 'orphaned'? He might find solace, like Mad Sweeney, in the momentary companionship of an animal or a weed or discover, like St Francis of Assisi, that creatures often possessed 'more Christian feelings' than humans. He seeks to be consoled in moments of despair by the poetry of the grass or the sight of the 'Evening Star over Jenny O'Toole's'. The grass could accommodate both his consolations and desolations. It would 'reflect the sun tomorrow and the wings of crows would be shadows upon it'.[41]

He regretted not having a more mountainous landscape where, like Myshkin, he might contemplate his situation more deeply. Here he might have experienced a greater intensity of beauty and been marked with deeper 'echo-corners' in his soul. He might even have known the madness of ecstasy:

If I had been born among the Mournes
Even in Forkhill,
I might have echo-corners in my soul
Repeating the dawn laughter.

I might have climbed to know the glory
Of toppling from the roof of seeing– *(Monaghan Hills)*

The Folly of Love

Kavanagh was a self-styled 'green fool' who had allowed himself become enslaved by the love of 'blue and green things'. His fields, he believed, had drugged him with their heady perfume and hedged him in with their whitethorn boundaries. He was laughed at for loving a field, a 'triangular field'. He loved stables, birds, trees, stones and weeds. There was 'a defect in him which these secluded fields developed',[42] loving 'even unto folly', a motto Kavanagh shared with no less a mystic than St Thérèse of Lisieux. Little things done with great love was her spiritual programme. In Kavanagh's words this becomes a theology of the ordinary:[43]

> nothing whatever is by love debarred
>
> The common and banal her heat can know.
>
> *(Lines Written on the Canal Bank Seat)*

An insignificant farmer attempting to scrape a living off poor land, while simultaneously involved in poetry and self-education, must have appeared foolish indeed to the learned parish priest Canon Maguire of Inniskeen. Fr Daly's words may have been wiser than he realised:

> 'This son of yours is a perfect fool, Mrs Flynn. A perfect fool. Yes, he takes on to know things that men have spent years in colleges to learn...'[44]

'Why should God choose you for these special graces and not me who has tried so hard to be worthy of his favours?' Kavanagh was in a position similar to Bernadette Soubirous whose novice mistress was envious of her special graces. He, like Bernadette Soubirous, knew that wisdom was not of the worldly kind yet he held secrets that were hidden from the 'wise'.[45] He, as 'child made seer', saw 'Christ transfigured' in a primrose and found him in a beggar's rags, while those of more respected religious observance failed to find him.

> And I whom men call fool ...
>
> Found Him whom the pieties
>
> Have vainly sought.
>
> *(Street Corner Christ)*

It was worth being a fool for such revelations. By contrast, Tarry Flynn's mercenary-minded neighbour, 'Charlie Treanor', served as a foil for the foolhardy poet with his fatal 'kink in the mind' for poetry. The poet wasted precious farming hours uselessly noticing 'clags and white butterflies ... dancing in the sun'. He felt it was his special job 'to puzzle out Eternity'. How foolish he seemed to Charlie Treanor! As a young man of twenty Patrick pondered over his 'foolishness' to see if there was anything of value in it. In his personal notebook he writes:

> When we are most foolish that is the time to study our real selves. That is the time to peer into the recesses of our minds and ask the question, 'where is my worth?' I write this because I played the seer and have been made a fool of by those whom I considered fools.[46]

His folly is seldom more poignantly felt than when, as poet-exile, he reflects on the foolishness of abandoning his 'childhood country' for a quixotic ideal:

> Out of that childhood country what fools climb
> To fight with tyrants Love and Life and Time?
> *(Peace)*

And yet, the decision to leave in the first place depicted one who was choosing the Way of the Cross. His poem 'Temptation in Harvest' establishes the unmistakeable parallel between Christ's temptation to renege on his passion and Kavanagh's temptation to abandon his dream. Could he, he asks himself, 'go over the fields to the city of the Kings?' Could he, like Christ, set his face on Jerusalem? He heard and saw all the danger signals: leaves 'spiked upon a thorn' foreshadowing the crowning with thorns, the sound of wood being cut, the wood of the cross. He saw the soldiers, the reserves – 'the flaggers in the swamp' – ready to 'ring him round' and arrest him. But in spite of the gentle seduction of weeds, trailing flowers and his own misgivings, he left the homeliness of Inniskeen for another love. He followed the wily seductress who 'winked' at him.

This poem is more sophisticated than might be suggested on first reading. The statement that it is 'what we love' and not 'what loves us' that 'we must make our own' is profound. Allegiance must be given, it suggests, not to the wily seduction of people and places who proffer us love, but to one's innermost 'calling'. Kavanagh states what modern psychologists now claim, that it is 'our desire' that constitutes our deepest identity and goal in life and not merely our duty or compliance with custom.

By following his desire Kavanagh saw himself a Christ-figure, condemned to suffer for his belief in poetry in spite of the pleas of those who begged him to remain on the land. Intuitively he knew that he was following a calling that would lead to crucifixation. We may not like Kavanagh's messianic stance, but it is there for all to see. He was foolish to leave and would have been equally foolish to stay. Kavanagh was born to lose, whichever way he chose. Ultimately poetry would both crown and crucify him.

Kavanagh: 'The Accused'

Kavanagh came from a litigious background. His father often entertained the family by reading aloud sessions from the House of Commons, as well as from court-case reports in the *Dundalk Democrat*. James Kavanagh would occasionally set up a mock-trial in the kitchen of his home before a local case was tried. The Kavanaghs had a talent for drama. It was often said of Lucy that she was wasted as a teacher and should have gone on stage. It is not surprising that Patrick includes a mock-trial in his novel, where Tarry Flynn becomes the defendant. Tarry had been accused of cutting bushes on the wrong side of Flynn's fence thereby infuriating his neighbour. A mock-trial was held in the plaintiff Finnegan's house. Tarry overhears the proceedings, in which he is subjected to cross-examination by the solicitor and ridicule by a neighbour, Petey Meegan, who attempts to mimic him:

> Solicitor: Your're a bit of a poet, Flynn, I believe? (laughter)
> Petey (attempting to mimic Tarry): There's a great beauty in stone and weeds (more laughter).[47]

Several years after the publication of *Tarry Flynn* (1948), a real court case arose (1954) where Patrick took the *Leader* to court on a charge of libel.[48] The claim against the *Leader* concerned an article entitled 'Profile: Mr Kavanagh' which appeared in print on 11 October, 1952. Kavanagh claimed that he had been 'held up to odium, hatred, ridicule and contempt, and had been gravely damaged in his reputation and profession'.[49] Consequently, he embarked on a lengthy and emotionally exhausting law-suit. He was called to defend himself as a poet, writer and literary critic, thereby evoking an uncanny similarity between the fictitious law-suit in *Tarry Flynn*, and what eventually happened between 1952 and 1954.[50]

The 'Profile' of Mr Kavanagh had indeed been a send-up. It described his person in mock-laudatory tones,'a pard-like spirit, beautiful and swift', so far from the truth that it poked fun at Kavanagh's actual awkwardness and ungainly appearance. Mr John A. Costello, as counsel for the defendant, cross-examined Mr Kavanagh the plaintiff:

> Mr Costello: 'Do you agree that the phrase "pard-like spirit, beautiful and swift" is a complimentary phrase'?
> Mr Kavanagh: I don't know it would get you a job.
> Mr Costello: 'That is not the point' – 'That is the keynote of modern living,' responded Mr Kavanagh,.
> 'Do you agree that it is a complimentary phrase?'
> 'Yes, with a strong note of starvation implicit in it.'
> Mr Costello: That may be the fate of poets.
> Mr Kavanagh: Nothing is a complimentary phrase which takes away a man's dinner.[51]

During his cross-examination Kavanagh repeatedly emphasised the poverty and plight of the writer, discounting the 'left-handed compliment' of being called 'our finest living poet'. His argument was stated bluntly: 'it doesn't buy butter or bread'. He also alludes to his own innovative prophetic role in Irish literature and feels unjustly maligned in spite of the pioneering work he has done for the nation. The report read as follows:

> Mr Kavanagh said that he knew quite well it was he who had

led a movement to weed out anything that was bogus. There
was a new thing growing up – a new fresh and lovely thing.
'There will be good writers in the country, and it will be due
to my work'.[52]

Continuing in this strangely prophetic manner, the plaintiff is
reminded of his own words on the subject of truth: 'The world is
full of Pilates asking the question which is always cynical,
"What is truth?" And every man who has in him something of
Christ will reply, "I am truth".'

> Mr Kavanagh: I don't see that I should disagree with that. I
> hope we all have something of Christ in us.
> Mr Costello: I believe we have.

Quoting further from Kavanagh's writing and continually challenging him on the meaning of his statements, Mr Costello reads
another excerpt from the poet's writing:

> Absolute truth is met with absolute hate. So in Ireland the
> only person who is likely to suffer till his heart is turned to
> stone is the writer – when such animal happens to appear.[53]

Mr Costello wondered if the plaintiff were not insinuating that
he had the ultimate truth. To this Kavanagh adds his often-quoted
phrase which confirms him in his Christ-figure role:

> It is difficult for a man who tells the truth. If I really told the
> truth they would take me up on a high hill and crucify me.[54]

Cronin believed that this overt messianic role expressed by
Kavanagh could easily degenerate into a martyr-complex. It
seemed to stem from the pathology of needing to be victim.[55]

The law-suit drew upon him exhaustive cross-examination.
Kavanagh was forced to defend himself publicly before a jury, in
matters that up to now had been part of what the poet called his
'humorosity' as a writer. Questions were asked regarding the
obscenity of certain passages in *The Great Hunger*. A previous
libel action taken by St John Gogarty pertaining to a passage in
The Green Fool, was resurrected and used in court to insinuate
that Kavanagh was accustomed to libellous action. Derogatory
words such as 'gurriers', 'buckleppers', 'firbolgs' were isolated
from their context and scrutinised in court. His unhappy rela-

tionship with Brendan Behan became an unexpected focal point
in the questioning. Clarification was sought regarding defamatory remarks written by Kavanagh, condemning 'the pigmy
literature that was produced by the so-called Irish literary re-
naissance'. His differences with past employers, his periods of
unproductiveness as a writer, even the ungainliness of his person, all became the focus of attention and matter for public questioning. Accounts of the trial were highly entertaining for the
public and eagerly read each day in the *Irish Times* over a period
of two weeks. Many who had never heard of Patrick Kavanagh
now knew of him because of this infamous court-case.

Kavanagh performed in court in his persona, apparently rev-
elling in the publicity. Called to defend his position as writer,
poet, and critic, his extreme vulnerability became excessively exposed. Under the glare of cross-examination, sometimes lasting
all day long, he sustained the mask, the bravado, while inwardly
his spirit ached. He had expected to gain substantial damages
because of the defamatory nature of the *Leader* article. Instead,
the jury found that Mr Kavanagh had *not* been libelled by the
article. Judgement was accordingly entered in favour of defen-
dants, with costs against the plaintiff.'[56] But Kavanagh was now
quite unwell. He had lung-cancer and within a few weeks was to
undergo major surgery.

His suffering and rejection during the whole of his Dublin
period became concentrated during the trial. This suffering and
intense hardship had had a double effect on the poet. On the one
hand, he became embittered, giving vent to satire, which was
clever and arrogant. Against the self-congratulory provincial
Dublin mentality, he had lashed out pitilessly, filled with sar-
donic wit:

> Outside this pig-sty life deteriorates,
> Civilisation dwindles. We are the last preserve
> Of Eden in a world of savage states.
> (*The Defeated*)

He had been equally scathing of 'Dublin's pretentious poet-
tasters' and 'bumptious intellectuals' denigrating them together

in 'The Paddiad' as a undifferentiated mob of massminded-ness.[57]

All the Paddies having fun
Since Yeats handed in his gun.
Every man completely blind
To the truth about his mind.

In stark contrast to the blinding satire of 'The Paddiad', he turns inward to confronts the truth about himself in 'Prelude', one of his finest poems. Struggling with the temptation yet again to satirise his enemies, he acknowledges his fault only to discover a new poetic and spiritual territory. He experiences the beginnings of catharsis, which he had previously exercised in 'The Great Hunger' without fully realising its enormously healing effects.

Ridicule, failure, serious illness, and the termination of relationship with a girl-friend of long-standing, brought Kavanagh, in December 1954, to stand alone before the shambles of his life. This period, in mystical language, could be called Kavanagh's Dark Night of the Soul:

Upon a gloomy night,
With all my cares to loving ardours flushed …
With nobody in sight
I went abroad when all my house was hushed.

He described the awfulness of the dilemma in which he found himself and his mood of utter desolation:

In all my life there is only one year in which I could say that I suffered a horrible desolation of spirit. This was the year 1954 when I was nurturing within my body that most celebrated of modern diseases – lung cancer ... It was the sickness of mind, the feeling of degradation.[58]

Hurt in his pride, his ego shattered, his spirit 'groping' for light 'under a low sky', he claws his way through his 'gloomy night', now more alone than ever before. Though much less reposed in his 'dark night' than St John of the Cross, Kavanagh's poetic 'dark night' is still one of surrender to darkness and unknowing. 'Making the statement is enough' is his wise solution to dealing with a host of unanswered questions concerning the cruelty of life:

Nineteen fifty-four, hold on till I try
To formulate some theory about you. A personal matter:
My lamp of contemplation you sought to shatter,
To leave me groping in madness under a low sky.
O I wish I could laugh! O I wish I could cry!
Or find some formula, some mystical patter
That would organise a perspective from this hellish scatter –
Everywhere I look a part of me is exiled from the I.
… there are no answers
To any real question …
(Ninteen Fifty-Four)

In mystical terms, this experience of total privation is a kind of mystical death. The spark of inspiration that has previously nourished the soul is no longer present. The sense of God is absent. A sense of helplessness and imperfection along with a feeling of 'degradation' contribute to the 'hellish scatter' experienced by Kavanagh. Mystically speaking, the ego is helpless, the will and intelligence impotent. The self must now become abandoned and wait upon God for solace.[59] The intensity and duration of this 'dark night' varies from one mystic to the next. Kavanagh's was of mercifully short duration.

The poem 'Prelude' was to mark a turning point poetically and spiritually for Kavanagh. The poem records an expression of self-purification, spiritually more effective than the self-inflicted crucifixion imposed by the trial. He finds a way to emerge from his 'dark night' into a new landscape and habitat, the 'inland' territory of his soul. He is blessed with a healthy level of self-knowledge. The veil is lifted from the ugly details of his *via dolorosa*. His life has become transfigured. In the transforming moment, 'the bits of road' he has ignominiously travelled have become 'eternal lanes of joy', his 'particular trees' are robed again in mystery, and happiest of all the 'millstone' he has bravely carried has miraculously become 'a star'. Henceforth, he will seek only the protection of love since it is 'lovers alone' whom 'lovers protect'.

Written partly during, and partly in the wake of, his unhappy law-suit, 'Prelude' is a kind of apologia for his life. Kavanagh views himself firstly through the eyes of others, a failed writer, unproductive, defeated. Early in the poem he moves with deft, satirical rhythm cleverly taking venomous aim at journalists, professors, bogus religion and art committees, while pretending in Popean tones to advise himself on how to succeed in life:

> Bring out a book as soon as you can
> and let them see you're a living man …
> Note well the face profoundly grave,
> An empty house can house a knave.

Midway the tone changes to a moment of self-revelation. He surrenders to it with intense lyrical fervour:

> But satire is unfruitful prayer,
> Only wild shoots of blossom there,
> But you must go inland and be
> Lost in compassion's ecstacy,
> Where suffering soars on summer air –
> The millstone has become a star.

Kavanagh is no longer foraging for inspiration in the poetic scrubland of clever and bitter satire, but luxuriating in the lush cadences of a fertile inland soil, the territory of his soul. It is here that he finds his surest poetic voice. 'Prelude' exemplifies the truth that, whatever Kavanagh pretended to be in his persona – arrogant, insulting, ungainly – he remained consistently honest, authentic, sincere (*sine cerum,* without wax) and surprisingly agile in his poetic technique. Nor did he fail to confront himself in the lonely 'cell of self-knowledge' which, mystically speaking, is the cornerstone of authentic self-purification.[60]

Kavanagh, the victim, the injured, the accused, must be seen not only in his genuine brokenness, but also in his almost pathological pursuit of ridicule. Though prophetic in many ways, he almost overplayed his role of having to defend and justify his position as a poet and writer. He enjoyed being a Christ-figure and felt an almost unhealthy security in being crucified. The position of defence was his favourite one, he liked the limits it set, the intransigence of its boundaries, the inescapable cornered sensation. Perhaps he felt, and with certain justification, that it goaded him into creativity.

Conclusion

Kavanagh was temperamentally suited to deal with negative experiences of God, to cope with emptiness, void, darkness, and nothingness which have been traditionally associated with the purgative stages of the mystical life.[61] 'Maybe the darkness is God,' says Matt Talbot in Tom Kilroy's play *Talbot's Box*, a sentiment with which Kavanagh would have concurred. He gravitated instinctively towards 'dark knowledge', God's absence, as a testing ground for the moment of revelation. He frequently denies himself access to brightness, except in the smallest measure: the slit, the chink, the tiniest aperture. Eventually, like Tarry Flynn, and the mystic, he sees best with his eyes closed. This is the darkness of interior contemplation.

Rejection and isolation served to leave him alone in the company of his muse. His alter ego, Tarry Flynn, is even more intensely a 'green fool' than his earlier precursor, inviting endless misunderstanding, ridicule and persecution. Kavanagh, though undoubtedly stigmatised, became excessive in his predeliction for the role of 'holy fool'. Nevertheless his spirituality of suffering was sound. To Richard Riordan, whom he later chose as best-man at his wedding, he confided that 'God sometimes enters the heart through a wound'. When one reflects on the profundity of such a statement, one realises that Kavanagh had access to an extraordinary depth of personal spirituality. Riordan acknowledges a lifelong personal indebtedness to Kavanagh.[62] This *via negativa*, though spiritually cleansing, could also degenerate on occasion into the darkness of paranoia, the plight of the sensitive soul who loses direction.

Kavanagh, nevertheless, could make light of his sufferings or see them as the price he must pay for poetry. Tarry Flynn is imbued with an inner sense of greatness which he feels could be endangered by intimacy with the 'girl he had dreamt of', convinced that to be great he must run away from things like this' ...

'he could never hope to hold this girl.[63] The greatness he sought was to become worthy of Divine Revelation, 'the flash of Divine Intelligence'[64] which he equated with true poetry. He would gladly suffer deprivation to keep this gift intact.

But for all his infatuation for women, Kavanagh may secretly have feared sexual intimacy. He loved passionately, but always from a distance, and always with a sense of hopelessness.[65] Had his father, victim of an irregular union, communicated an unconscious fear of sexuality? Or, as Kavanagh himself insisted, was he the 'poet or prophet' whose heart is so fixed on Parnassus that no human love can oust it?[66] Whatever goal possessed his heart, he was endowed, as many have said of him, with a certain quality of incorruptibility. He was a dogged follower of poetry through pain, poverty and occasional despair. His singleminded resolve has overtones of vocation and the will to follow it, come what may:

> … The main thing is to continue
> To walk Parnassus right into the sunset
> Detached in love where pygmies cannot pin you
> To the ground like Gulliver. *(Dear Folks)*

When he considered he had failed in this, his most cherished mission, he is badly shaken and turns to God in prayer:

> O God can a man find You when he lies with his face
> downwards
> And his nose in the rubble that was his achievement?
> *(From Failure Up)*

These lines, indicate a real desolation of spirit which come close to despair in 'On Reading a Book on Common Wild Flowers', written in the Rialto Hospital:

> Am I late?
> Am I tired?
> Is my heart sealed
> From the ravening passion that will eat it out
> Till there is not one pure moment left?

Though never as exposed in his despair as Hopkins, he nevertheless echoes something of the 'black' mood present in:

I am gall, I am heartburn. God's most deep decree
Bitter would have me taste: my taste was me;

Kavanagh's 'hell' of despair and self-disgust would eventually lead to the discovery of an answer to failure. His new knowledge would be gained at the cost of painful rebirth on the banks of the Grand Canal in the summer of 1955:

I learned, I learned – when one might be inclined
To think, too late, you cannot recover your losses –
I learned something of the nature of God's mind,
Not the abstract Creator but he who caresses
The daily and nightly earth; He who refuses
To take failure for an answer till again and again is worn.

(Miss Universe)

Kavanagh's moral strength was that he constantly learned from experience. He learned something new of God, of the world and of himself. Because his preoccupation was primarily metaphysical and not merely literary, his poetic journey like that of Hopkins and Eliot is also a spiritual one. Purification, however, was not in vain; it prepared him for those moments of illumination so characteristic of Kavanagh. Illumination was a further stage in the development of his mystical imagination.

CHAPTER 6

Illumination I

Intimations of Immortality

> I was in my mother's arms clinging with my small hands to
> the security of her shoulder. I saw into a far mysterious place
> that I long associated with Wordsworth's Ode on Immort-
> ality. I believed for many years that I had looked into the
> world from whence I came. And perhaps I had.
>
> *(The Green Fool)*[1]

The 'far mysterious place' of immortality which Kavanagh had
gazed into as a child was nothing more than 'the secret side of a
cupboard' whose 'not very accessible top-shelf was filled with
rent receipts and curtain rings'. Nevertheless, as an infant he
had unconsciously embarked on a journey of contemplation and
wonderment. He was entering the world of secret, barely accessible knowledge proper to the mystic.[2]

His visionary eye was further exercised by the view from the
hills that surrounded his home: Candlefort, 'Cassidy's hanging
hill', Rocksavage and Shanmullagh. These opened up magical
vistas into neighbouring counties.

> From the tops of the little hills there spread a view right back
> to the days of St Patrick and the druids. Slieve Gullion to the
> north fifteen miles distant, to the west the bewitched hills
> and forths of Donaghmoyne…[3]

As Kavanagh contemplates his landscape one sees in him something of a dreamer and a seer. 'Donaghmoyne' a few miles distant was the romantic place where Patrick Maguire and his
friends 'walked through the moon of Donaghmoyne ... seeking

adventure'. This moment summons up an image of transcendence, one of 'the brighter possibilities' which counterpoints images of a fallen world in 'The Great Hunger'.[4]

Depite the 'clay-strickenness' of Kavanagh's existence, he could imaginatively pierce the crust of the landscape with its cultural accretions, and be back with Sweeney the mad Gaelic poet, wrapt in 'primeval magic among the trees'. (*Lough Lerg*) His was a calling to be different, a source of frequent embarrassment which he attempted in vain to conceal with awkward displays of vulgarity and eccentricity. Instead of 'dancing at some cross-roads' as a youth, he wandered 'among the innocence of flower-land and tree-land' ... and remained true to himself and to the poetry and vision that were his.[5] His strong affinity with nature, together with his counter-cultural stance, gives him kinship with Sweeney who says:

I have lived among trees
Between flood and ebb-tide,
Going cold and naked

With no pillow for my head,
No human company
And, so help me, God,
No spear and no sword![6]

Kavanagh and Sweeney come close to the gospel theme of radical abandonment to divine providence, expressed in St Luke's gospel: 'Foxes have holes and the birds of the air have nests, but the Son of man has nowhere to lay his head.' (Lk 9:58) Being a poet made Kavanagh an outsider who saw clearly and was doomed to suffer the consequences of his prophetic vision.

To the infuriation of his parents and neighbours, he 'wasted' time gazing at the landscape and allowing the fields to stare at him. His comtemplation was involuntary. In mystical terms, this gazing might be ascribed to a state of inner quiet.[7] He enjoyed the 'wise passiveness' of the nature-mystic which allowed him possess his landscape interiorily:

Not everybody can have the fields and lanes stare at him as they stare at a man driving a cow to the fair.[8]

Of his fellow east-Ulster poets, Art Mc Cooey, Peadar Ó Doirnín and Séamus Dall Mac Cuarta, he said: 'they absorbed the little fields and lanes and became authentic through them'.[9] Kavanagh followed in their footsteps but went even further by absorbing the numinous quality of fields, lanes and cart-tracks. He dismantled old cliches and made Christianity 'young and new again', resurrecting it from 'old stables where Time begins'. (*Advent*)

>   What is this life, if full of care
>
>   We have no time to stand and stare?

With studied deliberateness Kavanagh alters W. H. Davies' famous lines, breaks with the familiar in order to make a new statement. He attributes life and spiritual vitality to earth and to things of earth, allowing them a life and movement of their own:

>   What is this life if, not full of care,
>
>   We do not let the cart-tracks stare
>
>   Into our hearts with love's despair?[10]

Through the medium of his character, Tarry Flynn, we find the poet, awkwardly wrapt in wonder, dumbstruck in the presence of an unearthly power staring at him from the fields and hedges:

>   … But if he did not look at the hedges or the dust of the road these things looked at him. Now he was caught in the stare of a huge boulder of whinstone that stood half way up the pass to Callan's house.[11]

Kavanagh exudes a primitive sense of awe reminiscent of the instinctive religious feeling which grips one in the presence of Ayer's Rock in Australia or Zuma Rock in Nigeria. He saw earth as a living organism and not merely an object of contemplation. Few would have suspected that this eccentric Co Monaghan youth was imbued not only with visionary knowledge but with a sense of contingency in the face of the eternal gaiety and superabundance of God. The illusory nature of worldly values and the transience of life were themes that struck at the heart of his poetic inspiration. He heard, with a mixture of awe and detachment, his 'pennies of time' numbered and counted in some eternal 'counting house', and was gripped by the awareness of life passing:

> You cannot keep the eastern sun
> On Cassidy's hill;
> You cannot stop the clock of Time
> On Adam's mill;
> You cannot slip down your vest
> Death's great pill;
> You must grow old Paddy Kavanagh
> So dream your fill. (*My Birthday*)

This early poem (1935) shows a sharpened awareness of life and death. But he was incapable of revealing his mystical gift in ways other than through poetry and writing. He was shy to speak of his belief in God except perhaps to his sister Celia who became a nun. Nevertheless he continued to be faithful to his own particular brand of religious practice, a fact which undoubtedly sustained his faith and enriched him symbolically. Despite his railings against institutional religion, Kavanagh's religious sense is strong. He had a natural awareness of the holy, of what Rudolf Otto calls the *mysterium tremendum et fascinans*.[12] He experienced 'the spirit-shocking wonder of a black-slanted Ulster hill' as well as the 'heart-breaking strangeness in dreeping hedges'. He was both awed and fascinated by the newness and strangeness in things around him. As early as 1933 he shows his ease with the sacred dimension of earth by contemplating the white seeds of spring-sowing. He uses a spiritually-laden metaphor in:[13]

> Now leave the check-reins slack,
> The seed is flying far today –
> the seed like stars against the black
> Eternity of April clay.
> (*To the Man after the Harrow*)

A sense of restrained awe emanates from this poem where the worker touches 'the formless void' of earth and partners God in the work of Creation. The poet stands reverently, placing what mysticism might call a 'cloud of forgetting' between the distracting power of those who stand 'on Brady's hill' and his absorption in and contemplation of the sacred.[14]

Forget the men on Brady's hill

Forget what Brady's boy may say ...

For you are driving your horses through

The mist where Genesis begins.

An enterprise in clay had begun which was not only earthy but mystical as well.

From the beginning, Kavanagh is richly endowed with a layer of pre-Christian religion. He is a genuine pagan, a word which derives its meaning from the French *paysanne* and the Latin *paganus*, meaning rustic. He is a man devoted to his *pagus* or district, fascinated with all that is 'unbaptised' and pre-Christian in it. He is at one with 'the poetic paganism of black-birds'.[15] Together, he and the blackbird become worshippers of the sun, eager to assimilate 'the rich colours and the mystical depths of the older faith'.[16] Along with 'Fr Mat', he cherished the opportunity to contemplate his landscape:

Stare through gaps at ancient Ireland sweeping

In again with all its unbaptised beauty:

The calm evening

The whitethorn blossoms,

The smell from ditches that were not Christian.

(Why Sorrow?)

Like mad Sweeney, he feared that institutionalised religion would rob him of his natural affinity for nature-worship. Filled with an awareness of the sacredness of the cosmos, he longed to be a part of a eucharistic banquet of life:

To your high altar I once came

Proudly, even brazenly, and I said:

Open your tabernacles I too am flame

Ablaze on the hills of Being. Let the dead

Chant the low prayer beneath a candled shrine,

O cut me life's bread, for me pour wine! *(Worship)*

'I too am flame' is a plea for the celebration of *his* life. He is not content to allow all worship and sacredness become the prerog-atives of church-centred eucharist. Kavanagh sensed in the Catholicism of his time an over-emphasis on the resplendence of heaven and an over-preoccupation with the unworthiness of humankind. His own religious preference seemed to retain hints of a more creation-affirming Celtic spirituality.

Something of the mystical light of prehistoric Newgrange flickers in the Kavanagh landscape. Newgrange is indeed neither geographically nor spiritually far removed from Inniskeen. The sun, for Kavanagh, as for neolithic man, was a source of revelation, healing and illumination. Sun-lit patches of landscape, 'the seat … that was a suntrap', 'the sun … lifting to importance (his) sixteen acre farm' *(Literary Adventures)*: these illumine Kavanagh's spirit as surely as the sun illuminated the pre-Christian Celtic world. Had he been alive then, Kavanagh would have rejoiced at winter solstice rituals, at sunrays penetrating ancient tombs, signalling immortality for dead spirits.[17] It was not the sun which captured his attention so much as its transforming power: its patterns on the little drumlin hills, its intimations of divine light, its radiance etched on everyday things within his contemplative range.

Kavanagh's affinity for pre-Christian religion derives from his strong sense of original innocence. There was for him a world of perfect innocence and beauty which predated the Fall, mythically recounted in the Bible. A residual unsullied radiance still remained, he felt, in the rural landscape, in the trees and flowers and in the stones and hedges. He wanted to recapture this lost innocence. Kavanagh's experiences of illumination, especially in his early poetry, stems from a conviction that he can recover his lost Eden and reverence again its virginal beauty.

The Innocence of Eden

Kavanagh's nostalgia for his lost Eden, his 'unworn world' is intense. Christmas is a painful reminder of 'the gay garden that was childhood's'. He longed to roam as of old, in 'the garden of the golden apples' and taste once again 'the luxury of a child's soul'. *(Advent)* The child, for him, epitomises mystical clear-sightedness, a way of seeing 'newness in every stale thing' and enjoying privileged insight. The poet warns the child to tread warily, lest he or she stray among 'the lean grey wolves' that lurk in 'the dark places of soul'. The child's rightful entitlement is gratuitous illumination – a glimpse of God:

> Child there is a light somewhere
> Under a star,
> Sometime it will be for you
> A window that looks
> Inward to God. (To A Child)

The poet intimates that a measure of illumination had been his from youth. Kavanagh's utopia is best captured in his 'Christmas Childhood', glittering with hoar-frost and tingling with magic. Here he glimpsed the 'transfigured face of a beauty the world did not touch'. Edenic images filter too, albeit reluctantly, through the dank atmosphere of 'The Great Hunger' carrying 'half glimpses of paradise', 'sunlight-woven cloaks' and 'chance windows of poetry and prayer'. Early in life the poet experiences a loss of this original poetic immediacy. Kavanagh is reluctant to become 'dis-illusioned' and to outgrow his Christmas childhood. He is slow to exchange the Divine Infant of illumination for the chastening purification of a God who 'delight(s) in disillusionment'. (Lough Derg)

Following the biblical imagery of the Fall, Kavanagh blames knowledge for his loss of innocence. It is clear that the poet is referring to some loss of mystical 'knowing' which has occurred through a more functional knowledge of life. Prior to eating from 'the Tree of knowledge', he enjoyed, like Adam and Eve, mystical powers and privileges. He knew 'the speech of mountains'; he could 'pray with stone and water', while his first dream 'had wings of light / And cherub witchery.' (To Knowledge) Having tasting the 'forbidden fruit' of knowledge, he feels that something within him has died. He struggles to recapture it in later poems such as 'Auditors In', 'Innocence' and especially in his Canal Bank poems. Some earthly knowledge shattered his 'Christmas Childhood' world so that his loss of Eden would continue to haunt him:

O you, Eve, were the world that tempted me
To eat the knowledge that grew in clay
And death the germ within it!
(A Christmas Childhood)

Although he longed for ideal love, Kavanagh resigns himself to a kind of fallen angelhood. What notion of perfect love tortured him so deeply that he feared love's consequences? A profound sadness lingers in the deceptive simplicity of 'Raglan Road' which warns that 'when the angel woos the clay he'd lose his wings at the dawn of day'. With similar death-dealing agony 'the clay hand was clapped across the mouth of Prophecy' strangling Tarry Flynn's life-enhancing dreams, while 'a layer of sticky soil lay between the fires of the heart preventing a general conflagration'. Images of clay become harbingers of death, especially in 'The Great Hunger'. The death of Eden is further accentuated by the presence of a ghostly figure, 'the apocalypse of clay', fiendishly haunting every corner of a land once allegedly idyllic and unspoilt.

By 1939, when he was beginning to be known as a poet, Kavanagh echoed Wordsworth's complaint that 'there hath passed away a glory from the earth'. This recurring idea that something had been lost is echoed in 'Primrose', when as a 'childhood seer' he had experienced 'one small flower flowering in (his) mind'. Clear-sighted vision reveals a 'page of Truth's manuscript made clear'. He finishes 'Primrose' (c.1939) with the Wordsworthean lament that

The years that pass
Like tired soldiers nevermore have given
Moments to see wonders in the grass. *(Primrose)*

But this was a false alarm. Kavanagh would become even more assured of the dynamism of his 'whitethorn hedges' and their role in recreating 'the heavenly place' within his poetic territory.[18] His Eden, which originated in the Monaghan landscape and which possessed his whole sensory and spiritual memory, was to become an inner disposition of the heart, a virginal landscape of which he can never be dispossessed. He would recover his

'placeless heaven' in the 'now', wherever he is, set firmly within
the parameters of everyday's 'bits and pieces'.

His earlier Eden had a less immanent quality to it. It possessed something of the illusiveness of AE's oriental landscapes:

The wheat is green on
The sidey hill-walk backwards up it:
There's a primeval plain to the south,
There's a flashing river mouth.
There's virgin soil – no flesh hand can crop it.
(*Possessing Eden*)

From the Heavenly Place to the Placeless Heaven

It is interesting to follow the transforming process, whereby the
poet's outer Eden became internalised as an inner oasis of peace.
The process begins first of all with the poet firmly rooted in his
sixteen-acre farm, 'bounded by the whitethorn hedges', becoming familiar with every detail of his territory. He knows his landscape not simply in its unchanging topography but also in its
'undying difference' and changing moods. He is enthralled by
its subtle blend of permanence and change. When he feels heaven
slipping from him he moves to recover his lost paradise by nostalgically trying to recapture in verse his lost home:

I came to Dublin in nineteen-thirty-nine. It was the worst
mistake of my life. The Hitler war had started. I had a comfortable holding of watery hills beside the Border. What was
to bate it for life![19]

Exile made him hanker continuously for a lost idyllic past; for
his 'childhood country' whose memory filled him with feelings
of peace. He regrets that now the grass and cocksfoot have over-
grown his familiar haunts. His treasured 'hollows' and 'rutted
cart-pass' are beginning to disappear in the undergrowth.
Worse still, like the writer Thomas Woulfe, he can no longer
fully come home again. He is a stranger among his own farming
neighbours who have continued to work at the perennial farming tasks. He feels he no longer belongs:

> And sometimes I am sorry when the grass
> Is growing over the stones in quiet hollows
> And the cocksfoot leans across the rutted cart-pass
> That I am not the voice of country fellows
> Who now are standing by some headland talking
> Of turnips and potatoes or young corn
> Of turf banks stripped for victory. *(Peace)*

Eden is disappearing, though still attainable through brief nostalgic memories of the 'packman' spreading his coloured wares across a country kitchen table:

> Here Peace is still hawking
> His coloured combs and scarves and beads of horn.[20]

Kavanagh becomes geographically separated from his sixteen-acre farm during his early years in Dublin. From 1942 to 1944 he wrote as a columnist for *The Irish Press* under the pseudonym of 'Piers Plowman'. The name he chose gave him licence to dream himself back to his Monaghan potato-fields and recapture their magic through the eyes of his alter-ego, Tarry Flynn:[21]

> On an apple-ripe September morning
> Through the mist-chilled fields I went
> With a pitch-fork on my shoulder
> Less for use than for devilment.
>
> …
>
> As I crossed the wooden bridge I wondered
> As I looked into the drain
> If ever a summer morning should find me
> Shovelling up eels again. *(Tarry Flynn)*

His territory, though earthy and mundane, is at the same time a spiritual land of the imagination. It is 'part of no earthly estate'.

The New Paradise

By 1951, it is clear that something significant has happened in the poet's life; he has become convinced of the primary significance of personal events. He has, in the words of his 'Epic', 'lived in important places' and at important times. He had begun to be aware that what is most intensely personal has universal

significance. Here in his home territory, the wrangling of neighbours over a patch of land has a stature all its own. The local undergoes transmutation under the influence of Kavanagh's poetic
alchemy. Mundane happenings becomes infused with Homeric
grandeur:

> I inclined
> To lose my faith in Ballyrush and Gortin
> Till Homer's ghost came whispering to my mind
> He said I made the Iliad from such
> A local row. Gods make their own importance. *(Epic)*

It is the poet who will thenceforth decide what is important in
life? Kavanagh's voice has a ring of assurance that augurs well
for his future work. 'Innocence', written at approximately the
same time as 'Epic', confirms this self-belief. He can freely ignore
his critics who considered him limited – a peasant poet –
'bounded by whitethorn hedges'. He now knows that he is right.
Little things encountered with great love are worthy subjects of
poetry. Something of his original innocence is still intact in his
public declaration of love for a 'triangular field':

> They laughed at one I loved –
> The triangular hill that hung
> Under the Big Forth. They said
> That I was bounded by the whitethorn hedges
> Of the little farm and did not know the world.
> But I knew that love's doorway to life
> Is the same doorway everywhere… *(Innocence)*

Kavanagh had found the key to a new world.

'Auditors In' marks the evaluation point where Kavanagh
recognises that he has eventually converted the outer beloved
landscape, his *pagus*, into an inner spiritual territory. This Edenic
land will be reclaimed, 'digged and ditched' to accommodate a
new poetic harvest, spiritually and rhythmically stronger than
before. Eden will no longer be merely culled from the dream-
blossoms of memory, but will grow out of present everyday
realities:

> Not mere memory but the Real
> Poised in the poet's commonweal.

The new Eden has a strange new location. It is in some interior place 'where the Self reposes/ The placeless Heaven that's under all our noses…' Heaney gives recognition to this spiritual event in his second appraisal of the poet. He acknowledges the fact that a unification of poetic subject and object has occurred in the later Kavanagh. This new Eden is primarily within.[22] Similarly John Jordan, well positioned to know the poet intimately, recognised as early as 1960 a growing serenity in 'the mature Kavanagh' who now, he admits, 'carries the paradise about within him'.[23] Kavanagh himself states openly that he is grateful to have come home to himself in such a manner that he finds his beloved Eden more present than ever. His new spiritual discovery involves a return to what he has always believed: that he is 'temple of the Holy Ghost' as he learned in his catechism at school but, unlike most, interiorised it in a radical way. The discovery of an Eden within has made the harrowing spiritual journey of recent years worthwhile. With relief he exclaims:

… I am so glad

To come accidentally upon

Myself at the end of a tortuous road

A new self-realisation has begun to dawn in the poems written at this period. Although his acknowledged rebirth (1955) is still chronologically some distance away, he has made significant progress in self-renewal. The radical re-appraisal of his life to date is a repossession of all that he previously held dear. No longer does he wistfully reconstruct the past in an effort to peek into Eden through 'a hole in Heaven's gable'. (*A Christmas Childhood*) He reclaims his first love with a new fervour: '*Now* I am back in her briary arms'. A sense of commitment to the present moment is heralded by the use of the word 'now'. Surrender to the present brings with it a new dedication to timeless, placeless moments and a glimpse into the poet's desire to achieve immortality:

The dew of an Indian Summer morning lies

On bleached potato-stalks –

What age am I?

I do not know what age I am,

I am no mortal age;
I know nothing of women,
Nothing of cities,
I cannot die
Unless I walk outside these whitethorn hedges.
(Innocence)

This instance of heightened awareness could be paralleled with a moment in Hindu mysticism when multiplicity dissolves and enlightenment occurs. It is the moment of undifferentiated unity when self-realisation is achieved. The poet seems to lose touch with his empirical self and, at that moment, finds his true Self.[24] 'What age am I?' 'I am no mortal age' 'I cannot die' – this language of apparent disorientation is close to that of St John of the Cross's intuition of God as 'I-know-not-what'. The poet's experience of 'Innocence' is not something logically *thought* out but something *known* as for the first time.

'Auditors In' further develops the implications present in the 'Innocence' experience. The poet's nostalgia, like the mystic's, is increased by a glimpse of the homeland.[25] There are hints of radical dispossession of all that impedes in the search for the ultimate good. Something akin to the '*nada, nada, nada*' of St John occurs, where nothing can substitute for the Ultimate which is God. For the poet, nothing satisfies but Eden itself. He must cut himself adrift if not 'on wings like Joyce's' (i.e. by complete physical exile), then at least his spirit will be free to fly onwards towards its goal. Relinquishing the things he once passionately sought – wealth, pleasure, acclaim, success – he turns at last to the greatest treasure of all, 'to where the Self reposes'. This is not the narrow empirical self which is ego-centred, but the 'whole' which has its being in God. It is this self that must be cherished as his greatest asset and where Eden resides – 'the placeless heaven that's under all our noses'.

A new self is being born from the old. This signals fresh phases of illumination and transformation. This change is more striking when one juxtaposes Kavanagh's new reliance on what Houston calls his 'landscapes of the heart' with the earlier objectless craving of Patrick Maguire. Not content with 'a primrose here and a daisy there', Maguire 'dreamt of the Absolute envased bouquet'. *(The Great Hunger)* To engage in futile reverie or to be scourged by 'a cursed ideal' was to miss the 'now,' the sacrament of the present moment, the God of everything and of everyday.

Illumined by the Holy Ghost

When Kavanagh first experienced unearthly beauty in the fields and hills, he spoke of this phenomenon with great simplicity and candour. This beauty, it seemed to him, emanated from Beyond. He felt that he was being moved, inspired by the Holy Spirit. Recognising that he enjoyed some kind of transcendent experience, he strove to express his vision in words:

> I saw upon the little hills and in the eyes of small flowers beauty too delicately rare for carnal words.[26]

This gift of poetry, bestowed by 'the Holy Spirit', carried with it considerable responsibility. The young poet had been allowed 'a glimpse into every tabernacle'. He felt he was already communing with the gods.

Subsequently, when faced with incomprehension, he was tempted to abandon his Muse and revert to the 'normality' of the crowd. He wanted to belong to the life of his neighbours in Inniskeen and later to that of his fellow-writers in Dublin. 'Try to be one of us,' pleaded the type-cast Davin with the young Stephen Dedalus.[27] Kavanagh's dilemma was similar. He was an artist with an individual mind, a poet among the people. Though ostracised because of his eccentricity, Kavanagh struggled to remain faithful to his vision and to the secret life of poetry which he strove to understand. He remained ambivalent all his life towards his cherished yet irksome gift. However difficult the stuggle he never abandoned his first love.

But how does one explain Kavanagh's visionary sense? Henri Bremond, whom I have quoted extensively in Chapter One, has made a careful study of both poet and mystic. He suggests that it is the mystical experience that best explains the poetic process:

> Is it not Shelley's experience that helps me know better the experience of John of the Cross, but conversely it is the experience of the saint that makes a little less obscure the mystery of the experience of poetry.[28]

Poet and mystic alike come under the transforming power of inspiration or, in some instances, of 'holy intoxication'. Both are smitten by a flash or spark of invisible power touching the spiritual substance of the self. This 'baptism' was clearly an experience which puzzled Kavanagh at the beginning of his poetic career.[29] He could only explain his experience in religious terms. He recounts how he asked a 'bearded man' whom he mistook for a mystic how he was to understand the things he saw. 'Of course, of course ye can see things,' he told him, 'sure any man that's a Catholic can see the Holy Ghost.' The bearded man persisted in his explanation:

> 'When a man's confirmed, doesn't the Holy Ghost come down on him? Sure the bishops can talk to the Holy Ghost any time they like. And the priests too if they want. Why, man, it's as simple as kiss yer hand.'[30]

The young poet was not convinced by the casualness of these answers. He was looking for a more metaphysical explanation for his vision of 'a beauty beyond beauty'. His experience, he thought, was being cheapened, trivialised into something commonplace. In desperation he returned to his catechism for help:

> I had learned from Miss Cassidy's catechism that there was only one unforgivable sin – the sin against the Holy Ghost. Now I understood.[31]

Whatever lack of understanding he experienced from those around him, he felt he had a sacred duty never to betray his vision. On the contrary, he must endeavor to be worthy of its divine visitation:

> The Holy Ghost will not enter a soul that has not within it a secret room, free from vulgarity.

Kavanagh's conclusion that the Holy Ghost was the author of his illumination made sense when placed in a Christian context. Like Bremond he had to look to religious experience as an explanation for his poetic inspiration. His was a divine gift, something of Gray's 'celestial fire', which was entrusted to him. He must serve it with devotion. This understanding of the action and role of the Holy Spirit in his life was quite extraordinary, especially when we consider the limits of Kavanagh's formal education and the current church teaching which lacked a vibrant theology of the Holy Spirit.

But it was the Holy Ghost Kavanagh felt, who also inspired him while reading from his favourite texts upstairs in his Parnassus room when the farming day was done. These texts ranged from newspaper-cuttings, *The Messenger*, to *Madame Bovary*.[32] Free at last from the chores he hated, he followed his usual ritual of reading a small amount at a time. Reading became one of those habitual occasions of inspiration when he was 'baptised again by fire and the Holy Spirit'.[33] At this moment he was ready to compose poetry of his own.

Inspiration also came freely to him when he listened to the unusual themes raised by the quarryman 'Bob'. At such moments, he felt his spirit enkindled. The 'damp wood' of his being came alight 'till sparks began to dance'.[34] The flame or spark of which he speaks is a biblical 'baptism by the Holy Spirit' where the intellect is enlightened and the will fixed on the object of desire. To be worthy of such visitations he had to maintain a place 'free from vulgarity', an inner sacred space – a secret room in his heart. Here he was freed from restriction. He was at home and at liberty to 'wander among the hills of a timeless world'[35] and experience, like Dostoyevsky's Myshkin, the holiness which pertains to loneliness.[36] It was at such moments as these that 'his little window lets in the stars'. (*My Room*)

Confirmation: The Sacrament of the Holy Spirit

An investigation of what Kavanagh learned in his 'penny catechism' regarding the Holy Ghost may throw some light on why this religious concept had left a lasting impression on his mind. The O'Reilly catechism was used in the diocese of Clogher up until the early 1950s.[37] Generations of Inniskeen people knew its short answers by heart. It can even today be recited by older people in the area. Bishop O'Reilly, author of the catechism, had one aim: to instruct his people in the sacrament of Confirmation, a sacrament which had been neglected during Penal times due to a dearth of bishops. One complete section of the Reilly catechism was dedicated to this end. It described how the Holy Ghost descended on the church and how we must pray that the Spirit 'ascend into our hearts', 'take possession' of us and 'cleanse our consciences from all filth of sin'. Kavanagh was sensitive, almost scrupulous, about sin. It was easier for him to appeal to the Holy Spirit for cleansing than to approach the priest in confession.

On 16 June 1913 Patrick Kavanagh was confirmed along with his sister Sissie. It must have been a memorable day for the Kavanagh household since the poet describes Confirmation day in his poem 'Why Sorrow?' in some detail. He writes:

The Holy Ghost descends
At random like the muse
On wise man and fool
And why should poet in the twilight choose?

'The descending Paraclete' becomes central to Kavanagh's idea of God. 'This was (my) God,' he says 'that brooded over the harrowed field… / The days my first verses were printed'. (*A View of God and the Devil*) The God who brooded over the earth in the Book of Genesis was the Holy Spirit. Likewise the breath of God over the soil in April facilitated new growth. The man who followed the pointed harrow-pins was partnering the invisible work of God in new beginnings. In faith he was entering 'the mist where Genesis begins'. (*To the Man after the Harrow*) Kavanagh had faith in a God whose power is as real but invisible as 'the rising sap' in springtime.

Besides the catechism, Kavanagh also learned about the Holy Ghost from the 'Sixth Book', which provided him with Dryden's poetic translation of the 'Veni Creator':

O source of uncreated light,
The Father's promised Paraclete!

Thrice holy fount, thrice holy fire,
Our hearts with heavenly love inspire

With Dryden, he yearned for the 'fire' of inspiration:

Refine and purge our earthly parts:
But, oh, inflame and fire our hearts![38]

In his meticulous preparation for the sacrament of Confirmation by his teachers at Kednaminsha, Kavanagh had learned to sing the 'Veni Creator' by heart:

Veni Creator Spiritus
Mentes tuorum visita
Imple superna gratia
Quae tu creasti pectora

(Come, Holy Ghost, Creator, come
From thy bright heavenly throne,
Come, take possession of our souls
And make them all your own.)

This hymn was sung by the assembled candidates as the Bishop entered the church for the Confirmation ceremony. The white-haired Bishop Mc Kenna was accompanied by the parish priest, Fr Maguire, ('Fr Mat'), Fr Gilmartin and perhaps even the outsider, Fr Pat. It was a gala day in the life of a rural parish when boys and girls, dressed in their new suits and white dresses, awaited the moment of anointing with chrism. Apart from the religious dimension of the sacrament, a carnival atmosphere prevailed in the village. 'Standings' were erected for the occasion and sweets, buns and lemonade as well as religious souvenirs were on sale. Confirmation made an impression on Patrick, since he frequently returns to this keenly anticipated event at St Mary's Church in his verse.[39] The parish was ahum with activity:

The bishop of that diocese came that way.
He christened the children and slapped their humble cheeks
In token of the descending Paraclete. *(Why Sorrow?)*

The sacrament of Confirmation may well have been a milestone in the poet's life. It was a moment he imagined to have shared with the poetic priest 'Fr Mat' when together they found the 'the secret of a different deity written…' What 'different deity' was found at Confirmation and how did it affect the poet's life?

Was this the moment when Kavanagh first discovered that the Holy Spirit not only christened the confirmant but also imbued the landscape with divine radiance? The 'alder trees'were clothed in 'white Confirmation dresses' as if they too participated in the occasion. Clay, which once had the capacity to imprison and stifle, could now also become pregnant with mystical life and energy. A new awareness of the possible marriage between spirit and clay became apparent in the notion that 'the Holy Spirit consummates' in some mystical encounter with earth. When he is fired by mystical thoughts, Tarry Flynn's clay-bound environment seemed to quicken with new life:

> Ah clay! It was out of the clay that wings were made. He stared down into the dry little canyons in the parched earth and he loved that dry earth which could produce a miracle of wings.

Above all months of the year, Kavanagh associates April with the Holy Ghost, an idea which he got from the monthly *Messenger*.

Kavanagh's theology of Pentecost derived in part from reading the little red monthly magazine published by the Jesuit fathers in Gardiner Street, Dublin. Joyce was a student of the Jesuits and described in his *Portrait of the Artist as a Young Man* how the Holy Spirit moved Dedalus. He saw the Holy Ghost as:

> the unseen Paraclete, Whose symbols were a dove and a mighty wind, to sin against Whom was a sin beyond forgiveness, the eternal mysterious secret Being to Whom, as God, the priests offered up mass once a year, robed in the scarlet of the tongues of fire.[40]

Kavanagh was schooled in a similar theology. The Jesuits at that time were engaged in the consolidation of the faith in Ireland. They fulfilled this mission not only through their schools at Belvedere and Clongowes Wood, but also through their monthly *Messenger* which offered a simple digest of Catholic spirituality. This publication reached far and wide into the rural parishes of Ireland, to Donaghmoyne, Inniskeen and Crossmaglen. Kavanagh was hungry for reading material. He read the *Messenger* each month, often taking it with him to the fields so that he could read in peace.[41] It was, as Dedalus explains, a particular Jesuit custom to dedicate each day of the week to a different patron:

> Sunday was dedicated to the mystery of the Holy Trinity, Monday to the Holy Ghost, Tuesday to the Guardian Angels, Wednesday to Saint Joseph, Thursday to the Most Blessed Sacrament of the Altar, Friday to the Suffering Jesus, Saturday to the Blessed Virgin Mary.[42]

The *Messenger* took this practice a step further by also dedicating each month to a particular patron: April to the Holy Ghost, May to the Virgin Mary, June to the Sacred Heart, October to the Holy Angels and November to the Holy Souls etc. The Jesuit writer[43] in the May edition 1921 explained how fitting it was that May be dedicated to the Virgin Mary:

> The sombre days of November seem appropriate to the special remembrance of the dead, the bright sunshine of June may typify the glory of the Sacred Heart, but the pure fresh beauty of the May-time, the hopeful promise of budding trees and flowers, the break from tentative spring into summer splendour – this belongs to Mary. May is the morning of the year, it drives away the lingering shadows of winter...
> (*The Messenger*, May, 1921)

To accentuate the themes of dedication Brian O'Higgins[44] was engaged to write a series of pious verses entitled 'Songs of Consecration', in which he dedicated each month to its appropriate patron.[45] The April edition 1922 has in large caption, 'April, 1922 – Dedicated to the Holy Ghost', followed by a two-page instruction on the doctrine of the Holy Spirit. The instruction was simple and theologically sound. In this edition Brian O'Higgins' verse reads:

> The earth is awake at the call of Spring,
> There are flowers on hill and lea,
> A tender breeze with a song of hope
> Steals in from the mighty sea.
> The life that seemed gone in the winter drear
> Stirs now in the greening sod,

> As we turn with hearts that are glad, to give
> Our toil to Thee, Heart of God.

We can be sure that Kavanagh read this edition with care. He admits to having followed O'Higgins closely each month. He tried his hand also at this time to write for the Holy Poet's Corner in *The Weekly Irish Independent*,[46] thinking that his muse was guiding him to 'holy' verse. Even after he had abandoned 'holy poetry' and Higgins' verse, he was obliged to concede that whatever his topic, his poetic inspiration was closely associated with the Holy Ghost's power to generate new life in inert matter. He continued to celebrate the months of the year as the *Messenger* had taught him, but in his own unique style.

The Maiden of Spring is with Child

Kavanagh's references to the earth as a mother and bride are well documented in 'The Great Hunger'. He envisages the meadows in spring as a virgin or maiden, made pregnant with new life. In Christian terms, he is conversant with the Incarnation and the Virgin Mary with Child by the Holy Spirit. Fecundity in nature also fills him with intense mystical energy. Phoenix-like spring raises itself out of the ashes of winter; in the words of Jeffrey in the 'Sixth Book', 'it is the renovation of life and of joy to all animated beings, that constitutes this great jubilee of nature'.[47] April at the heart of spring becomes a source of double inspiration for Kavanagh. He prepared to slough off the torpor of his winter-bound spirit for the new life and 'fire' of spring:

> Now is the hour we rake out the ashes
> Of the spirit-fires winter-kindled.
> This old temple must fall,
> We dare not leave it
> Dark, unlovely, deserted.
> Level! O level it down!
> Here we are building a bright new town. *(April)*

Here Kavanagh's language breaks with Victorian schoolbook vocabulary of 'spirit-fires' and 'winter-kindled' and surrenders to a new transparency of language. Does he perhaps at the same time relinquish his pagan affinity for ancient temples? He emerges alone and victorious with idiom and fully appropriated Christian mythology intact. He announces himself unashamedly a Christian poet. Theme, language, metaphor conspire to effect a new annunciation or, more appropriately, a new incarnation.

> The old cranky spinster is dead
> Who fed us with cold flesh.
> And in the green meadows
> The maiden of Spring is with child
> By the Holy Ghost.

Paul Vincent Carroll, a Dundalk playwright, on reading these lines was deeply impressed: 'When I read … the final couplet (quoted above) … I knew for certain that here was a poet that might easily steal the mantle that AE passed on to Fred Higgins'.[50] AE had recognised Kavanagh's spiritual leanings. He sought to encourage his protege toward eastern mysticism. But their literary paths only touched; they would later diverge. Illumination for Kavanagh, unlike AE, proceeds along specifically Christian lines. It is the Spirit who unseals the poet's eyes to the mystery of hidden beauty of forms in life around him. This is particularly evident in the short poem 'Plough Horses', chosen to represent him in *Fifty Years of Modern Verse* (1938). The poet is awakened to the beauty of horses through the power of the Holy Spirit. Sunlight plays a transforming role as the 'flying splinters of the sun' are reminiscent of the Spirit's 'tongues of fire'. The rhythmic movement of couplets imitate the measured pace of a two-horse team:

> Their glossy flanks and manes outshone
> The flying splinters of the sun.
>
> The tranquil rhythm of that team
> Was as slow flowing meadow stream.
>
> And I saw Phidias's chisel there –
> An ocean stallion, mountain mare –
>
> Seeing with eyes the Spirit unsealed
> Plough horses in a quiet field. *(Plough Horses)*

It is the light of the Holy Ghost which radiates with even greater authority, from the well-constructed sonnet 'Primrose'. The poet encounters in a single flower the transfigured face of Christ whose presence is reassuring, tender and kind. The moment is authenticated by the signature in flame at the heart of the flower:

> And where the Holy Ghost in flame had signed
>
> I read it through the lenses of a tear.

This epiphany is fleeting as any genuine divine visitation. Subsequently the poet's eyes 'grew dim', forecasting new stages of purification of spirit.

It is interesting to ask to what extent the Holy Spirit is a poetic experience and to what extent spiritual? At root, the Holy Ghost seems to be an effective symbol in Kavanagh's hands. Moreover, at times the symbol achieves an even higher level of reality. It is, to use Yeats' terminology, 'a moving symbol' of both emotional and intellectual stature whereby 'one is mixed into the shadow of God'. 'The soul moves among symbols and unfolds in symbols.' Kavanagh's soul seems to unfold in the symbol of the Holy Spirit. Unlike Joyce, who ponders 'the divine gloom and silence wherein dwelt the unseen Paraclete', Kavanagh was at home with the Holy Ghost and became inspired by it.[49] Though he became easily entranced, 'lost to potato-fields', like Milton, the Holy Ghost was the only Muse worthy of invocation when engaged in the sacred task of poetry:

> Sing Heavenly Muse, that, on the secret top
>
> Of Oreb, of Sinai, didst inspire
>
> That shepherd who first taught the chosen seed
>
> In the beginning how the heavens and Earth
>
> Rose out of Chaos:...[50]

Indeed, the Holy Spirit, traditional source of spiritual and poetic inspiration, became Kavanagh's only available muse. Firmly rooted in his Catholic tradition, he appropriated the symbol, was personally touched by it and used it to express his poetic and religious experience.

The Holy Spirit is on the Fields

Perhaps the strongest evocation of the power of the Holy Ghost at work in Kavanagh's landscape comes from a passage in *Tarry Flynn*. Tarry has been moulding his potatoes while thinking of the 'strange girls that would be coming to the Mission'. His mind was cooled by the clay 'running through his mind'. Absorbed by the beauty of his finished work he became suddenly rapt in the presence of the Holy Ghost in the landscape:

> The Holy Ghost was taking the Bedlam of the little fields and making it into a song, a simple song which he could understand. And he saw the Holy Spirit on the hills.
>
> With the cynical side of himself, he realised that there was nothing unusual about the landscape. And yet what he imagined was hardly self-deception. The totality of the scene about him was a miracle. There might be something of self-deception in his imagination of the general landscape but there was none in his observation of the little flowers and weeds. These had God's message in them.[51]

Here the Holy Ghost is depicted traditionally as the divine creative power which brings order out of chaos. He takes the 'the bedlam of little fields' and weaves it into a song. The scriptural role of 'descending Paraclete' which gave unlettered men the gift of tongues at Pentecost is implied in Tarry's ability to understand what he has witnessed. This Holy Spirit has at the same time the authority to instruct and inspire and is invoked by poets such as Milton and Dryden. Tarry Flynn is in the grip of a palpable presence. He is filled with a song, simple, mysterious, holy. Fearing self-deception, a state as damaging to the mystic as the poet, he is impelled to seek confirmation for his experience. He chooses his mother as confidante, recognising in her sound common sense a discerning charism. He needed her earthy wisdom as ballast for his rapt giddiness. Kavanagh, now a writer of some sophistication (1947), may have had other literary purposes in introducing the down-to-earth pragmatism of Mrs Flynn. She had in many ways the attributes of Brigid Quinn, Patrick Kavanagh's mother, who had a special understanding of her poet son:

'The Holy Spirit is in the fields,' he said in even cold tones. He was unemotional, for these strange statements did not lend themselves to any human emotion. The mother who had one shoe off and her foot on a stool did not seem to have heard. 'There's a curse o' God corn on that wee toe and it's starting to bother me again.'

Here, Kavanagh significantly juxtaposes a moment of extraordinary banality, that of Tarry paring his mother's corn, with the strange pronouncement: 'The Holy Spirit is in the fields'. The tone of Tarry's exalted mood is swiftly rocketed earthwards by his mother's exclamation: 'There's a curse o' God corn on that wee toe and its starting to bother me again.' This jolt back to earth for the reader throws the mystical moment into relief, emphasising it all the more by stark contrast. The unlikely counterbalancing of the Holy Ghost and his mother's corn adds an hilarity to the incident, but also gives it theological significance. Was Kavanagh so deeply incarnational as to deliberately juxtapose the banal and the spiritual in one hilarious moment? Did he genuinely see the broken human condition going hand in hand with the sublime, as part of the same redeemed universe? If he did, and I believe he did, he was enlightened beyond the ordinary.

Like Fr Daly, modelled on Canon Maguire of Inniskeen, Kavanagh strove to combine humour with seriousness to achieve 'that appearance of not being too earnest'. This was the real sign of sincerity, he mused.[52] The twinkle in his mother's eye 'that was half-humorous and half-terror' assured him of the validity of what he had seen on the hills. The allusion to madness 'not being on her side of the house' was a subtle admiration for her son's poetic aspirations which she acknowledged had not come from the Quinns. Mention of anything holy only gave Mrs Flynn an opportunity to promote attendance at the forthcoming parish mission. She was a conventional Catholic, strong in religious observance, faithful to the institutional church. Tarry, on the other hand, epitomised Kavanagh's own unusual dedication to the sacred commonplace, brightened by those illusive but genuine moments of vision.

Tarry Flynn's prompt return from mystical reverie of the Holy Spirit to the gross daily realities of 'hens' dishes' and 'Callan's ducks', shows Kavanagh's firm belief that 'revelation comes as an aside'. The ordinary, for him, was to become more and more the material garment of transcendence. Moreover, 'being too serious (about religion) meant it was not integrated into his ordinary life'.[53] In spite of his humourous approach Kavanagh struggles towards an integrated religion. He gradually fashions 'a little way' of his own, like that of the mystic St Thérèse of Lisieux, whose 'little way of perfection' consisted in 'doing little things with great love'. Kavanagh's God-in-the-bits-and-pieces-of-everyday, which had originated in 'The Great Hunger', now becomes more actual. Its fullest expression comes in the wake of his hospitalisation when he realises that 'Nothing whatever is by love debarred'. *(The Hospital)* Commonplace events like a 'walk in summer along the canal' become mystical events, when the poet's gaze is filled with vision and 'the evening is lifted up and in Eternity poised'. *(Cool Water Under Bridges)*

The several allusions to the Holy Spirit's presence in the landscape point to the fact that Kavanagh was not a pantheist, nor had he leanings in this direction, beyond his initial attempts at impressing his early pantheistic mentor, AE.[54] Kavanagh's sacramental sense of God in nature resembled more that of Baron von Hugel who sees the Christian mystic as a 'pan-en-the-ist'; one who perceives God-*in*-nature. Such authentic Christian mysticism sees God in flowers, in the fields, 'seeing in all created things God's 'energies', yet moving always beyond them towards the Transcendent 'essence'.[55]

Kavanagh was often palpably moved by the strength of God's energy in nature, in the smallest flower, in the riotous colour of the bog in full bloom, in the beggarman who sold ballads at street corners. Nevertheless, there is no conscious theological schema in his allusions to God, to Trinity or indeed to the Holy Ghost. His theology like his revelation 'comes as an aside'. His was an innate charism that defied systematisation. It is the 'ordinary plenty' of life: weeds, fields and streets that gave him hints of God. He was a poet in love with the life of things around him; they spoke eloquently to him of God's delight in creation.

Conclusion

Kavanagh made a long inner journey in his search of the happiness that always seemed to elude him. He drew on a variety of symbols to enshrine one of the most important themes of his poetry, Eden, paradise, heaven, the 'underworld' of grasses, the whitethorn hedges. In these he finds some of his finest moments of illumination, moments destined 'to endure'. He believed that the innocence of a child holds the secret of 'possessing Eden'. By gazing at the landscape without ownership, the child possesses of it forever.

> We should be like children and not try to possess it
> And that way it will be ours forever. *(Possessing Eden)*

His personal return to innocence parallels a state of gospel simplicity: 'Unless you change and become like little children you will never enter the kingdom of heaven.' (Mt 18:3) Kavanagh's hold on heaven derived ultimately from his ability to recover and preserve the eyes and inner dispositions of a child. He was aided in this by his extraordinary comprehension of the Holy Spirit as the key to his poetic inspiration and the subsequent illumination of soul.

We have seen how, from an early age, the Holy Spirit's brooding presence found a special kinship with Kavanagh. The Spirit brooding over the fields called up images of poetic fecundity. He felt a kinship with Gray's unsung hero whose 'heart (was) once pregnant with celestial fire'.[56] Kavanagh identified with pregnant images and with the poet's feminine role of incubating hints of God in 'the womb of poetry' so as to deliver them to the world. He appreciated the spark or fire that baptised him with inspiration. The poet's role, however, was to be situated squarely in the commonplace of everyday, intent on 'the final fusion of all crudeness into a pure flame'.[57] The power of the Holy Ghost, the female principle of God, the *ruah* or breath, was undoubtedly one of his sources of inspiration. At times when money was scarce, he was perhaps too arrogantly sure of the Holy Ghost's insignia on his work, especially when he outrageously claims:

It is a bank will refuse a post-
Dated cheque of the Holy Ghost.
(To Hell With Commonsense)

Kavanagh's non-viable cheques were notorious. But his theology of the Holy Ghost was sound and at its best when casual, whimsical or as an aside.

In summary then, Kavanagh had endorsed his point of view that the poet is a theologian entrusted with the task of restoring the world to God. In an analogous way, though devoid of explicit religious sentiment, Heaney sees the poet as diviner involved in the 'restoration of the culture to itself'.[58] This work of restoration was frequently achieved by Kavanagh's instinctive technique of epiphany, whereby simple everyday things and events, like the 'thorn-tree' for Wordsworth, were restored to the status of 'impressive objects'. In the final chapter we will examine Kavanagh's mystical imagination at work in some of these epiphanies.

CHAPTER SEVEN

Illumination II

I find a star-lovely art
In a dark sod.
Joy that is timeless! O heart
That knows God!
(Ploughman)

Epiphanies in Kavanagh

It was through the *Irish Statesman*, AE's newspaper, that Patrick Kavanagh first became aquainted with the work of James Joyce. He found in Joyce 'a strange intangible quality ... something which enlarges the imagination (and) excites the reader creatively'.[1] *The Portrait of the Artist as a Young Man* (1916), Kavanagh believed, was 'Joyce's testament'. Nevertheless, it was *Ulysses* (1922), first encountered in 1937, that he counted among his three favourite books. These were: *Moby Dick*, *Gil Blas* and *Ulysses*, with Knut Hamsun's *Wanderers* fighting for a place. He read his favourite books 'scores of times', finding them 'new' at each reading.[2] *Ulysses*, he considered, was 'only incidentally about Dublin and fundamentally the history of a soul'. Kavanagh tended to be dismissive of all writers except those who explored this sacred spiritual territory. Melville's *Moby Dick*, he considered, was 'one of the great epics of all time' because it too was only 'incidentally about the sea and fundamentally about the soul'.

The spiritual function of art is a topic introduced in Joyce's *Portrait*. The notion of art as 'epiphany' had been developed by Joyce in a manner that would have delighted Kavanagh. Through the character of *Stephen Hero* (1944) he explains how an object, a moment, an event, is suddenly recognised by the artist as being 'that thing which it is' and thus 'achieves its epiphany':

Its soul, its whatness, leaps to us from the vestment of its appearance. The soul of the commonest object ... seems to us radiant.[3]

An epiphany was further explained as 'a sudden spiritual manifestation' in speech, gesture or 'phase of the mind itself'. It was, Stephen believed, 'for the man of letters to record these epiphanies with extreme care, seeing that they are the most delicate and evanescent of moments'.[4] Richard Ellmann holds that although Joyce did not see 'epiphany' in specifically Christian terms, as the showing forth of the Godhead to the Magi, yet he feels it is 'a useful metaphor for what he had in mind'.[5] But even with Joyce one can never be sure that there is not an implicit religious allusion lurking in the back of his mind.

Kavanagh's instinct for Epiphanies

Whatever about Joyce, Kavanagh had an instinct for epiphanies. One of his poetic strengths lay in his spontaneous capacity for 'loving to the heart of any ordinary thing'. *(Moment on the Canal)* It was in this way that he grasped the essence of experience. His epiphanies have a wide range, beginning on a small tillage farm in Co Monaghan. An early poem, 'Ploughman', sets an example:

I find a star-lovely art
In a dark sod.
Joy that is timeless! O heart
That knows God! *(Ploughman)*

Here he uncovers a translucent beauty in the normally opaque density of 'a dark sod'. On other occasions he notices 'fantastic light' in the 'eyes of bridges' and an eerie brightness in the 'moonlight that stays forever in a tree'. *(On Looking into E. V. Rieu's Homer)* These moments of illumination are what Ellmann describes as 'moments of fullness and passion'. They also suggest something of Hopkins' *inscape*: the inner 'pattern or order' hidden in the external form of a sod, a bluebell or tree. This sensation of inscape is perceived in a 'mysterious instant', an instant of *claritas* which Joyce's Stephas Dedalus translates as 'radiance'.

Kavanagh's epiphanies occur when he experiences what he calls his 'Divine flash' of insight. In Hopkins' language this could be described as *instress* – a sensation of inscape – or a 'quasi-mystical illumination, a sudden perception of that deeper pattern, order, and unity which gives meaning to external forms'.[6] For Kavanagh, this mystical illumination can be prompted by a section of the Iliad in translation, E. V. Rieu's Homer. Moved by his reading, he experienced a fresh, unprecedented encounter with 'the Far Field Rock', an already familiar 'external form' which now suddenly becomes luminous:

The intensity that radiated from
The Far Field Rock – you afterwards denied –
Was the half-god seeing his half-brothers
Joking on the fabulous mountain-side.

Kavanagh liked to quote Chesterton, who held that 'the arts exist to show forth the glory of God'. He himself held firmly to his belief in the poet as a theologian, whose destiny it is to 'scrape away convention' in order to reveal 'the miracle of ordinary life'. Joyce's sense of epiphany is similar in many aspects. 'The artist,' Joyce felt, 'was charged with such revelations, and must look for them not among gods but among men, in casual, unostentatious, even unpleasant moments.' His proper task was the 'artistic discovery and representation of the divine purpose in anything'.[7] One of Kavanagh's strengths as a poet was his ability to capture moments of 'divine purpose', the glow of Shelley's 'fading coal' or, in his own words, to 'snatch out of time the passionate transitory'. (*The Hospital*) Moments of passion such as these in Kavanagh are usually charged with considerable lyrical strength and beauty of language.

Such a moment of illumination and epiphany comes in 'The Great Hunger' in a landscape starkly bespectred by apocalytic visions. This milieu of 'mechanised scarecrows' and 'ragged sculpture(s) of the wind' is made momentarily resplendent with a magnificent fullness and vision. The scene grows into a splendid theophany when simple peasants are surprised by a glimpse of Trinitarian life on a small unpretentious farm in Co

Monaghan. The moment is superbly timed to give a momentary brightness within the darkened narrative of 'The Great Hunger'. Kavanagh had himself experienced the tedium of farming, its relentless drudgery, its treadmill monotony. October, December, winter: these have constricted the diminishing spirit of the fictitious Paddy Maguire who is dying of unlived life – pursuing a dismal existence of 'quiet desperation' to the end. Formalised religion, a mere candle lit for him 'on a June altar', has left Maguire cold and unmoved.

> Maguire watches the drills flattened out
> And the flints that lit a candle for him on a June altar
> Flameless.

Kavanagh the artist, or the occasional cameraman, as John Nemo astutely points out,[8] now adjusts his light to achieve the full radiance of a spring epiphany. A new season makes its entrance into this townland with scenes of ploughing attended by a 'blackening' March east wind. Maguire is unperturbed; he is part of the landscape, with the ideal 'uncaring' attitude, like 'a slack wire paling', available for whatever symphony might happen to play. For the artist, revelation happens, as Joyce intimates, 'in casual, unostentatious, even unpleasant moments'.[9] For Kavanagh, it occurs 'when the sun comes through a gap'. In this gift-moment, the faith-life of a simple community is mystically uncovered by a sudden shaft of winter sunshine. There ensues one of Kavanagh's most magnificent epiphanies which, like the prayers of 'Lough Derg', takes the approximate shape of a sonnet:

> The pull is on the traces it is March
> And a cold black wind is blowing from Dundalk.
> The twisting sod rolls over on her back –
> The virgin screams before the irresistible sock.
> No worry on Maguire's mind this day
> Except that he forgot to bring his matches.
> From every second hill a neighbour watches
> With all the sharpened interest of rivalry.
> Yet sometimes when the sun comes through a gap
> These men see God the Father in a tree:

> The Holy Spirit is the rising sap,
> And Christ will be the green leaves that will come
> At Easter from the sealed and guarded tomb.

Here Kavanagh almost nonchalantly compresses a positive, well-honed theology of the Trinity into a short lyrical passage. By contrast, Joyce in his *Portrait* assigns distinct attributes to the persons of the Trinity, prompted by 'the books of devotion' which were available to him as a young man in a Jesuit school. But Joyce's Trinity is spiritually lifeless:

> The imagery through which the nature and kinship of the Three Persons of the Trinity were darkly shadowed forth in the books of devotion which he read – the Father contemplating from all eternity as in a mirror His Divine Perfections and thereby begetting the Eternal Son and the Holy Spirit proceeding out of Father and Son from all eternity...[10]

Joyce's Trinity is self-absorbed, cerebral, gloomy, intellectually viable but denuded of radiance and vision. Kavanagh has no such agenda. He moved in a more Celtic frame of mind, ready to understand and compassionate with his rural milieu, and portrays its ordinary tasks momentarily illumined in the name of the Great Three.

The poet knew the sturdy quality of rural Irish faith, symbolised in the ageless permanence of trees, the excitement occasioned by the rising sap, and the miracle of green leaves escaping the tooth of winter. In this epiphany Kavanagh gains access to a lived faith, personal and communal, as well as into the secret life of a self-renewing God whose dynamism 'renews the face of the earth'. His own 'three-cornered heart', with its propensity for intermittent radiances, is also glimpsed in the process.

Kavanagh was familiar with the legend of St Patrick, who was said to have picked a shamrock to illustrate the doctrine of Three Persons in One God – three leaves on a single stem. He may well have sought to portray the Trinity in his own way, just as St Patrick his patron did, by taking his metaphor directly out of the context of people's lives. In a similar way he would re-invent the Christmas story in rural Irish idiom transforming the familiar Bethlehem account into a local event. 'Three whin bushes' on a Monaghan skyline were the guise of the three wise kings – the Magi following a star to Mucker. Epiphany had been re-enacted in his home and on his doorstep, all transfigured now into 'a Christmas townland'. 'Cassiopeia', the familiar local star 'over Cassidy's hanging hill', had been transformed into 'the star of Bethlehem'.

Early Epiphanies in the Making

Kavanagh's instinct for penetrating to the heart of an event may well have begun while recalling memories of school life in his autobiographical work *The Green Fool* (1938). One such incident is noteworthy for the manner in which it shows the beginnings of a revelatory quality to his storytelling. Miss Cassidy, his teacher, was apt to become so totally absorbed in catechetical in-struction that nothing could distract her attention from it. This obsession, Kavanagh believed, was responsible for the partial destruction of her prized cloak which was, on this occasion, 'hanging a-drying on a pair of stools by the fire'. It was incidents such as this that made Kavanagh trust the integrity of his own experience.

Severe though her reputation was, Miss Cassidy allowed her pupils to dry themselves in turn on wet days by the fire. In the last batch of pupils was the author himself who witnessed the spectacle of the burning cloak at close range:

> The truth is Miss Cassidy's beautiful black cloak was on fire, and a hole was spreading from its centre, slowly spreading outwards.
>
> Miss Cassidy was at the bottom of the schoolroom; she must have been teaching the catechism; no other subject would have shut her senses off from some inkling of this dis-aster. We now and then gave a look from the cloak to its owner. She hadn't noticed or sensed anything, though there was a fine flavour of burning wool in the place.[11]

Though her pupils laughed at her misfortune, Kavanagh saw a humourous side to the incident. He felt a sudden kinship with

Moses' vision of God in the burning bush of the Old Testament where 'the angel of Yahweh appeared to him in the shape of a flame of fire, coming from the middle of a bush'. (Ex 3:1-6) In the classroom, before his eyes, Patrick saw 'a merry pagan god' appear in 'Miss Cassidy's burning cloak'. She did not slap her pupils since 'the thing was too serious for that'! A three-foot hole in her good woollen cloak was a serious personal loss. For Patrick it was perhaps one of his earliest inklings of epiphany; his ability to see a light break through the crust of an event. It was also perhaps an early manifestation of his comic muse. The seriousness of religion and of classroom discipline became unexpectedly shot through with humour, perspective and even spectacle!

A similar ability to penetrate to the quintessential can be noted in the pig-killing incident also recounted in *The Green Fool*.[12] The scene is set for the anticipated massacre which, despite its bloody nature, was also a celebration of plenty for the family larder! The 'rattle of the fan-bellows' bringing the fire alight to prepare the necessary quantities of boiling water. 'The sound of boots crossing the railway sleepers' as the pig-killers arrived. The clean table set out with 'knives and hammers' ready for the 'pig-carcasses'. The pigs 'one by one' gaffed on the doorstep. Kavanagh's ability to put the gory details into perspective and release the inherent celebration of the moment is achieved by his unusual technique of juxtaposing the bloody incident with the beauty of sunrise over the drumlin hills:

> It was a memorable morning; the blood of dawn was being poured over the hills, and that other blood we only thought how much black pudding it would make. Our talk had the romantic beauty of reality. We were as close to life and death as we could be. I was part of that existence.

Revealing what is Concealed

But it was in poetry that Kavanagh best succeeded in unveiling the small miracles of life. His poetry relied strongly on his technique of revealing what is concealed in the ordinary. He continued therefore, to pursue illumination with all the hunger of the mystic. Epiphany was for him 'a moment of Beatific vision', 'the divine flash' which was the hallmark of his poetic calling. Recalling and re-membering an external form, an event, a cameo of his personal past or moments that live on as personal history: these became epiphanies under the influence of his pen. They resurrected from within his own personal vision intimations of a personal encounter with God:

> This was my God who made the grass
> And the sun.
> And the stones in streams in April;
> This was the God I met in Dublin
> As I wandered the unconscious streets.
>
> This was the God that brooded over the harrowed field –
> Rooneys – beside the main Carrick road
> The day my first verses were printed –
> *(A View of God and the Devil)*

Kavanagh's God is once again Trinitarian: The Father, the Creator 'who made the grass...', the Son who walked the streets of Dublin, the Holy Spirit, source of his poetic inspiration, 'the un-seen guest' who 'brooded over the harrowed field – Rooneys...' Kavanagh gives a precise time and location for his meeting with God: 'beside the main Carrick road / The day my first verses were printed'. A red-letter day for the poet had undoubtedly the finger of God in it. God and poet were to become joint partners in this work.

By 1951 Kavanagh had become skilled at creating epipha-nies. 'Epic' is essentially the development of an epiphany from an impassioned memory. Kavanagh recalls an incident from his townland which he discovers has all the inner hallmarks of an epic. Through it he struggles to fashion rural consciousness and gradually dispel the temptation to sink into anonymity and loss of belief in the personal.

> I have lived in important places, times
> When great events were decided, who owned
> That half a rood of rock, a no-man's land

> Surrounded by our pitchfork-armed claims.
> I heard the Duffys shouting 'Damn your soul'
> And old McCabe stripped to the waist, seen
> Step the plot defying blue cast-steel –
> 'Here is the march along these iron stones'
> That was the year of the Munich bother. Which
> Was more important? I inclined
> To lose my faith in Ballyrush and Gortin
> Till Homer's ghost came whispering to my mind
> He said: I made the Illiad from such
> A local row. Gods make their own importance. *(Epic)*

He slowly re-assembles the past, captures its dramatic tension, ruminates upon its rugged textures of 'pitchfork-armed claims', 'iron stones' and 'blue-cast steel'. He hears its earthy dialogue and gradually uncovers the heroic hidden in the local. The grand scale of human passions of which literature is made lies in wait, made authentic in an Irish townland as in ancient Troy. People roused by hate, greed, love, lust, anger, desire, envy are the stuff of literature, be they natives of 'Ballyrush and Gortin' or ancient Greece and Rome.

Kavanagh reaches out effortlessly from the local to the universal; from 'parish to universe'. This is a fine example of what Patrick Rafroidi calls Kavanagh's imaginative capacity 'to explode the atoms of (his) ordinary experience'.[13] Such explosions release magnificent illuminations. They transpose 'black hills' into 'Alps', a 'local row' into an epic, and the familial 'Mucker fog' into a world-come-to-life touched by 'the God of imagination'. Each revelation explodes meteor-like and continues its speaking power beyond the written word, silently challenging the epiphany to 'renew the face of the earth'.

Epiphany in a city setting

In Dublin, Kavanagh finds a new locus for his epiphanies. He startles us with his rare luminous moments of city life:

> Girls in red blouses,
> Steps up to houses

> Sunlight round gables,
> Gossip's young fables,
> The life of a street. *(Is)*

Similar revelations appear in 'the mystical view of Leeson Bridge' and 'those sunsets that look back at me from Crumlin' when 'the evening is lifted up and in Eternity poised'. *(Cool Water Under Bridges)* But he is not a city dweller at heart. He is more illumined by 'the undying difference in the corner of a field' or the sudden 'far-frighted surprise in a crow's flight'. *(E. V. Rieu's Homer)* He is more a stranger on the streets of Dublin than ever he was in Inniskeen. An epiphany or cluster of epiphanies of this 'strangeness' becomes immortalised in his unusual ballad, 'If ever you go to Dublin Town'.

Kavanagh experiences a ghostly movement within his spirit when, on Baggot Street and Pembroke Road, the crust of the years crumble and he projects himself forward into the future century.

> On Pembroke Road look out for my ghost,
> Dishevelled with shoes untied,
> Playing through the railings with little children
> Whose children have long since died.
> *(If ever You Go to Dublin Town)*

This ballad is the work of a man who once again feels the sting of contingency as he did once before in his 'Birthday' poem of 1935. Now he deals with the experience in the spirit of what he calls his 'humorosity' that characterises some of his better work. He seeks to make his own self-assessment as he confronts death. He skillfully pens his perceived reputation: 'queer', 'dangerous', 'nice', 'eccentric', 'proud', 'vain', 'slothful' and 'alone'. Yet it is his humour, his detachment and unfailing insight that speak most eloquently under cover of a jingling ballad. The piece has a surreal quality, a tinge of liminality, a blend of tragic and comic elements. Its tone embraces both the eerie and the actual. He cleverly counterpoints the commonplace: 'playing through the railings with little children', with the imponderable: 'whose children have long since died'. Time and afterlife are cleverly superimposed. Kavanagh in the illumined state can wander in and out of time, a quality that must have contributed to his uneasy inhabitance of his body and the noticeable awkwardness of his gait.

Kavanagh's Dublin ballad was not an attempt to reveal Dublin or to depict his life there except as an aside. It is rather an epiphany of his own idiosyncratic self: what he was like, how he lived both externally and internally, and something of the legend that surrounded his daily peregrinations between Pembroke Road and Baggot Street.

Kavanagh's Dark Night

Kavanagh acknowleges that 1954 was the worst year of his life. He sensed that he had somehow lost his verve, his belief in life. He resorts to becoming more philosopher than poet, asking fundamental questions of life. His epiphanic power has waned and he is uncertain where he might look for new inspiration. His allegiance to clay had been severely tried by poverty and ridicule so that he had been urged to fight for a precarious poetic existence 'on the rocky present'. Though he had many hungry years in Dublin, this year was different. It marked also the low-point of his spiritual 'dark night'.

> Nineteen fifty-four hold on till I try
> To formulate some theory about you. A personal matter:
> My lamp of contemplation you sought to shatter,
> To leave me groping in madness under a low sky …
> Everywhere I look a part of me is exiled from the I.
> *(Nineteen Fifty-Four)*

The poet's dilemma is serious. Worst of all, his 'lamp of contemplation' is shattered and to compound the problem he is inwardly in turmoil and at variance within himself. For one who had always kept a strong grip on life, who could always negotiate for at least 'something to wear as a buttonhole in heaven', it is saddening to see despair writ large over his life.

Unknown to the poet, this was the spiritual desert that would eventually blossom and bear fruit in the Canal Bank poems. All Kavanagh could do was to articulate it. He was undergoing an intense phase of frustration and purification. He had experienced, in quick succession, the ignominy of a lost public law-suit, serious lung cancer, and the disturbing thought that death might be imminent. Not least of his mental tortures was the niggling suspicion that he had failed as a poet. To crown it all he was also depressed by the fact that he might never marry, never 'reproduce himself' which was to be one of his secret life-long regrets.[14] Despite this period of darkness, and perhaps even because of his honesty in dealing with it, a fuller poetic illumination awaited him.

Rebirth

It must be admitted, despite the frequent occurrence of epiphany in Kavanagh's early work, that the fullness of illumination is most evident in his later poems. The moment that signals the beginning of this period of poetic well-being occurred during the exceptionally warm summer of 1955 when, with a blend of mischievous humour and recovered self-confidence, he reports in *Nimbus* magazine on an 'exclusive' news-item relating to himself: He has escaped death and is recuperating from his surgery for lung-cancer. This was how he experienced his rebirth or 'hegira':

I lay on that grass in an ante-natal roll with a hand under my head. And because that grass and sun and canal were good to me they were a particular, personal grass, sun and canal. Nobody anywhere else in the world knew that place as I knew it. There was a branch in the water and it is still in the immortal water in my mind; and the dent in the bank can never be changed nor the wooden seat. When I raised myself on my elbow I saw Leeson Street Bridge. Only by a miracle could anyone ever see Leeson Street Bridge as I saw it. I report too on the corner of St Stephen's Green (The Grafton St entrance) where between the hours of two and four every day last summer I lay in the same ante-natal roll. I could see the clock over Robert's cafe from here. It would never rain again....[15]

This exclusive vision of grass, sun and water began a healing, il-luminating and transforming process which would bear fruit in the Canal Bank poems (1956-60). Kavanagh knew exactly when the moment of his 'rebirth' occurred, its exact location 'on the banks of the Grand Canal between Baggot and Leeson Street bridges' and the detailed circumstances of his life at this time. The poems that ensue have all the hallmarks of mystical illumi-nation. As well as heightened awareness, there is a conscious-ness of divine presence, intense emotional and spiritual passion, and radiant splendour in his immediate world. Added to this, there was an unforgettable sense of interior change, a personal spiritual catharsis, a rebirth! Thus it was, he says, that 'as a poet, I was born.'[16]

The strength of the poems composed at this time was first recognised by Stephen Spender and published by him in *Encounter*, 1958. He acclaimed the poems as 'violently beautiful'. Peter Kavanagh, recognising the exciting 'new twist' in his brother's work, decided 'to start a private Press' for the sole purpose of printing them.[17] The letters exchanged between the brothers at this time capture something of the momentous nature of the canal-bank happening. Patrick's mood is one of expectancy and delight that his work has taken a 'new start'. In more than one letter he remarks on 'his good form' and new feeling of energy. Peter is affirming of his brother's new 'exotic' phase of creativity. He commends this exciting new change in his work which he finds colourful, warm and enthusiastic.

Moments of Fullness and Passion
Mystical fullness is the mood in which the Canal Bank poems are written. Kavanagh is in love again, loving with the abandon of a child and lover:

> … O mother
> Grass, mother me the poet's faculty
> Of loving to the heart of any ordinary thing
> (*Moment on the Canal*)

He thrills at each opportunity to make love again with Miss Universe who is more God-Woman than of earthly origin.

O the sensual throb
Of the explosive body, the tumultous thighs!
Adown a summer lane comes Miss Universe
She whom no lecher's art can rob
Though she is not the virgin who was wise.

His 'leafy-with-love banks' respond to him with overwhelming redemptive intimacy. He wallows in a new baptism effected by 'the green waters of the canal' which 'pour redemption' for him. He is at one with God, with nature and with 'Miss Universe' in a kind of mystical marriage. Kavanagh's nuptial evocations, and humorous disapproval of 'the (un)wise virgins' of the gospel, who declined to share their oil, evokes an ambience of sensuous generous love reminiscent of the biblical 'Song of Songs':

You ravish my heart,
My sister, my promised bride,
you ravish my heart
With a single one of your glances
With one single pearl of your necklace.
(Sg 4:9-10)

In the throes of mystical desire, the poet craves fulfillment for 'the gaping need of (his) senses'. This love-affair will be further ratified in his poem, 'The One' where, luxuriating in divine ardour, he expressed his triple affirmation of God the beautiful One:

… beautiful, beautiful, beautiful God
Was breathing His love by a cut-away bog. (The One)

The Language of Mysticism

Sacred lyrical language in Kavanagh's late poems urges the necessity of a more careful reading of the Canal Bank poems in the light of the mystical events that gave birth to them. Kavanagh's mystical-nuptial language is expanded even further when in a late poem, he speaks with eager anticipation of 'the opening of that holy door'. (Thank You! Thank you!) This image might be seen as bringing to completion a period of mystic 'blessedness' along with an awareness of gratitude for having being able to 'bring home' his harvest of new poems. On a more historical note, the 'holy door' may refer to the solemn ceremony of opening the Holy Door in the Vatican in Rome to celebrate the Marian Year of 1954. Perhaps Kavanagh felt his 'holy door' and his 'holy year' had finally opened. Those of Kavanagh's interpretors who are preoccupied with seeing this merely as a sexual metaphor, may be unwilling or unable to recognise the mystical propensities of the poet, this expert of 'holy love'. They fail to see the entranced visionary hidden beneath the raucous rantings of a frustrated bachelor.

'It is October over all my life'
The poem 'October' manifests something of this overflowing sensibility, coupled with an interior detachment and self-confidence hitherto absent in Kavanagh's work.

> O leafy yellowness you create for me
> A world that was and now is poised above time,
> I do not need to puzzle out Eternity
> As I walk this arboreal street on the edge of a town.
> The breeze too, even the temperature
> And pattern of movement is precisely the same
> As broke my heart for youth passing. Now I am sure
> Of something. Something will be mine wherever I am.

Kavanagh had at this point communed with eternal voices. He walks with the assurance of one who glimpses 'eternity' and is confident of his new contemplative role: 'To look on is enough/ In the business of love'. *(Is)* Caught in the mystical stare of October's 'leafy yellowness', he is scarcely able to withstand its mystical impact. A light from beyond suffuses itself throughout the poem. An aura of transendence envelops the autumnal setting as he is caught in 'this arboreal street on the edge of a town'. Mellow in mood and colour, the poem moves beyond finite realities into the realm of the universal, the eternal, the permanent. Kavanagh's personal autumn is beautiful, his harvest of poems assured. The confident assertion that 'Something will be mine wherever I am' has about it the ring of prophecy.

When the poet further exclaims that he wishes to 'throw (himself) on the public street without caring / For anything but the prayering that the earth offers', it is clear that he is enraptured. He can abandon himself 'without caring' to the 'prayering' of the earth with its penetrating power. The 'stare' of transcendence has caught him in its mystery. These are significant expressions in the total context of the poet's writing. But now they demonstrate sureness of technique in one who feels he has touched the quintessential spirit. As his poetic hazel rod[18] twitches under the rich poetic vein of October symbols, his mood and disposition respond fully to this 'kairos' – moment – a moment of divine visitation. If ever Kavanagh achieves 'weightlessness' it is here. He is undoubtedly 'airborne'.[19] Disciplined over the years to counter starriness with earthiness, he returns to his roots and to the place where it all began, in faith, with the 'man after the harrow' where

'a man is ploughing ground for winter wheat...'

By deliberately recovering contact with the past, with ordinary farm work, he momentarily relinquishes the transcendent, trusting implicity in the sonnet's grounding powers as well as in its transcendent possibilities. Equilibrium restored, the aura of illumination remains rich and exotic in colour and texture.

'It is October over all my life' is a statement that can stand alone. This is a man who stands tall in grateful humility before his completed life's work. The poem's last lines presents an unexpected, comic confrontation of past with present when his new-found sense of completeness is juxtaposed with the once naive simplicity of:

'and my nineteen years weigh heavily on my feet'.

A lifetime's dream has been fulfilled in this setting of harvest and thanksgiving. Spring had been a metaphor for uncertain beginnings in the darkness of faith – Genesis. Now October becomes a powerful metaphor, bringing Kavanagh's life's work to completion – the Parousia. This harvest month moves him momentarily back to his beginnings, a nineteen-year-old youth in a Monaghan field, and to his father's death in October 1929 which strangely heralded the beginning of his poetic career. 'October-coloured weather' with its 'kind brown earth' has always had an appeal for Kavanagh. In October the earth would be warm after the summer months, an ideal time to dig a grave. Rural people think of such things:

> Over the kind brown earth we bend
> Knowing how warm a grave must be
> In October. O Death send
> In October-time your warrant for me. *(October Warrant)*

But this is a brand new 'October', bringing with it a late harvest of poems – all celebrated in the poet's unconquerable comic sense of life. 'October' could serve as his epitaph in that now, in the autumn of his life, he has come home within himself and, like Eliot, 'sees the place for the first time'.

Transformation

Kavanagh has struggled to be transformed into a self-abandoned lover of life, much as the mystic struggles to come home to her/himself. While proclaiming his new vision to the world, his ego still wrestles. He is torn between pride and humility, between being freed of 'self-necessity' and wearing 'the arrogant air that goes with a yellow vestment'. The vestment, a priestly garb, is his imagined poetic cloak. He yearns for recognition yet acknowledges his unimportance except as the namer of objects. Arrogance and humility vie for supremacy as he sees himself 'cavorting on mile-high stilts' above 'crowds looking up with terror in their rational faces'. *(Come Dance with Kitty Stobbling)* Sureness of vision and a new interior calm purify him inwardly as he steers his soul 'by night unstarred' past madness into mysticism.

Torn also at times between pride and self-pity, he finds the true evocation of his self-worth in an old religious medieval story frequently told by preachers at Missions in the early part of this century. 'Our Lady's Tumbler' [20] was the medieval tale that prompted a moment of personal gratitude and self-affirmation in the wake of his canal-bank harvest. Kavanagh identifies with the simple unlettered monk who, unable to pray the psalter in Latin, discovered how best to praise God. Nightly he performed sommersaults in an empty church before the altar. He had been a circus-tumbler before entering the monastery. Tumbling was what he knew best. Likewise Kavanagh, aware of his gift at last, renewed his dedication to poetry and presented his offerings to the one whom, years before at the end of a school day, he had hailed as 'Queen of Heaven', confident then as now that she 'has prayed for me and guided my wanderings'.[21]

> I come to you to verse my thanks
> To parks and flowers and canal banks
> I bring you this verse interlude
> Our Lady's Tumbler's gratitude.
> *(Our Lady's Tumbler)*

Under her patronage, he would remain faithful to 'personal visions', grateful for opportunities to 'get to know new blades of grass' and celebrate 'the view / That happened to no one else but you'.

A Return to Simplicity

By 1959, it seems clear that Kavanagh returned to simplicity of vision, to recording 'love's mystery without claptrap'. *(The Hospital)* Moreover, his simple vocation to love would transform his life into a more 'shapely form'.

> I will have love, have love
> From everything made of
> And a life with a shapely form
> With gaity and charm
> And capable of receiving
> With grace the grace of living... *(The Self-Slaved)*

This newly acquired simplicity has been dearly bought. Assessing himself in his *Self Portrait,* he says:

> There are two kinds of simplicity, the simplicity of going away and the simplicity of return. The last is the ultimate in sophistication. In the final simplicity we don't care whether we appear foolish or not. We talk of things that earlier would

embarrass. We are satisfied with being ourselves, however small.[22]

T. S. Eliot spoke of a similar state at the end of 'Little Gidding' as a 'condition of complete simplicity / (costing not less than everything'), an achievement only at 'the end of all (his) exploring'. Evelyn Underhill sees the mystical simplicity of a child as the ultimate fruit of the spiritual life. It is a condition of humility, equanimity, and personal integration.[23] Kavanagh never reached the consistent 'not-caring' attitude to life which he desired. Nevertheless at heart he was content with himself and content with his new role in life to bless, to be grateful and 'to die in harness' with his renewed mission to love.

He refers to a new phase of 'blessing' in his life. He has escaped the tyranny of dispiriting idealism and can say sincerely:

With Auden I was forced to bless

What is, whatever be its dress. *(Along the Grand Canal)*

Theology of the Commonplace

Kavanagh strongly identified with Auden's search for a spirit of blessing, though Auden himself could aspire only to this happy inner state. Kavanagh seemed to arrive there as its special guest while Auden's cry is still one of a soul astray:

'O look, look in the mirror,

O look in your distress;

Life remains a blessing

Although you cannot bless'.

(As I walked out one evening)

He could also identify with Yeats who, in his 'Dialogue of a Self and Soul', strikes a note of fellow feeling:

We must laugh and we must sing

We are blest by everything,

Everything we look upon is blest.[24]

The transformed Kavanagh found blessedness everywhere. His was the blessedness of simple things, the 'anonymous performers' of life. His vindication of the ordinary and humble belief in his own unique vision is pre-eminent. Overwhelming gratitude

for his new harvest of poems indicates that his consciousness
has been transformed in a manner proper to the saint and mystic. Overwhelmed with thanks for the gift of illumination,
Kavanagh's ego is humbled:

> I sat me down upon the grass
> And asked what have I paid for this
> Why should I be allowed? (*Along the Grand Canal*)

The earlier Kavanagh of 'The Great Hunger', like his anti-hero
Patrick Maguire would have become easily wearied of the occasional 'primrose here and a daisy there'. He would have idly
dreamt of 'the Absolute envased Bouquet'. The later Kavanagh
is humbled into daily, moment by moment surrender to 'the
wonders of holy love'. His new role is one wearing the priestly
poet's vestment so that he may consider 'for love's sake ... whatever widens the field of the faithful's activity'. Constantly returning to the posture of gratitude, and in the guise of 'Our
Lady's Tumbler', he is imbued with a profound thanks to 'parks
and flowers and canal banks'. This new abandonment to 'what
is', to 'the everydays of nature', marks the serenity of one who is
familiar with what spiritual writers call 'the sacrament of the
present moment'. More than ever now his is a theology of the
commonplace.[25]

Fascination with 'light staring' is a marked feature of these
late poems. They contrast noticeably with the younger Kavanagh, who shyly averts his gaze from the acknowledged beauty
of bluebells and only glimpes snatches of light through chinks
and lattices. The mature poet, who has somehow been united to
Reality, is open to the no longer escapable 'stare' of Being.
Moreover, he is capable of giving expression to this experience.
It is impossible to evaluate the full significance of the canal-bank
rebirth. There is little doubt that it has about it an aura of mystical communion, combined with an undeniable transformation
of life.

Illumination is now also attended by new levels of spiritual
awakening and insight gained from a transformed consciousness. The poet is confident now that true knowlege is gained

through contemplative loving and not through mere scholarly activity:

> The only true teaching
> Subsists in watching
> Things moving or just colour
> Without comment from the scholar. *(Is)*

His renewed belief in contemplation implies a simultaneous denunciation of a laborious 'wisdom plodded together by concerned fools'. Making a strong plea for transcendent knowledge and its eternal significance, he strikes a note of combined comic and lyrical strength at the end of 'To Hell with Commonsense'. Kavanagh can trust his intuitive power fully and express it with confidence and humour:

> And I have a feeling
> That through the hole in reason's ceiling
> We can fly to knowledge
> Without ever going to college.

Interior Change

Transformation, however, is never complete. Despite his desire to be 'uncaring', Kavanagh remains susceptible to retaliating with stinging indignation when unfairly criticised. Even in his Canal Bank poems he is never far from satirising his 'pigmy' critics and denouncing those who would share Parnassus, the mount of true poetry, with him. Nevertheless he emerges from his rebirth with some foundational convictions in place. He is firmly rooted in 'a world man's world cannot shake'. His resolution to avoid satire as 'unfruitful prayer', made years earlier in 'Prelude', is reaffirmed. He struggled to be inwardly free to avoid self-pity, one of poetry's counterfeits:

> Me I will throw away.
> Me sufficient for the day
> The sticky self that clings
> Adhesion on the wings
> To love and adventure,
> To go on the grand tour

A man must be free
From self-necessity. *(The Self-Slaved)*

Rebirth for Kavanagh, as for Joyce, was a dark process. Kavanagh had already grappled with 'the nets' flung at the soul to 'hold it back from flight'. He had resolved his conflicts with religion, idiom and nationality. The poet, he had discovered, transcends nationality. Deftly skirting 'the matter of Ireland', which remained alive in the wake of Irish Literary Revival, he freed himself from conventions and continued to 'wrest his idiom bare-handed out of a literary nowhere'.[26] Religion, however, was innate. It could be sifted through but not sloughed off nor sidestepped. The greatest enemies of Kavanagh's rebirth came from within: self-pity, loneliness, pride and arrogance, along with an over-preoccupation with those who envied him. These 'nets' he now dispelled with a sense of abandonment and resurgence of his comic spirit. Life had imparted its wisdom and become his teacher:

For what it teaches is just this
We are not alone in our loneliness,
Others have been here and known
Griefs we thought our special own
Problems that we could not solve
Lovers that we could not have
Pleasures that we missed by inches.
Come I'm beginning to get pretentious...
(Thank You, Thank You)

But the question remains: did Kavanagh change his life radically as a result of the inner vision which he experienced on the banks of the Grand Canal? Outwardly it might appear not, but who is in a position to judge? Inwardly he had triply confessed to his discovery of a new image of God. 'I learned, I learned when one might be inclined to think, too late!...'/I learned something of the nature of God's mind...' *(Miss Universe)* The vehemence with which he states his position gives us to understand that what he has experienced is radical. He had come to terms with life and with God in a new way. Spiritually speaking, when our image of

God changes radically, as Kavanagh's does, we suspect that something monumental has occurred interiorly. Kavanagh had changed from an abstract notion of God to a personal God who loved him eternally in all aspects. This God was:

> Not the abstract Creator but he who caresses
> The daily and nightly earth; He who refuses
> To take failure for an answer till again and again is worn.
> (*Miss Universe*)

This new definition of God is at the same time a new affirmation of a redeemed self in a redeemed world: 'There are no recriminations in Heaven'. He is already in Paradise since he has experienced 'a sensational ... and almost incredible flowering of (his) catharsis'. Kavanagh's God is feminine, affirming, beautiful, forgiving, caressing yet unfathomable: 'the Mind that has baulked the profoundest of mortals'. His own life has undergone healing; he is content. James Liddy, who knew him in these latter years, gives confirmation of this inner equanimity:

> When I knew him, his health had given way, and he perhaps used alcohol too much as a form of day-long liturgy, yet he had content in his work and was content with his life. His domicile moved more frequently than his pub but he was well rested in the signposts of his mind. I take him to have been a Christian; he had the secret quality of real traditional religion...[27]

The notion that Kavanagh was content with his God comes also from Katherine Moloney, whom he married a few months before his death. She frequently said of him with conviction: 'There goes all I know of God',[28] and Liddy further attests to something sacred that emanated from the man:

> ... my life was changed by the evangelisation of Kavanagh in McDaid's and elsewhere, even on very bad coughing and sweating days. The soul goes marching on![29]

Last Days

Little is known concerning the details of Kavanagh's last days. He collapsed at a performance of *Tarry Flynn* in the Town Hall in

Dundalk. The producer, Thomas Mac Anna, was working at The Abbey Theatre Company at this time. As a Dundalk man he was suited to be one of the first producers of this play. The performance was scheduled to take place from Thursday 23 November to Saturday 25 November. On Wednesday 22 November, Patrick came from Dublin and stayed overnight at the Imperial Hotel in Dundalk to be present at the opening night. He collapsed in the theatre lounge before the performance but sat through the play beside his sister Mary who was a nurse. Later he retired to Mulligan's pub where, apparently recovered, he expounded on drama and other topics in the company of some of his friends. He was taken home to Inniskeen that night. During the night his condition deteriorated.[30] Next day his wife Katherine and her sister Judy came to take him by car to what was then The Merrion Nursing Home at No 21, Herbert Place in Dublin.[31] He was suffering from pneumonia and was obviously very ill. He received expert attention in the Merrion Nursing Home with supplementary private nursing to ensure that he was at no time without medical care. Since it was a private establishment there was no permanent Roman Catholic chaplain in attendance. The curates from Westland Row parish, however, served this hospital on request. The sick-call book at the church in Westland Row contained a single entry for 28 November 1967. It read, 'Merrion Nursing Home: "A Patient"' and was signed by the priest who attended, a Fr Joe Stone. It was Fr Arthur Larkin, curate at Westland Row Parish in November 1989, who showed me this historic sick-call book. He explained that it was customary for the priest on duty at that time to record every sick-call made during his time of duty. Recently these books were destroyed.

I have been unable to verify with exact certitude that this anonymous patient attended by Fr Stone was in fact Patrick Kavanagh. Father Drumy, stationed at Westland Row parish at that time, considers it very probable.[32] He remembered Fr Stone remark in passing that Patrick Kavanagh had in the end made his peace with the church. Richard Riordan who attended

Patrick Kavanagh's funeral. L to R: Kieran Markey, Andrew Quinn,
Patrick Moloney, the undertaker, Sr Celia Kavanagh, Packie Quinn.
Photo courtesy Hugh Brady, Inniskeen

Patrick as his doctor and later signed his death-certificate, asked
Patrick if he wished to see a priest. He had nodded consent. Who
the priest was, he did not know. Kavanagh's friend Leo Holohan
is reported to have been at his friend's bedside and to have heard
him repeatedly say: 'O God, I believe.' His brother Peter, reflecting on this afterwards, says that this has the ring of truth.[33]

At Kavanagh's death-bed the special nurse employed to attend him on the night of 29 November 1967 was Mrs Flo
Connaughton-Riordan. She recalls his 'almost saintly smile' as
he opened his eyes to find her ministering to him. He had difficulty breathing and she adjusted his oxygen mask to make him
more comfortable. Remembering the incident she writes:

> I will never forget that special moment with Patrick
> Kavanagh, it was God's love shining through ... I do remem-
> ber attempting to describe this to my mother sometime later
> – it was as if even on his death-bed one could see his bril-
> liance – he was no ordinary person.[34]

She also recalls being informed by the nurse whom she replaced
that her patient 'had been attended by the priest', a phrase
which indicated that he had received the sacrament of Extreme

Unction, presumably from Fr Stone. Patrick Kavanagh died at one thirty on the morning of 30 November.

The account of the last moments of Patrick Kavanagh's life, recounted by nurse Flo Connaughton, confirms the fact that the transformed Kavanagh only became visible at rare moments. Apart from his poetry, where illumination is most obvious, the 'inner man' kept himself to himself. Briefly and unforgettably on occasion he impressed those who were privileged to know him more intimately. He shared with them his spirituality, his insight and his humour.

Conclusion

Kavanagh the poet believed that illumination was essential to true poetry. A real poem contained, he believed, the 'flash' of 'Beatific Vision', thus it took wings, was possessed of 'weightlessness' and became 'airborne'. His spiritual nature was frequently haunted by the 'light that might be mystic or a fraud'. This salutary self-doubt he shared with mystics as much as the poets. There is only the finest line of difference between Kavanagh the poet and Kavanagh the mystic. There are moments when it seems that he is both. Like Hopkins perhaps, the poet in him gives voice to the mystic. It is difficult to discern any note of dissonance between them. Kavanagh's life-long dedication to integrity, to self-knowledge, to self-doubt, as well as to self-affirmation, would have us believe that he *is* in harmony with his vision. Genuine graced moments of spiritual illumination have been his and, what is more, they have transformed him.

Once he began to trust his experiences of illumination, he discovered the accompanying technique of executing them poetically. His early Christian formation, both in doctrine and in genuine practice of his faith, guided him in the knowledge of what it meant to be illumined by the Holy Spirit. This gave him a strong spiritual and doctrinal context in which to ground his 'intimations of immortality' and his daily poetic baptisms 'by fire and the Holy Ghost'. The Holy Ghost on the fields or in the bog forecast further illumining epiphanies. Kavanagh learned the simplicity of being present to record such personal 'exclusive news items'.

Religious mysticism provided Kavanagh with the framework from which he could operate as a poet. His lone and fiercely individual spirit brought him face to face with periods of intense purification which inevitably lead to a transformed consciousness. He makes friends with the cracks and chinks of life that let the light in. Practised in restricted vision, he not only 'sees into the life of things', but also observes creation's plenitude with Hopkins whom he admired greatly. Both are able to 'deal(s) out that being indoor each one dwells'. Kavanagh was mentally and physically strong enough to sustain the impact of his eternal visitations. As a poet he was a subtle enough technician to deliver some of the finest lyrical language to ensure the permanent illumination of 'bits of road', 'particular trees', and 'the dew of an Indian summer morning ... on bleached potato stalks'. Like his 'moonlight that stays forever in a tree', Kavanagh was an assured technician of illumination. He hung lights in rural Ireland for others to find, by which they in turn became illumined. He was fascinated with the earth, the great festival of nature, the fecundity of clay, and the seasons. As Jordan says, 'he is, first and foremost a celebrant of life'. But Kavanagh was the true alchemist of life. His mystical imagination refined what he saw into a pure flame. And for this, I believe, we must confer on him the mystical mantle or vestment that is his due.

Once Kavanagh has tasted the mystical 'bread of angels' he is no longer content with prose. He is involved in a lifetime of yearning and longing which is characteristic of the mystic. His journey to Eden and back again is a familiar mystical/poetic route outlined by Jordan. It involves 'departure, disillusion and bewilderment, enrichment and return'.[35] His journeying, however naïve in its early stages, leaves the reader with no doubt that the poet has journeyed interiorly as well as exteriorly to the outer limits of his (un)'earthly estate'. His 'candle of vision' waxes at times to a flame and wanes to a flicker towards the very end of his life when he becomes a chronically ill man. Without his 'lamp of contemplation' he cannot live. More than physical disability, his loss of the 'spark' of inspiration robs him of his zest for life.

Kavanagh saw himself as holy, not in any orthodox meaning of the word, but as one fascinated by God. He knew there was in him a winged life, a poetic and/or spiritual spark that sought expression. In his latter period of inner repose he stopped wrestling with 'the nets flung out to trap him' and settled for mental equanimity. His final battle with ill-health, alcohol and burn-out was a losing one. His poetic journey was over but his 'holy door' had opened. When he died, he was, one could say, almost content. Some attendant angel, witnessing his passing might have glimpsed his tragi-comic soul:

Swaggering celestially home to his three wishes granted.

(*The Great Hunger*)

The Word Becomes Flesh

'Something to wear as a buttonhole in heaven'
(From Failure Up)

Having released the twists and turns of Kavanagh's lifelong dialogue with the divine presence in the phenomenological world, one must ask what that enterprise amounted to in terms of his life's work? Or more specifically, where does the argument of self and soul eventually lead him?

It is clear from the beginning that a personal odyssey is under way, a path destined to be trod by him to the bitter end. Lured by his early visionary powers, he is easily enamoured of his ability to peek into nature's tabernacles. He boldly asks for 'faith' to be 'alive' to witness 'April's ecstasy'. In love with the magic of spring, he is caught up with the newness of life and its dancing capabilities. Moreover, he is unusually awake to his colourful Monaghan environment whose 'yellow flame-blossoms of the whin, lit bonfires all over the landscape…'[1] Kavanagh was perplexed at times by being privy to revelations of a mystical light that played on the hills. Caught in the ardour of such moments, he held divine conversations with flowers and weeds. Misunderstood even at home, at school and in his rural neighbourhood, he mused alone among the drumlin hills. People who watched him thought he was mad.

Very early in his poetic life he tended toward an idealistic stance in tone and imagery. He wanted to escape from the ordinary; to taste the exotic 'bread of wisdom' that 'grows in the other lands'. He knew what he wanted would not be bought cheaply. He entertained exalted aspirations to 'rise amongst

starry fields/ on winged dust', and envisaged himself in splendid isolation 'on the world's rim', 'stretching out hands to
Seraphim'. Under the influence of his early reading of Joyce, he
demands the sacred vestment worthy of a priest of 'the eternal
imagination':

I too am flame

Ablaze on the hills of Being...

O cut for me life's bread, for me pour wine. *(Worship)*

Just as *Stephen Hero* leaves the Catholic priesthood for the poetic
priesthood of 'transmuting the daily bread of experience into
the radiant body of everlasting life', so would Kavanagh be attracted to a similar mission to the commonplace.[2] He would
covet this role without, however, relinquishing his Catholic
roots. Because Kavanagh chose the more difficult route of re-
maining true to his religious convictions, he would undergo a
thorough purification in the pursuit of his dream.

His early desire to dance with the April's 'white-thorn tree' is
idyllic but this too will undergo a long and thorough transformation. However appealingly his 'white-thorn tree' as a sign-
post to his 'childhood country', it will eventually have to be
spiritually up-rooted and re-planted through a harrowing inner
process. This transformation is made possible only through the
agility of his mystical imagination. Kavanagh's imaginative
landscape would take on a timeless, placeless quality, increasing
in size and stature as it grew into an interior space. From his
pioneering work, a new generation of Irish poets would be born
and nurtured. The immortality he craved would derive from his
unwavering commitment to his landscape and to his soul.

Similarly, his external 'stony grey soil' will in time become an
'inland' territory which is taken in hand, 'digged and ditched'
until it bears the harvest proper to 'authentic land'. Through
straitened circumstances Kavanagh succumbed to selling his
'sixteen acre farm' in the spring of 1949, knowing full well that
his 'hungry hills' would live forever in his imagination.
Whoever came to 'own' the hills of Shancoduff would never
'own' them as he had. For him they would always be something

more than a place 'that the waterhen and snipe might have for-saken'. The transformation process that effected this conversion was attained only at the end of 'a tortuous road'. Patrick Kavan-agh had to learn with the mystic that 'the longest journey is the journey inward'.[3] But he *did* learn it while commuting the short geographical distance between Monaghan and the Grand Canal.

Although he was smitten with an early innocent passion for primrose banks, which 'smiled (at him) with violets', he learned to temper passion with patience. In poetry he practised the deli-cate poetic art of falling in love with nature. He courted blue-bells 'under the big trees' and revelled in the romance of 'hold-ing November in the woods'. He enthused nostalgically over 'the dandelions at Willie Hughes's' as well as over the 'rotted shafts of a remembered cart', but acknowledged eventually that mere aesthetic pleasure yielded a host of inner questions about the real role of the poet in society. His early love-affair with na-ture is soon seen for what it was: 'merely a point of departure for the play'. The poet, now mature, speaks the language of humility, of ageless love, of timeless beauty and of spiritual self-emptying. 'There are no answers to any real questions,' he discovers. He is at home in this land of un-knowing: 'I do not know what age I am/ I am no mortal age', and yet he knew his immortality lay somehow enscribed in his native 'whitethorn hedges'. These words of his poem, 'Innocence' (1951), herald a new sense of self and of poetry. The innocence of youth has become the innocence of mature vision.

Throughout his poetic journey Kavanagh danced or 'buck-lepped', as the case may be, in tandem with the drama of his per-sonal life. He struggled, as many poets and artists do, to find the necessary relationship between art and life. In an early poem, 'Four Birds', he sees something of the true artist in 'the kestrel', the 'stately dancer' in his 'sky ballroom'. Kavanagh wanted to dance with life. As early as 'Inniskeen Road' (1936), he wistfully envies his neighbours who so easily converge on the local dance. His lot is rather to engage in his own solitary side-step in time with a singular tune and rhythm. His dance would become more varied than the kestrel's. It would at times have the lively physicality of a jig or a polka and occasionally the measured grace of a slow waltz. His dance with the fictitious 'Kitty Stobbling' would be part of his mad celebratory cavorting 'on mile high stilts', lost in the pleasure of being alive. By contrast and in more lyrical mood, his canal-bank dance would have the poise and stately elegance of a gavotte.

'How can we know the dancer from the dance?' was Yeats' cry to the artist in 'Among School Children' (1927). Kavanagh's work consistently confronts this issue while contemplating his own multi-angular soul in his attempt to attain poetic integrity. Contemplating his four birds, he identifies at times with the 'night-winged' owl and its mystical predilection for darkness. Or the sweet-throated lark, the 'morning star / Announcing the birth / Of a love-child'. He cherished an ambition to be a poet of love, secret love in particular. More often he found he was the wilderness-loving corncrake, rare, raucous, prophetic and un-prepossessing.

Aspects of his rugged outer world at the same time con-tributed to the fashioning of his angular inner disposition. The 'Monaghan hills' with their 'hundred little heads' were not de-signed, it seemed, for making him a poet. A permanent darkness clings to these north-facing drumlins that 'have never seen the sun rising'. This darker aspect of landscape filtered through his work even in his sunniest poems. At times he looked enviously towards Slieve Gullion, the Mourne Mountains, 'even Forkhill', and wished for the 'echo-corners' they might create in his soul. Like it or not, he had to dance with his angular fields and watery drumlin hills. It was an ambivalent partnership but one that made him who he was.

Kavanagh's search for Perfection
Kavanagh admits that he was tempted to covet a conventional style of self-perfection. He states this clearly in his prose-poem 'The Gift'. This poem could serve as a summary poem to exem-plify the movement that occurs in Kavanagh between the early and later phases of his life.

One day I asked God to give
Me perfection so I'd live
Smooth and courteous, calmly wise
All the world's virtuous prize.

So I should not always be
Getting into jeopardy,
Being savage, wild and proud
Fighting, arguing with the crowd...

The tone changes as he moves away from self-preoccupation to self-insight. He creates a jingling rhyme appropriate to self-mockery as he sketches the derelict condition of his state of mind: 'being poor, sick, depressed, / Everywhere an awful pest...' These lines carry overtones of the biblical Book of Lamentations:

Listen to my groaning
there is no one to comfort me.
All my enemies gloat over my disaster:
this is your doing. *(Lam 1:21)*

The self-recriminatory note becomes quickly supplanted by the surprising announcement that God will deign to answer Patrick Kavanagh's request. True to form, Kavanagh plays both roles in this small dramatic interlude!

And God spoke out of Heaven
The only gift in my giving
Is yours – Life. Seek in hell
Death, perfect, wise, comfortable.

Outrageous though it may seem, Kavanagh manifests a profound grasp of divine wisdom. He counsels himself to accept his original selfhood with its kinks, foibles and idiosyncrasies. Acceptance at God's hands of the self-that-one-is is the foundation of a sturdy spirituality. This personal struggle becomes the possibility of his own idiosyncratic 'word' becoming 'flesh'.

Kavanagh learned further lessons of self-acceptance from his continuous study of the human condition. Once more he counsels the students of UCD in 1956:

The weakness, unhappiness and frustration of men springs
from the fact that they are dissatisfied with the person that

God has made. In other words, they do not love God. And
unless you love God you cannot be happy.[5]

Nature has taught him to cherish not only the beauty of God but
the irreducible integrity of his own originality. He notices how
the humblest weed in a hedge is not envious of the rose but
loves and is grateful to the God who made it.

And Kavanagh is more than the humblest weed! A calmer,
more spiritually insightful Kavanagh has eventually succeeded
in climbing the 'unending stair' of asceticism and exuding a wisdom learnt from experience. His 'humble trade' of poetry has
served him well in the unfolding of his personal destiny.

Chinks and Buttonholes

Perhaps it is Kavanagh's personal woundedness which becomes
one of his most valuable artistic assets. 'God sometimes enters
the heart through a wound' is his lived spirituality. Was this a
spirituality derived from the belief that 'art is life squeezed
through a repression'? Was it his own brokenness that led him
to the conviction that suffering squeezed through chinks, cracks
and buttonholes could be transformed into something beautiful? – even radiant? Whatever his repression, Kavanagh's art
flourished in adversity. Whatever hidden hurt gripped his soul,
he used it as ballast for his soaring imagination.

Before he asked his famous question regarding poetry in
'Auditors In' (1951), 'Is verse an entertainment only?', he was
convinced of the answer. Poetry was

... a profound and holy
Faith that cries the inner history
Of the failure of man's mission.

Here he gives us the key to understanding his belief in poetry as
prophecy and transparency. His verse would emerge from the
pain of failure and remain as proof that, with its help, the soul
triumphs over darkness.

He explored the chinks and cracks of his life and landscape
so thoroughly that he was assured that even out of 'the dead
clod of failure' he could still salvage something beautiful to

wear as 'a buttonhole in heaven'. The buttonhole image is useful as a composite symbol of restriction and openness. A hole has all the properties of a wound, yet in ideal conditions becomes a means of disclosure. Buttonholes plucked from the landscape became for Kavanagh items of perennial celebration. However dire the circumstances, he remains close enough to earth, to the humus, to grow something he can wear with a modicum of triumph, 'something humble as a dandelion or a daisy'. Nothing incarnate, he believed, not even failure was too base to be transformed. With the aid of his epiphany-technique, he simply uncovered the inherent beauty of things. Kavanagh believed with unshakeable faith that he, too, would swagger 'celestially home', wearing something beautiful salvaged from the brokenness of his existence.

He had learned that equanimity in the face of failure cannot be achieved without prayer and self-direction. His habit of self-guidance through self-disclosure was an exercise begun in his 'Diary' published in *Envoy* (1949-51) and gradually woven into the textures of his later poems. The old habit of talking to himself, which he had initially learned from his father, became a form of self-counselling, an interior dialogue between self and soul. In 'Auditors In' he counsels himself against combating the 'looney ghosts that goad/ The savages of Pembroke Road ...' with weapons other than with poetry and prayer. In gratitude for his 'humble trade of versing' which 'restore(s) (his) equanimity', he invites himself to pray: 'Bow down here and thank your God.' Prayer and poetry have engaged him fully in the dual tasks of purification and illumination.

Shedding illusions as a final twist to his life, he is willing to start at the bottom, ignoring all would-be flatterers and false-worshippers. Poetically and spiritually he has travelled far since his youthful dalliance with the 'smooth, courteous' externals of perfection. His early unrealistic demands have been at least partially won through self-acceptance and growing self-confidence. More mystically inspired, he now takes flight 'on wings like Joyce's' wearing, not 'second-hand clothes' like those prepared by Dedalus' mother,[6] but 'brand new clothes' laid out by 'Mother Earth'. Characteristically he does not forget a carefully selected 'buttonhole'!

> Away, away on wings of Joyce's
> Mother Earth is putting my brand new clothes in order
> Praying, she says, that I no more ignore her
> Yellow buttons she found at bargain prices.
> Kelly's Big Bush for a button-hole. Surprises
> In every pocket –

This is no escape but rather a new commitment to everything that exists. He has come home within himself. 'I have a home to return to now. O blessing/ For the Return in the Departure'. Outwardly nothing has changed. He will continue to be as described in 'Gift': 'savage, wild and proud/ Fighting, arguing with the crowd'. Inwardly, however, his mystical imagination has glimpsed the 'home' of repose on which he has fixed his gaze. In this relative calm of surrender the final ascent to Calvary has only begun. The mocking 'hysterical laughter of the defeated' that peopled 'The Great Hunger' will become 'the terrifying yell' of 'the defeated' in the Dublin pubs. Defeat follows him, parried only by a self-destructive mordant satire which serves to augment the all-pervading sense of the 'failure of (his) mission'. Is he the 'Son of God' then? Kavanagh, one feels, is tempted to answer: 'Thou has said it.' He seeks to escape Calvary but will never quite irradicate the cry of those who want him to be the Christ-poet and therefore to shed his blood to the last drop.

In his messianic ambitions, as in other areas of his life, the poet struggles to reconcile polarities within himself. He is at pains to harmonise the Christ and anti-Christ within him, the ascetic and the hedonist, the lover of rural life and the hater of vision-dampening clay, the church as the sure measure of life, and the cruel spoil-sport institution that unfairly 'cuts all the green branches'. Kavanagh lived on a knife-edge of unresolved ambivalences, and yet within this tension he produces moments of exquisite beauty. The 'agonising pincer-jaws' of life were, for him, of heaven's making. They helped him achieve his earthly redemption and within their agonising grip he still somehow seemed to sing most sweetly.

Resurrection was slow in coming. The chrysalis was slow to open. His renewed inner life was tardy in finding its assured mystical wings. The apparent disintegration poetically and biographically of 'Nineteen Fifty-Four' (1954) signalled the death-throes that forecast rebirth. To discover a life more radiant than before 'at the end of a tortuous road' is an unexpected bonus for a sick, disspirited writer. Kavanagh's Christian faith is confirmed in his perceived 'hegira' which, however thinly disguised, will be a thoroughly Christian rebirth. In effect, the Christian images skilfully deployed in his new poems show more kinship with the Pauline notion of shedding the 'old man' (Col 3:9-10) and putting on 'the new cloak of immortality' (1 Cor 15:53) than with the Muslim ritual of 'hegira'. This was indeed a foretaste of heaven. But the poet has not died – he is simply reborn.

Kavanagh exults in his renewed sense of Incarnation. Clay, so long sterile and 'mouth-gagging' for the 'stricken' poet of the past, is now reconciled with God whose 'Word (is) eloquently new and abandoned'. The renewed earth is engaged in 'building a nest for the Word'. These images highlight the poet's commitment to earth and flesh. The hero-courageous tomb has in reality been a life-giving womb.

As earth and self are reborn, so too is the divine presence that illumines them. His former deity, the *deus ex machina* who could deliver or deny perfection at will, is now the beneficent God of the Universe and of humankind. 'Miss Universe' announces the presence of a God, fully incarnational, endlessly forgiving, radiant with life and grace. This is the voluptuous delicious God of the Rhineland mystic Meister Eckhart, who with nuptial undertones conspires with the poet to make love to the earth and its people.

The poet has come full circle. His landscapes, be they of Monaghan, Dublin or London, are made holy through a visible conspiracy between God and poetry. The divine presence, no longer in a stance of control and judgement, is now fully committed to the earth and to earth's collaborators. Kavanagh's new-found catharsis is universally cleansing, healing the self and its milieu. The poet's task is no longer intent on perfection but on contemplation. 'To look on is enough/ in the business of love'. However tempting the worldly images of 'the beautiful unbroken', they are to be waived as distractions 'from the main purpose' which is a profound and unwavering commitment to the ordinary:

> count them the beautiful unbroken
> And then forget them
> As things aside from the main purpose
> Which is to be
> Passive, observing with a steady eye.
> *(Intimate Parnassus)*

The mood and images of repose and contentment which filter through the poet's mature work are established. 'Not caring,' he says, 'is really a sense of values and feeling of confidence. A man who cares is not the master.' This note of equanimity makes of Kavanagh a wisdom figure for the students at UCD in 1956. In a fatherly way he shares with them what life has taught him:

> For what it teaches is just this
> We are not alone in our loneliness
> Others have been here and known
> Griefs we thought our special own
> Problems that we could not solve
> Lovers that we could not have
> Pleasures that we missed by inches
> Come I'm beginning to get pretentious...
> *(Thank you, Thank you)*

There is no final formula for perfection. Kavanagh may easily slip into old postures. But he returns more readily now to the hard core of his poetic integrity and to the 'shapely (inner) form' which is 'capable of receiving / With grace the grace of living...' *(The Self-Slaved)* His earliest aspiration to be truly 'alive' has

come close to being realised. Blessing in a Christian context returns all reality to God in delight and mutual appreciation.[7] It
has taken Kavanagh a lifetime to achieve this sense of blessing.
Gratitude is the mood which now characterises his work and is
the secret of the extraordinary self-confidence he expresses in
one of the many sayings which he assembled in his *Collected
Pruse* as one of the 'Signposts' for his life:

> No man need be mediocre if he accepts himself as God made
> him. God only made geniuses. But many men do not like
> God's work...[8]

Kavanagh did not always like the type of genius he was. His
specific poetic task was to penetrate the divine purpose in himself and in everything around him. In this way the poet found
God's will for his life. His Christian faith was 'not of the
Lourdes-Fatima variety' he said. This was understandable. It
was nonetheless genuine. He embarked on his own mythical
'crossing over' to the world of God and art, only to return with
radiance in his person and in his poetry. 'The real trouble with
the world today is,' he says, 'that it wants to believe in God and
cannot.'[9] Kavanagh penetrated to the heart of the of 'the gay
imaginative God' through whom he believed everything became 'happy and young again and filled with sublime hope'.[10]
'Only the Eternal (is) worthwhile' was his perennial gospel of
life and one with which he could rest easily:

> So be reposed and praise, praise, praise
> The way it happened and the way it was.
> (*Question to Life*)

These lines have brought us full circle, back to the simplicity
which inspired the poet in the first place, but which has cost him
everything.

Kavanagh a Mystic?

Was Kavanagh a mystic then? Was he Franciscan in his spirituality, devoted to the praise of God's creatures and singing his
own 'Canticle of the Sun'? Was he a 'holy fool', 'a Matt Talbot of
Monaghan', trapped into a life of extraordinary self-sacrifice?

Was he a Christ-figure, 'foolishly' given to the fulfilment of his mission as poet and prophet, but held by many as a figure of fun? Was he a Julian of Norwich who saw the mystery of God in 'something as small as a hazelnut', yet focused at the same time on the Creator who held it in being? Did Kavanagh vie with Julian in his insight into God who was father and mother in one? Surprisingly, he was one of the first Irish theologians to recognise the femininity of God in his memorable line, 'Surely my God is feminine'. *(God in Woman)* Or was Kavanagh rather something of the ascetical St John of the Cross who searched for the Ultimate Essence of God? He did indeed see himself at work '... like a monk / In a grey cell/ copying out (his) soul's/ queer miracle'. *(Poet)* Finally, one might ask had he not kinship with St Thérèse of Lisieux, who was totally abandoned to a 'little way of Divine Love'. Here, as in the later Kavanagh, the smallest item embraced with great love was capable of infinite value.

Not surprisingly, no *one* of these suggestions adequately encompasses Kavanagh's charism. Each suggestion in turn might seem ludicrous, since Kavanagh is an unlikely candidate for canonisation! I hope I have not made the unforgiveable mistake of appearing to canonise him. Yet I believe that I have succeeded in proving that beneath his external awkwardness of character there is an unmistakeable Christian mystical dimension to his work. Moreover, his mystical imagination gifted him with rare instances of divine revelation. This artistic disclosure became his messianic mission to society. He was prophetic in that he reasoned for a God who embraced the human condition in all its vagaries and imperfections. He embodied a dedication to earth and to earth's commonplaces. He surrendered to incarnation against the tide of current teaching within a Catholic Church strongly tainted with Jansenism. His 'word' speaks the truth for the unconscious soul of the Irish psyche which continuously seeks to be made 'flesh'.

And so the poet proceeded from the situation of one who 'dabbled in verse' to one who had a life-commitment to poetry. This commitment eased the pain of his existence and helped him achieve his mission. The flashes of radiance that buttonholed the drabness of his existence will outlive him. He aimed at nothing cultivated or manicured, but glimpses, splashes of colour: primroses, violets, coltsfoot, daisies, dandelions, whins, wild iris, bluebells, whitethorn – trimmed and festooned with an amalgam of weeds and grasses. Here was a poet in love with an Eden of his own making, intent on making his soul through poetry. There were times when he skirted the walls of hell, and found himself 'lying with his nose in the rubble that was his achievement'. Yet he dared to hope that despite failure he would don his poetic mantle with the rest and wear his contribution proudly as 'a buttonhole in heaven'.

Notes

INTRODUCTION

1. Patrick Kavanagh, *The Complete Poems*, ed. Peter Kavanagh, Newbridge, Ireland: The Goldsmith Press, 1984. Unless otherwise stated all quotations are from this edition.
2. All Biblical references are taken from *The Jerusalem Bible*, London: Darton, Longman and Todd, Ltd, 1966.

NOTES TO CHAPTER 1

1. Evelyn Underhill, (Mrs Steward Moore), *Mysticism*, New York: E.P. Dutton and Co, Inc, Dutton Paperback ed., 1961, pp. 70-94.
2. St John of the Cross, 'The Spiritual Canticle' in *The Collected Works of St John of the Cross*, trans. Kieran Kavanaugh, O.C.D. and Otilio Rodriguez, O.C.D., Washington, DC: Institute of Carmelite Studies, 1973, p. 712. All further references to the writings of St John are taken from this edition unless otherwise stated.
3. Underhill, pp. 1-2.
4. Underhill, p. 48
5. Joseph de Maistre quoted by Henri Bremond, *Prayer and Poetry*, London: Burns Oates and Washbourne Ltd,1927, introductory quotations, n.p.
6. From the prayer *Anima Christi*, 'Blood of Christ, inebriate me'. See Underhill (1911), p. 235.
7. Roy Campbell trans., 'Upon a Gloomy Night', *Collected Poems*, III London: The Bodley Head Ltd, 1960, p. 47.
8. 'East Coker,' *Four Quartets*, New York: Harcourt, Brace and World, Inc., 1943, pp. 27-8.
9. William Johnston, *The Inner Eye of Love*, London: William Collins and Sons Ltd, 1978, p. 16.
10. Underhill, *Practical Mysticism*, New York: E.P. Dutton and Co, Inc, 1915, p. 9.
11. Brendan Kennelly ed., Joseph Mary Plunkett, 'I See His Blood Upon the Rose', *The Penguin Book of Irish Verse*, London: Penguin Books, 1970. p. 301.
12. William Johnston, p. 39.
13. Underhill (1911), p. 94.
14. Bremond, pp. 187-200.
15. Bremond, p. 187.
16. Underhill, p. 74. Blake's words are also quoted by W.B. Yeats,

Essays and Introductions , London: Macmillan and Co Ltd, 1961, p. 117.

17. W.B. Yeats, 'Under Ben Bulben,' *Collected Poems*, ed. Augustine Martin, London: Arrow Books Ltd. An Arena Book, 1990 p. 342.

18. William Blake, 'Jerusalem,' in *Poetry and Prose of William Blake*, ed. Geoffrey Keynes, Bloomsbury, The Nonesuch Press, 1927, iii, pp. 649-702.

19. Quoted by Bremond, p. 199.

20. Bremond, p. 84 and p. 90.

21. Harvey D. Egan, *What are they saying about Mysticism?* New York: Paulist Press, 1982, pp. 42-50.

22. Gerard Manley Hopkins, *Poems and Prose*, H. Gardner ed., Middlesex, England: Penguin Books, 1953, p. 27.

23. Underhill, pp. 169-70. See also S. Foster Damon, *William Blake: His Philosophy and Symbols*, Gloucester, Mass., Peter Smith, 1958, p. 2. Here the five states of mystical development are successfully applied to the poetry of William Blake.

24. Mircea Eliade, *The Forge and the Crucible*, tr. Stephen Corrin, New York: Harper and Row, 1962, p. 142-4.

25. Martin Heidegger, 'What are Poets For?' in *Poetry, Language, Thought*, New York: Harper and Row Publishers Inc., 1971, p. 91.

26. Harvey Egan, *What are they saying about Mysticism?* New York: Paulist Press, 1982, p. 42.

27. Bremond, p. 187.

28. John Jordan, 'Mr Kavanagh's Progress,' *Studies*, 49 (Fall, 1960), p. 297.

29. The science of spiritual guidance practised in religious traditions east and west, had as its aim the discernment of true and false spirits.

30. Egan, p. 43.

31. Patrick Kavanagh, *The Green Fool*, London: Penguin Book, 1975, p. 201. All quotations are from this edition.

32. Patrick Kavanagh, *Tarry Flynn*, London: Penguin Books, 1978, p. 29. All quotations are from this edition.

33. *The Green Fool*, p. 194.

34. *Collected Pruse*, London: Martin, Brian and O'Keeffe, 1964, p. 198.

35. *The Green Fool*, p. 123.

36. Bremond, p. 88.

37. The edition of this poem entitled 'The Long Garden' published in *Collected Poems* by Brian and O'Keeffe in 1972 is preferable, to the edition as it appears in the long poem 'Why Sorrow?' as edited by Peter Kavanagh in *The Complete Poems*, New York: The Peter Kavanagh Hand Press, 1972.

38. *The Green Fool*, pp. 200-201.

39. William Johnston, ed. *The Cloud of Unknowing and the Book of Privy Counseling*, New York: Image Books, 1973.

40. *Sixth Reading Book*, Dublin: Alex Thom and Co, Ltd, 1889, Notes, p. 421, often referred to as the 'Sixth Book'.

41. Kavanagh refers to his 'third eye' in a poem entitled 'Remembered Country', p. 49. The notion of 'the third eye' is Indian in origin and denotes enlightenment. It is represented in Indian culture by the round spot painted on the forehead, the eye of true vision, contrasted with the illusory world of the flesh. See Johnston, pp. 143-151.

42. Kavanagh may have borrowed the reference to the Greek sculptor from 'Under Ben Bulben' by W.B.Yeats. It is more likely that he learned of Phidias from the 'Sixth Book', one of the Royal Readers, Dublin: Alex Thom and Co, Ltd, 1889, which he read after he had left primary school. The first lesson in this reader is a piece by Addison entitled 'Education compared to Sculpture', pp. 1-2. Aristotle's doctrine of substantial forms is referred to. He tells us that 'a statue lies hid (sic) in a block of marble',... 'The figure is in stone, the sculptor only finds it.' Phidias (432 BC) and Praxiteles (324 BC) are named as master-sculptors gifted with 'nice touches and finishings'. Explanatory notes in these readers provided comprehensive information.

43. Mircea Eliade, p. 144.

44. *Collected Pruse*, p. 33.

45. *The New Oxford Book of Irish Verse*, ed. Thomas Kinsella, Oxford: OUP, 1986, No. 19, p. 30.

46. *The Green Fool*, p. 74.

47. ibid., p. 180.

48. English magazines filled with snippets of information. *Titbits* is still being published at Stamford Street, London, SE1 9LS. The contents of these publications were the subject of conversation around the shoemaker's bench in the Kavanagh home.

49. *The Green Fool*, p. 154.

50. St John of the Cross, 'Stanzas Concerning an Ecstasy experienced in High Contemplation.' p. 719.

51. *Collected Pruse*, p. 195.

52. 'Is', 'Spraying the Potatoes' and 'The Long Garden' are among the poems to which I refer here.

53. For a further example of ritual naming see Brian Friel, 'Faith Healer', *Selected Plays*, London: Faber and Faber, 1984, pp. 327-376 at 332. Here the repetition of 'Kinlochbervie, Inverbervie,/ Inverdruie, Invergordon,/...,' acts as a kind of incantation whose very mention can effect healing.

54. St John of the Cross, 'A Romance on the Psalm "By the Waters of Babylon"', p. 733.

55. For the historical background to this poem see Peadar Livingstone, *The Monaghan Story*, Enniskillen: Clogher Historical Society, Watergate Press, 1980, p. 179. Kavanagh's information is accurate.

56. See Chapter Five for a full account of this incident.

57. Interview with Kieran Markey, nephew of the poet, January, 1991.

58. *The Green Fool*, p. 125.

59. *Irish Farmers Journal*, Sept 1, 1962.
60. 'Moments As Big As Years', *Creation*, July, 1957.
61. From an interview with Mr Terence Lennon, Hackballscross. August, 1990.
62. *The Green Fool*, p. 150.
63. *November Haggard*, Peter Kavanagh ed., New York, 1971, p. 16.
64. *Self Portrait*, p. 28.
65. *The Green Fool*, p. 123.

NOTES TO CHAPTER 2

1. Eric Cross, *The Tailor and Ansty*, Dublin, The Mercier Press: 1970 (1942).
2. *Lapped Furrows,* New York: The Peter Kavanagh Hand Press, 1969, p. 2.
3. James Collins a local historian from Monalty, recalled that his mother went to school in Tiercork in the 1880s. Her teacher was Miss Anne Farrelly, well respected for the way she conducted her school.
4. A Celtic cross marks the Cassidy grave in Kilmainham Wood cemetery. The names inscribed there are: Patrick (father) died September 1890, Mary (mother) died July 1875, Philip (brother) died 1912, Julia (sister) died 1918, Mary Ann died 1928, Alice (sister) died 1938.
5. Report dated April 29 1915, Education File (Ed/9 27780), National Archives, Bishop Street, Dublin. See also annual reports of the Board of Education, 1903, NLI, for reference to 'Carlyle and Blake' award.
6. *The Green Fool*, p. 26.
7. From a personal interview, November, 1989. (She died May 8th, 1990).
8. Patrick Kavanagh, introd. to Peter Kavanagh, *Irish Mythology*, Newbridge, Co Kildare: The Goldsmith Press, Ltd, 1988 (1958), p. 3.
9. *The Green Fool*, p. 88.
10. Interview with Mrs Briege Mc Caughan, daughter of the late Brigid Agnew (Miss Moore), September, 1989.
11. Peter Kavanagh, *Patrick Kavanagh Country*, The Curragh, Ireland, 1978, p. 18. A note written to Miss Cassidy dated September 26th, 1917, indicates that the cause of absence from school was that he was helping to draw home the corn.
12. *The Green Fool*, p. 88
13. ibid., p. 85.
14. ibid., p. 11.
15. See Chapter Five for a full account of the Patrick Kevany story, (1826-1896).
16. *The Green Fool*, p. 12.
17. Hugh Oram, *The Newspaper Book: A History of Newspapers in Ireland, 1649-1983*, Dublin: Mount Salus Press Ltd,1983, 'A brand new name in publishing in 1902 was *Ireland's Own*, born in Wexford as an off-spring of the *Wexford People*. The Walsh family who owned the latter

paper believed that there was a market in Ireland for an Irish publication to counteract the flood of English magazines, such as *Titbits* and *John O' London's Weekly* into the country'. p. 98.

18. *The Green Fool*, p. 11.
19. *Lapped Furrows*, p. 28.
20. *The Green Fool*, p. 11.
21. *Tarry Flynn*, p. 76
22. *The Green Fool*, p. 196.
23. ibid., p. 20.
24. *Lapped Furrows*, p. 18.
25. *Collected Pruse*, p. 283.
26. *Tarry Flynn*, p. 60.
27. *The Green Fool*, pp 207-208.
28. John Nemo, *Patrick Kavanagh*, Boston, Massachusetts: Twayne Publishers, 1979, p. 58.
29. Nemo, p. 69.
30. Parish records in Inniskeen date back to 1837.
31. John Nemo points this out in his essay 'Patrick Kavanagh: Notes Towards a Critical Biography', *The Journal of Irish Literature*, Robert Hogan ed., 6 (1977), pp. 4-21 at 4.
32. Margaret Drabble ed., *The Oxford Companion to English Literature*, London: Oxford University Press, 1987. The error appears as recently as Douglas Houston's 'Landscapes of the Heart: Parallels in the Poetries of Kavanagh and Auden' in *Studies*, Winter, 1988, pp. 445-459.
33. Manuscript No. 3220 in The National Library of Ireland.
34. Registry of Births, General Register Office, Lombard Street, Dublin 2. The birth was registered on November 11th, 1904, three weeks after the actual birth, another reason why the date might have been inaccurately recorded.
35. Katie Campbell (nee Mc Geough) was in the same class as Patrick Kavanagh and had reliable memories about her schooldays until her death May 8th, 1990.
36. The Catholic Directory confirms that Fr Treanor was curate in Inniskeen from 1913-1915, which coincides with the date of Kavanagh's Confirmation.
37. *Parishes of Clogher*, p. 411.
38. My source here is the late Bishop Mulligan, Bishop of Clogher. Interview, November, 1988.
39. *Tarry Flynn*, p. 15
40. ibid., p. 142.
41. From an interview with Mary Mulholland, September, 1988. She comes from a family who has had longstanding roots in the parish.
42. From an interview with Kevin McKeown, Magoney, Inniskeen, (November, 1989), who served Mass for Canon Maguire as a youth and attended his Mass regularly while he was Parish Priest.

43. Interview with Mary Mulholland.

44. *Collected Poems*, London: Martin Brian and O Keeffe, 1972, p. 61.

45. *Beyond Affection*, p. 47.

46. *Tarry Flynn*, p. 142.

47. *The Standard*, October 5th, 1945.

48. Interview with the late Bishop Mulligan, Diocese of Clogher. It is said that it was an Irish Bishop, recently transferred from Rome, who had asked for two priests from every diocese, to assist him in his work in Sidney, Australia. The venture is said to have been, for the most part, unsuccessful.

49. *By Night Unstarred: An Autobiographical Novel*, Newbridge, Ireland: The Goldsmith Press, 1978, p. 98.

50. *The Green Fool*, p. 32.

51. Interview with Elizabeth Gregory (nee Cassidy) 1986, and *Lapped Furrows*, p. 15.

52. The late Monsignor Séamus Morris, Carrickmacross recalling Fr Pat wrote, January 12th, 1987:
     Fr Pat was suspended for drink off and on, but was a very popular priest. One story I know of him – and you'll pardon me for telling it – a young fella went to Confession and said he had bad thoughts. Fr Pat's comment was 'Ah, them's the buggers'!

53. The late Mrs Katie Kirke-Campbell (Nee McGeough) who was at school with Kavanagh, claimed that she was healed by Fr Pat during a difficult pregnancy. Interview, December, 1989.

54. *The Green Fool*, pp. 45-50.

55. 'Literature', *Kavanagh's Weekly*, April 19th, 1952, p. 7

56. *Lapped Furrows*, p. 14.

57. 'Journeymen Shoemakers: Recollections of Other Days', *Irish Times*, Thursday, July 14th, 1936.

58. *The Green Fool*, p. 16.

59. ibid., pp. 89-97.

60. 'The Sixth Book', *Irish Times*, April 11th, 1940.

61. John Gallagher, reared in Dungloe, Co Donegal recalled how in the 1950s his Father, John Dan, recited poems from the 'Sixth Book' to him while footing turf in the bog.

62. *The Green Fool*, pp. 185-186.

63. ibid., p. 185.

64. ibid., pp. 185-186.

65. Anthony Cronin, *Dead as Doornails*, Dublin: Poolbeg Press, 1976, p. 96.

66. *The Green Fool*, p. 240.

67. Barney Rooney's sister Catherine was married to Pat Mc Hugh, (also spelt Mc Cue), James Kavanagh's half brother. They went to live in Sunderland, England. From the Family Record Book (Kavanagh Papers, UCD, Kav/D/5) there is evidence that Rooney was Annie Kavanagh's godparent. Further information regarding this family connection appears on a page containing some notes

which Patrick Kavanagh was using to prepare for a radio broadcast on Co Down for the BBC, Kav/ D/13. It reads: 'Barney Rooney's sister was wife of Pat Mc Hugh…'

68. *The Green Fool*, pp. 169 and 170.
69. For further development of this theme see Kevin Danaher, *Gentle Places and Simple Things*, Cork: The Mercier Press, 1964.
70. *The Green Fool*, p. 239.
71. James E. Mc Kenna, *Parishes of Clogher*, 2 vols, Enniskillen: 1920, Vol I, p. 412.
72. *Collected Pruse*, p. 64.
73. *Irish Mythology*, p. 1.
74. *Collected Pruse*, p. 33.
75. George Steiner, *Heidegger*, London: Fontana Press, 1978, p. 123.

NOTES TO CHAPTER 3

1. 'Schoolbook Poetry', *Kavanagh's Weekly*, 10 May 1952.
2. I am indebted to Mr Charles Cassidy now residing at Celbridge, Co Kildare, for identifying this field as being one of the fields taken for conacre by the Kavanaghs on the Rocksavage estate.
3. *Tarry Flynn*, p. 19.
4. The statistics for County Louth were similar as indeed were those nationwide.
5. A copy of this reader can be found in the Church of Ireland College of Education, Research Area, Upper Rathmines Rd., Dublin. It is an exact replica of the reader owned by Mrs Katie Campbell.
6. 'Schoolbook Poetry'. I have not succeeded in locating the exact excerpt from 'Locksley Hall' quoted here by Kavanagh in any of the schoolbooks available to me at present. I am satisfied, however, from interviews conducted with those who attended school at this time that an earlier edition of their class reader did in fact contain this piece.
7. See *The Green Fool*, p. 84 and *Tarry Flynn*, p. 142.
8. *Tarry Flynn*, p. 157 and p. 165.
9. ibid., p. 122.
10. Selections from the 'Sixth Book' are still known by heart, by those who learned them from their fathers while working in the field or bogs, or while doing household tasks with their mothers.
11. Interview with Mrs Patrick Hamill, Knockbridge, June, 1991.
12. 'Schoolbook Poetry'. This is an excerpt from 'The Children's Hour' by Longfellow, found in the Brown and Nolan Sterling Readers, Intermediate Book. It's cover was bright orange (yellow?) and also contains the coloured illustration of 'The Birds of Paradise' alluded to in 'The Great Hunger'.
13. Mangan's 'A Vision of Connaught in the Thirteenth Century' does not appear in the older school anthologies. The inclusion of poems by Irish writers came later. If Kavanagh heard the poem in school,

(*The Green Fool*, p. 83), he heard it from a junior rather than a senior class. It was certainly included in Professor Corcoran's schoolbooks which Lucy Kavanagh used in St Louis Convent, Carrickmacross (c. 1918-1924).

14. *The Green Fool*, p. 83.
15. *The Green Fool*, p. 84.
16. The only schoolbooks, to my knowledge, which contain this poem are the series of readers called *School and College Series*, Third Reader and *The New School and College Series*, Senior Book, ed. Rev T.A. Finlay, SJ, Dublin, n.d.
17. *Tarry Flynn*, p. 157-8.
18. *The Irish Farmers Journal*, 24 October, 1959.
19. *Tarry Flynn*, p. 10. Kavanagh makes an error in the title of this poem. It is entitled 'And then No More' and not 'The Nameless One'.
20. *Tarry Flynn*, p. 133.
21. *The Green Fool*, p. 84.
22. 'Schoolbook Poetry'.
23. Interview with Charles Cassidy, October 1990. Mary Kavanagh who died July, 1991, also provided similar information in September, 1989.
24. This song was heard from Katie Campbell (1903-1990), Charlie Cassidy (1898-) and Mary Kavanagh (1900-1991), who were at school at that time. The present writer heard it also from her father, John Agnew (1905-1985) who learned it at Shelagh NS.
25. Editions of Moore's Melodies were freely available, many of them designed for use in schools.
26. *The Green Fool*, p. 84.
27. *Dead as Doornails*, p. 92.
28. Interview with Mrs Briege McCaughan, daughter of Brigid Agnew, September, 1989.
29. *Tarry Flynn*, p. 17.
30. ibid., p. 15.
31. Douglas Houston, 'Landscapes of the Heart,' p. 449.
32. Patrick Kavanagh who was a friend of Ronnie Drew and the Dubliners, asked Luke Kelly to be the official singer of his song 'Raglan Road'.
33. Interview with Katie Campbell, January 1990.
34. The school Register for Kednaminsha shows that although he had completed fifth class, his entrance into sixth class was not sanctioned. He was marked 'Not Promoted'.
35. *Tarry Flynn*, p. 165.
36. *The Green Fool*, p. 208.
37. ibid., p. 208.
38. ibid., p. 187.
39. ibid., p. 10.
40. See Patrick Kavanagh, 'I sing the praise of Farney' in *Ireland of the Welcomes*, March, 1952.

41. The Bard McEnaney was well-known for his verbal contests with another local versifier, Jackson Blake from Ardee. This contest was printed in the *Dundalk Democrat* in 1902.

42. These poems are printed in *Patrick Kavanagh: The Complete Poems*, New York:The Peter Kavanagh Hand Press, 1984, pp. 369ff.

43. *The Green Fool*, p. 197.

44. William Carleton, *Traits and Stories of the Irish Peasantry*, London: George Routledge and Sons., Ltd, n.d. This was on of the few books to which Kavanagh had access while he was growing up. Peter says there was a copy of it in the Kavanagh home. *Beyond Affection*, p. 22.

45. Editorial of *The Irish Homestead*, Dublin, 1 (March 9th, 1895), Price: a penny halfpenny.

46. *The Green Fool*, p. 194.

47. ibid., p. 194.

48. *Sacred Keeper*, p. 232.

49. Monk Gibbon, 'AE', in *The Living Torch: A.E.*, ed. Monk Gibbon, London: 1937, pp. 3-81 (p. 45-6).

50. Monk Gibbon, p. 44.

51. Gibbon, p. 12.

52. Gibbon, p. 19.

53. Alan Warner, *Clay is the Word: Patrick Kavanagh 1904-1967*, Dublin: 1973, p. 49.

54. Paul Vincent Carroll, in a letter quoted by Warner, p. 133.

55. *Collected Pruse*, p. 263.

56. St John Ervine, 'A.E. – The Man and the Writer' from *John O' London's Weekly*, 9 August, 1919.

57. Warner, p. 86.

58. *Sacred Keeper*, pp. 48-49.

59. *Tarry Flynn*, p. 178.

60. *The Green Fool*, p. 244-5.

61. *Tarry Flynn*, pp. 178.

62. *The Green Fool*, p. 245.

63. Jean Leclerq, *The Love of Learning and the Desire for God*, trans. Catherine Misrahi, pp. 76-93.

64. *Patrick Kavanagh: Man and Poet*, ed. Peter Kavanagh, Newbridge: The Goldsmith Press, 1987, p. 242. See also *November Haggard*, p. 67.

65. *Collected Pruse*, p. 231.

66. Larry Morrow, 'Meet Mr Patrick Kavanagh', *The Bell*, April, 1948. See also *Collected Pruse*, p. 234.

67. 'Schoolbook Poetry'.

68. *The Green Fool*, p. 8.

69. Peter Kavanagh, *Irish Mythology; A Dictionary*, from the Introduction by Patrick Kavanagh, Newbridge, Ireland: 1988, p. 1.

70. 'Schoolbook Poetry'.

71. Seamus Heaney, *The Tribune*, 1990.

72. 'Schoolbook Poetry'.

73. *Self Portrait*, p. 173.
74. *Tarry Flynn*, p. 173.
75. Soren Kierkegaard, *The Point of View for My Work as an Author: A Report to History*, trans. Walter Lowrie, New York, 1962, p. 135.
76. Irish Writing, December, 1947.
77. *November Haggard*, p. 71.
78. T.S. Eliot, *Four Quarters*, New York: Faber and Faber, 1943, p. 59.
79. Patrick Kavanagh, *Patrick Kavanagh Country*, foreword.
80. *Collected Pruse*, p. 223.
81. *Tarry Flynn*, p. 21.
82. When Canon Maguire visited the school he would often spend time explaining why one should say be careful to say: 'In the name of the Father etc... and not the mindless, frequently mumbled version: '...Name of the Father etc...'
83. John Jordan, *Hibernia*, January, 1968. Richard D'Alton Williams' poem is identified as 'From a Munster Vale they Brought Her' by Anthony Cronin in *Dead as Doornails*, p. 92.
84. To his friend Eoin Ryan he wrote the following note: 'I'm sorry over the other evening. You cannot fully understand how I've been suffering from loneliness. I'm naturally social and not a hermit and the frustration is terrible'... Addressed 62, Pembroke Rd., July 27th, 1949.

NOTES TO CHAPTER 4

1. *The Green Fool*, p. 11.
2. ibid., p. 168.
3. Esther de Waal, *Celtic Vision, Prayers and Blessings from the Outer Hebridees*, Darton Longman and Todd, St Bede's Publications, USA, 1988.
4. Patrick Corish, *The Irish Catholic Experience: A Historical Survey*, Dublin, 1985, p. 197-201.
5. *The Green Fool*, p. 168.
6. 'The Wonder of Easter', *Irish Farmers Journal*, 1 April, 1961.
7. *The Irish Catholic Directory*, p. 596.
8. ibid., p. 596.
9. Ronald Knox, 1950, p. 596.
10. Published in *Kavanagh's Weekly* entitled 'Sex and Christianity'. He republished it in *The Irish Times*, 10 June, 1965. The piece is entitled 'George Moore', *Collected Pruse*, London, 1967, pp. 257ff.
11. *Collected Pruse*, p. 258.
12. Paddy Kierans, (d. 1995), resident at Annavackey, remembered the deck there. He was one of the committee-members. They commissioned a local carpenter to make the wooden platform and from the weekly contributions of the dancers, paid their small overhead and weekly expenses.
13. Peadar Livingstone, *The Monaghan Story*, Enniskillen, 1980, pp. 444-5.
14. *Collected Pruse*, p. 258.

15. Ronald Knox, *Enthusiasm*, Oxford: Clarendon Press, 1950, pp. 204-230.

16. *Kavanagh Weekly*, 21 June, 1952, p. 7.

17. *Tarry Flynn*, p. 32.

18. 'The Light that Fails', *Kavanagh Weekly*, 21 June, 1952.

19. John Jordan, 'Mr Kavanagh's Progress', *Studies*, Autumn, 1960, p. 297.

20. Under the pseudonym P.J. McCabe, *Kavanagh's Weekly*, 26 April, 1952.

21. For this information I am indebted to Father Basil OSB, student at Milltown Institute, Dublin, Spring Term, 1991, from his research carried out while studying 'The Great Hunger' in class.

22. *Kavanagh's Weekly*, 'Finnegan's Wake', 10 May, 1952.

23. The townlands of Corduff, Mulladuff, Cregganduff in this area are also north-facing.

24. *Collected Pruse*, p. 278.

25. 'Suffering and Literature' *Collected Pruse*, p. 278. The emphasis is mine.

26. *Tarry Flynn*, p. 31.

27. St John of the Cross, *Complete Works*, trans. Kieran Kavanaugh, Washington, DC, 1973, p. 69.

28. *The Green Fool*, p. 12.

29. *Reilly Catechism*, (Dublin, 1855 and 1949), Part 4, Lesson III, p. 37, p. 36. Both editions of the Reilly Catechism have identical texts, unchanged over a century except for the slight change in page numbering. I have chosen the catechism edition of the text rather than the Bible reference (Mt 5:3) or (Lk 6:20-23).

30. *November Haggard*, p. 62.

31. 'The Lilies of the Field', *Irish Farmers' Journal*, May 16, 1959.

32. *Collected Poems*, p.xiii. In *Dead as Doornails*, Dublin, 1976, Anthony Cronin dates this period as 1950-51, p. 79.

33. *Tarry Flynn*, p. 165.

34. St John of the Cross, p. 46.

35. *The Green Fool*, p. 178.

36. *Tarry Flynn*, p. 14.

37. St John of the Cross, p. 437.

38. Mary O'Driscoll, *Catherine of Siena: Selected Spiritual Writings*, New York: New City Press, 1993, p. 16.

39. *Kavanagh Papers*, UCD, from Patrick's school exercise-book.

40. *November Haggard*, p. 65.

41. Fr Corcoran's book is mentioned in *The Green Fool*, p. 187. See chapter Three for further information on Fr Finlay's schoolbooks. Reference here is to Wordsworth's 'Scorn not the Sonnet'.

42. 'Moments as Big as Years,' *Creation*, July, 1957, p. 79.

43. St Stephen's Magazine, Dublin: Autumn 1962.

44. This was his position on the local Innisken football team during the early 1930s.

45. *The Green Fool*, p. 7.

46. ibid., p. 7.

47. Oscar Wilde 'The Nightingale and the Rose', in *The Fairy Stories of Oscar Wilde*, London, 1990.

48. *Self-Portrait*, p. 10.

49. ibid.

50. ibid., p. 15.

51. *The Green Fool*, p. 88.

52. *X Magazine*, 1961 and *November Haggard*, pp. 79-87.

53. Robert F. Garratt, *Modern Irish Poetry: Tradition and Continuity from Yeats to Heaney*, Berkeley, 1989, p. 141.

54. *Lapped Furrows*, p. 44.

55. ibid., p. 45.

56. Kavanagh was offered a job in T. C. Martins, building contractors, through the influence of John Charles McQuaid, but he considered this job to be beneath his dignity. It is also true that he viewed football matches in Croke Park from the branches of nearby trees through lack of money.

57. Anthony Cronin, *Dead as Doornails*, Dublin, 1980 (1976), p. 76.

58. *Lapped Furrows*, p. 55.

59. *Collected Pruse*, 'Kavanagh v The Leader and Others', p. 165. *The Leader* profile was published October 11, 1952.

60. *Tarry Flynn*, p. 28.

61. *Collected Pruse*, 'Kavanagh v The Leader and Others', p. 166.

NOTES TO CHAPTER 5

1. *Beyond Affection*, p. 14.

2. *The Green Fool*, p. 12.

3. There are no state registers of births until the early 1860s. Official records depend on parish registers. The Inniskeen Parish Register (1837–) is available on microfilm in the National Library of Ireland.

4. The Griffith's Valuation of Rateable Property published in 1858 shows that Owen Kevany, was in possession of 32 acres in the townland of Castletown, Co Sligo. Owen was Patrick Kevany's father. He married Brigid Malloney and they had five sons: John, Lawrence, Philip, Owen and Patrick. Brigid died in February 1867, while Owen died on 6 May 1870 aged 81 years. His tombstone, erected by his son John, is in the old Catholic graveyard in Easkey.

5. See *Albert Agricultural College Centenary Souvenir*, 1838-1938, for a full account of the history, development and status of this institute for over one hundred years. A copy of this booklet is available both in the National Library as well as in the UCD Archives

6. Mr Edward Howley, Justice of the Peace, and Deputy Lieutenant, resided with his brother Thomas Howley at Beleek Castle, Ballina. They are both named among the nobility and gentry in Ballina in *Slater's Directory*, 1846. Local tradition remembers them as kindly land-agents, concerned for the people's welfare. Thomas Howley was Kevany's mentor when he applied for a teaching job at

Owenbeg NS. He also financed his education at Glasnevin, paying the five pounds yearly fee.

7. The earliest records for the Royal Albert Institute, including the Register of Pupils, are kept in the UCD Archives, Belfield, Dublin 4. The original agricultural Institute has changed its name and function with the years. It is now Dublin City University.

8. Tristram Kennedy was then agent of the Bath Estate in the area of Carrickmacross, Co Monaghan. He resided at Essex Castle, which is now a St Louis convent and secondary school. From the castle he administered his estate which extended to Kednaminsha, Drumlusty and Blackstaff.

9. The ruins of McEnteggarts still stands. It was a few hundred yards from the school. Owen Mc Entegart, (spelling used in the registers of the Commissioners of Education, Ed 2/102 folio 82) succeeded Kevany in Kednaminsha. He was appointed from January, 26th, 1856 and remained their until 1874. He is buried in Knockbridge graveyard. He is mentioned in *The Green Fool*, p. 72.

10. Tithe Applotment Books for Mucker, 1829, indicate that Mary Callan owned one acre of land valued at fifteen shillings.

11. As Manager of the school, he had retained the right of dismissal.

12. Education Register, Ed 2/102, folio 82, in the National Archives, Bishops Street, Dublin. These registers and folios contain information regarding Kednaminsha NS Roll No. 5498, 1848-1876.

13. *The Green Fool*, p. 247.

14. Mrs Mary Jo Feeney (nee Kevany) of Fortland, Easkey stated in interview October 1994, that her father, also Patrick Kevany, was insistent on this particular spelling of their name.

15. *Tarry Flynn*, p. 104.

16. Mentioned among the top ten South Monaghan names in 1970 by Livingstone in *The Monaghan Story*, Enniskillen, 1980, pp. 575-608.

17. *The Green Fool*, pp. 12-13.

18. Seamus Heaney, 'From Monaghan to the Grand Canal', *Preoccupations: Selected Prose*, 1968-1978, London/Boston, Faber and Faber, 1980.

19. An early poem, entitled 'Pioneers' refers to his having 'no name'. Could this be a reference to his lost lineage or does it simply allude to the fact that he had, as yet, no reputation as a poet?

> They hungered as they went the sharp-stoned road,
> And only one small lamp above them glowed…
> I too have eaten of the holy bread,
> A crust they spared for me who no name had.
> (Pioneers)

20. *Tarry Flynn*, p. 11. It was Corcoran's *Intermediate Poetry Book*, which Lucy Kavanagh used at the St Louis Convent in Carrickmacross, that introduced Patrick to a number of poems by Mangan and Ferguson. Earlier schoolbooks carried only translations from the German by Mangan.

21. *Tarry Flynn*, p. 106. As well as having no paternal relatives, his mother's family, the Quinns of Tullyrain lived in the next parish, too far distant to be of immediate help.

22. *Lapped Furrows*, p. 75. Writing to Peter who was touring Ireland by bicycle in 1942, he asked: 'You passed through Tullamore. Did you make any enquiries about our relatives?'

23. Kevany became Master of the Workhouse in Tullamore in 1861 and married Mary Molloy from Urney in April 1873. She was also in workhouse employment in Mountmellick. They had four children, two boys and two girls. It is not known whether this family knew of James Kavanagh's existence in Inniskeen.

24. From an interview (1992) with Eileen Molly, niece of Mary Molloy, Mrs Patrick Kevany of Tullamore. Eileen only barely knew her cousin Patrick and the two Mercy nuns in Galway since they were much older.

25. *The Green Fool*, p. 10.

26. *Tarry Flynn*, p. 104.

27. *Beyond Affection*, p. 13.

28. *The Green Fool*, p. 11.

29. ibid., p. 199.

30. *Sacred Keeper*, p. 16.

31. *Tarry Flynn*, p. 82.

32. ibid., p. 102.

33. *The Green Fool*, p. 10.

34. Lennart Ryden, 'The Holy Fool', in *The Byzantine Saint*, Sergei Hackel ed., London, 1981, pp. 106-113 (p. 106).

35. Literally, this Russian word means 'odd'.

36. Louis Bouyer, *A History of Christian Spirituality*, 3 vols, London, 1969, III, 32-35.

37. John Saward, *Perfect Fools: Folly for Christ's Sake* in *Catholic and Orthodox Spirituality*, Oxford: Oxford University Press, 1980, p. 34.

38. Seamus Heaney, *Sweeney Astray*, Derry, A Field Day Production, 1983.

39. Fyodor Dostoyevsky, tr. David Magarshack, *The Idiot*, Penguin Classics, London, 1955.

40. *The Idiot*, p. 359.

41. *Tarry Flynn*, p. 115.

42. ibid., p. 99.

43. It is quite possible that Kavanagh identified with St Thérèse, since she was the patroness of those who suffered from lung disease. During Kavanagh's stay in hospital, he spent much of his time with lung patients. In the wards St Thérèse was frequently invoked.

44. *Tarry Flynn*, p. 143.

45. As film-critic, Kavanagh would have seen 'The Song of Bernadette' which was popular at this time.

46. 'Notebook,' National Library of Ireland Ms. 3218.

47. *Tarry Flynn*, pp. 119-120.

48. *Collected Pruse*, pp 163-219.

49. ibid., p. 164.

50. For a synopsis of the trial see *Collected Pruse*, pp 163-219.

51. ibid., p. 180ff.

52. ibid., p. 192.

53. ibid., p. 211.

54. ibid., p. 215.

55. Anthony Cronin, *Dead as Doornails*, Dublin, 1976, p. 180.

56. *Collected Pruse*, p. 219.

57. Brendan Kennelly, 'Patrick Kavanagh', *Irish Poets in English: The Thomas Davis Lectures in Anglo-Irish Poetry*, ed. Sean Lucy, Cork and Dublin: The Mercier Press, 1973, p. 171. First published in Ariel, I (July, 1970), 7-28.

58. Patrick Kavanagh, public lecture given at UCD, Fall, 1956. Also in *November Haggard*, p. 71.

59. Underhill, pp. 380-412.

60. Underhill, p. 200.

61. Underhill, pp. 198-231.

62. Interview with Richard Riordan who shared the apartment at 41 Fitzwilliam Place with Kavanagh.

63. *Tarry Flynn*, p. 95.

64. *Collected Pruse*, p. 195.

65. Cronin, p. 83.

66. *Tarry Flynn*, p. 21.

NOTES TO CHAPTER 6

1. *The Green Fool*, p. 13.

2. William Johnston, *Silent Music*, p. 16. Mystic knowledge was originally secret, the mystic (mustes) being sworn to keep his mouth shut (muein).

3. *The Green Fool*, p. 8.

4. Augustine Martin, 'The Apocalypse of Clay: Technique and Vision in The Great Hunger' in *Patrick Kavanagh: Man and Poet*, Peter Kavanagh ed., Newbridge, Ireland, 1987, pp. 285-293.

5. *The Green Fool*, p. 200.

6. Seamus Heaney, *Sweeney Astray*, Derry, 1983, p. 24.

7. Underhill, p. 245.

8. *Collected Pruse*, 'Shirley Monaghan'.

9. A well-known school of poets, often referred to as the Sliabh Gullion poets, who once benefited from the patronage of the O'Neills of Clandeboy. Places immortalised in poems such as 'Úr-Chill a' Chreagáin' and 'Úr-Chnoc Chéin Mhic Cáinte' can be seen locally. Patrick Kavanagh admitted to the Irish writer and scholar, Seán Mac Réamoinn, that had he been born some fifty or sixty years earlier he would undoubtedly be writing in Gaelic.

10. *Collected Pruse*, p. 63.

11. *Tarry Flynn*, p. 134.

12. Rudolph Otto, *The Idea of the Holy*, trans. John W. Harvey, London: Oxford University Press, 1950, pp. 5-11.

13. The parable of the sower (Lk 8:4-15) was, during Kavanagh's lifetime, the gospel for Sexagesima Sunday. This was the Sunday which occurred sixty days before Easter, usually in early spring. Kavanagh served Mass regularly as a youth and enjoyed Canon Maguire's learned sermons. The Canon, being a keen horticulturalist and part-time farmer himself, would undoubtedly have commented on this gospel and related it to spring-sowing. The parable was also part of Kavanagh's catechism programme at school. *The Catholic Child's* and *Youth's Bible History*, New Testament Part, compiled by the Sisters of Mercy Downpatrick, first published in 1898 was used in all schools. There were numerous reprintings of this text, the last one being in 1949.

14. The anonymous author of *The Cloud of Unknowing*, a Middle English mystical classic, counsels the need for leaving 'beneath a cloud of forgetting' those distracting thoughts which prevent one piercing 'the cloud of unknowing' which is God.

15. *The Green Fool*, p. 263.

16. ibid., p. 168.

17. The well-observed position of the sun on a kitchen dresser, served as a clock for rural people. From *The Green Fool*, p. 99, we note the following incident: 'Pat looked at the dresser. "It's not six yet", he said. "It's not six till the sun shines on the second of them blue plates".'

18. Douglas Houston, 'Landscapes of the Heart: Parallels in the Poetries of Kavanagh and Auden', *Studies*, Winter, 1988.

19. *Self Portrait*, p. 11.

20. The packman was a feature of country life in Kavanagh's time. He would go from house to house by bicycle, displaying his goods: aprons, scarves, combs and beads. Tinkers' wives also came around with coloured flowers, and baskets of haberdashery which they sold from door to door.

21. This poem was first published in the *Irish Press*, 27 September 1943, entitled 'A Reverie of Poor Piers'. For further information see Antoinette Quinn ed., *Patrick Kavanagh: Selected Poems*, Penguin Books, 1996, p. 164.

22. Seamus Heaney, 'The Placeless Heaven: Another Look at Kavanagh', *The Government of the Tongue*, London, 1988, pp. 3-22.

23. John Jordan, 'Mr. Kavanagh's Progress' in *Studies*, Autumn, 1960, p. 299.

24. Walter T. Stace, *The Teachings of the Mystics*, New York, 1960, pp. 30-33.

25. Underhill, p. 378.

26. *The Green Fool*, p. 201.

27. James Joyce, *A Portrait of the Artist as a Young Man*, Middlesex, England: Penguin Modern Classics, 1960 p. 202.

28. Bremond, p. 84.

29. *The Green Fool*, pp. 195-203.

30. ibid., p. 201.

31. ibid., p. 202.

32. See *The Green Fool*, p. 244-5 and *Tarry Flynn*, p. 177-8.

33. *The Green Fool*, p. 245.

34. ibid., p. 185.

35. ibid., p. 194.

36. ibid., p. 263.

37. See Michael Tynan, *Catholic Instruction in Ireland 1720-1950: The O'Reilly/Dunlevy Catechetical Tradition*, Dublin: Four Courts Press, 1985. Tynan tracing the use of the Reilly catechism established that it was 'the Duffy/O'Reilly (Duffy was the publisher then operating from Westmoreland St Dublin) which 'was used in the diocese of Clogher to the 1950s when catechisms throughout the country were gradually replaced by the national text'. (p. 40) The people of Carleton's Clogher had memorised the exact same catechism with slight variations in wording. See William Carleton, Volume I, 'The Station' London, 1990, p. 167.

38. *Sixth Reading Book*, p. 89.

39. A classmate of Patrick Kavanagh's, Mrs Katie Campbell, now deceased, recalled that she was confirmed with the poet in June, 1913.

40. *A Portrait*, p. 149.

41. Austin Clarke once complained to the poet Paul Marray OP, that Kavanagh refused the books he had offered to lend him. 'The only thing he will read' said Clarke, 'is T.S. Eliot and *The Messenger*'!

42. *A Portrait*, p. 147.

43. The editor was Fr Joseph Mc Donnell, SJ, who had assisted the great Fr James Cullen in the editing of *The Messenger of the Sacred Heart*, founded in January 1888.

44. Brian O'Higgins wrote pious verses regularly for *The Messenger* from 1910 until 1922. He worked for a time in Dundalk. Christmas cards including verses by Brian O'Higgins were printed locally in the Examiner Office, Dundalk.

45. *Tarry Flynn*, p. 19.

46. *The Green Fool*, p. 189, p. 194, p. 369ff.

47. Jeffrey, 'On Beauty', *Sixth Reading Book*, p. 314.

48. Warner, 'Appendix – A Letter from Paul Vincent Carroll', *Clay is the Word: Patrick Kavanagh 1904-1967*, Dublin: The Dolmen Press, 1973, p. 133.

49. W.B. Yeats, 'The Symbolism of Poetry' in *Essays and Introductions*, London, 1961, pp. 153-164 at 162.

50. *Paradise Lost*, I (The Invocation, 5-10).

51. *Tarry Flynn*, p. 29-30.

52. ibid., p. 33.

53. ibid., p. 43.

54. The pantheist identifies God with the universe; nature takes on the

properties and stature of a god. The Buddhist differs by being 'panenhenic', a state whereby the soul is oned with nature

55. John H. Davies, 'Mysticism – Nature', in *A Dictionary of Christian Spirituality*, Gordon S. Wakefield ed., SCM Press Ltd, 1983, pp. 274-5.
56. Finlay, *Sixth Reader*, pp. 72-6.
57. *Collected Pruse*, p. 225.
58. Seamus Heaney, *Preoccupations*, London, 1980, p. 60.

NOTES TO CHAPTER 7

1. *Collected Pruse*, 'James Joyce', p. 262.
2. ibid., pp. 263-265.
3. *Stephen Hero*, London / Glasgow / Auckland, Grafton Books, p. 190.
4. ibid., p. 188.
5. Richard Ellmann, *James Joyce*, Oxford: Oxford University Press, 1983, p. 83.
6. W.H. Gradner ed., *Poems and Prose of Gerard Manley Hopkins*, 'Introduction', p. xxi.
7. *A Portrait*, p. 212.
8. Augustine Martin, *Patrick Kavanagh: Man and Poet*, p. 293.
9. Ellmann, p. 83.
10. *The Green Fool*, p. 30.
11. ibid., p. 30.
12. ibid., pp. 180-181.
13. Patrick Rafroidi, 'A French Tribute', *Patrick Kavanagh: Man and Poet*, Newbridge, Ireland: 1987, p. 325.
14. Deirdre Manifold, Galway, Ireland, has recently revealed that 1954 marked the moment when her relationship with Kavanagh came to an end. They had been going out together for some time, when it slowly became clear to her that he had no means of marrying her. She left Dublin and later married the late Mr Manifold. Kavanagh, she knew, regretted the circumstances of her departure, but knew it was inevitable.
15. *Nimbus*, 1962. Also *November Haggard*, p. 45.
16. *Self-Portrait*, p. 27.
17. *Lapped Furrows*, pp. 209ff.
18. *See Preoccupations*, p. 48.
19. *Self Portrait*, p. 27.
20. *Aucassin and Nicolette and Other Medieval Romances and Legends*, tr. Eugene Mason, New York: E.P. Dutton and Co, 1958.
21. *The Green Fool*, p. 29.
22. *Self Portrait*, p. 25.
23. *Mysticism*, p. 443.
24. W.B.Yeats, 'A Dialogue of Self and Soul', Augustine Martin ed., p. 242.
25. John Jordan, 'Mr. Kavanagh's Progress', *Studies*, Autumn, 1960, p. 297.
26. Heaney, *Preoccupations*, p. 116.
27. James Liddy, 'A Memoir of Parnassus', *Patrick Kavanagh: Man and Poet*, p. 298.

28. From an interview with Richard Riordan who was Katherine's friend until she died in 1989.

29. Liddy, p. 300.

30. *Sacred Keeper*, p. 187.

31. For an account of his last days see *Love's Tortured Headlands*, New York: The Peter Kavanagh Hand Press, 1978. This is a sequel to *Lapped Furrows* and contains some intimate family letters. The Merrion Nursing Home was privately owned and now belongs to the Barrett Foundation. It is now run as one of the Cheshire Homes which cares for the disabled. I have been unable to find any written records of his hospitalisation there. Accounts of his illness have come from his doctor Richard Riordan and his private nurse Florence Connaughton.

32. Based on personal correspondence from Fr Drumy, curate at Westland Row in 1967 and now Parish Priest at Brakenstown, Swords, Co Dublin. He writes:

> It was the custom to record every single call in the sick-call book. Most frequently it was done under the name 'patient'. We did not get many calls to the Merrion so it is highly probable and possible that the call Fr Stone attended that night was indeed to Patrick Kavanagh. I have a vague recollection of Fr Mc Carthy and Fr Stone speaking about the death of the poet in this context. (Extract from letter received by the present writer November 17th, 1989).

33. *Beyond Affection*, p. 188.

34. Letter from Mrs Flo Connaughton-Foley, May 30th, 1990 from her home in New Jersey, USA. She was employed by Katherine, Patrick's wife, through a nursing agency, to attend Patrick on the night he died, Nov. 29th-30th, 1967.

35. *Jordan*, p. 304.

NOTES TO CONCLUSION

1. *The Green Fool*, p. 8.

2. Ellmann, p. 298.

3. Dag Hammarskjold, tr. Auden, W.H. and Leif Sjoberg, *Markings*, London: Faber and Faber, 1964, p. 65.

5. UCD Lecture Notes reproduced in *November Haggard*, p. 57.

6. From Stephen's diary in, *A Portrait*, p. 253.

7. Daniel W. Hardy and David F. Ford, *Jubilate*, London: Darton, Longman and Todd, 1984, p. 81.

8. 'Signposts', *Collected Pruse*, p. 28.

9. *Envoy*, January 1950.

10. *The Standard*, May 8th, 1942.

Selected Bibliography

PRIMARY SOURCES

1. Poetry
A Soul for Sale, London: Macmillan, 1947.
Collected Poems, London: Martin Brian and O'Keeffe, 1972.
Come Dance with Kitty Stobling and Other Poems, London: Longmans,
    Green and Company Ltd, 1960.
The Complete Poems of Patrick Kavanagh, Peter Kavanagh (ed),
    Newbridge, Ireland: The Goldsmith Press, 1984.
*The Complete Poems of Patrick Kavanagh with commentary by Peter
    Kavanagh*, New York: Kavanagh Hand Press Inc, 1996.
Lough Derg, with foreword by Paul Durcan, London: Martin Brian and
    O'Keeffe, 1978.
Ploughman and Other Poems, London: Macmillan and Company Ltd, 1936.
Selected Poems, Antoinette Quinn (ed), London/New York: Penguin
    Twentieth Century Classics, 1996.

2. Prose
By Night Unstarred, Peter Kavanagh (ed), Newbridge, Ireland: The
    Goldsmith Press, 1977.
Collected Pruse, London: Mc Gibbon and Kee, 1967.
Kavanagh's Weekly, with Peter Kavanagh, Newbridge, Ireland: The
    Goldsmith Press, 1981.
Self-Portrait, Dublin: Dolmen Press, 1964, from a Telefís Éireann
    documentary, produced by Jim Fitzgerald, October 30, 1962.
Tarry Flynn, Middlesex: Penguin Books Ltd, 1978 (1948).
The Green Fool, Middlesex: Penguin Books Ltd, 1975 (1938).
November Haggard, Uncollected Prose and Verse of Patrick Kavanagh,
    selected, arranged and edited by Peter Kavanagh, New York: Peter
    Kavanagh Hand Press, 1972.

3. Letters
Kavanagh, Peter ed., *Lapped Furrows*, Correspondence between Patrick
    and Peter Kavanagh 1933-67, New York: The Peter Kavanagh Hand
    Press, 1969.
Kavanagh, Peter (ed), *Love's Tortured Headland*, New York: The Peter
    Kavanagh Hand Press, 1978.

4. Contributions to Newspapers, Journals in order of publication:
'Journeymen Shoemakers: Recollections of Other Days', *The Irish Times*,
    Thursday, July 14, 1936.

'The Sixth Book', *The Irish Times*, April 11, 1940.
'Croagh Patrick', *Irish Independent*, July 29, 1940.
'Pilgrim without Petrol: Patrick Kavanagh Goes to Knock', *The Standard*, May 8, 1942.
'When You Go to Lough Derg', *The Standard*, June 12, 1942.
'The Church and the Poets', *The Standard*, July 3, 1942.
'Sisters of the Grey Veil', *The Standard*, September 11, 1942.
'Returning I Heard the Lark', *The Standard*, December 18, 1942.
'Ethical Standards', *The Standard*, April 2, 1943.
'Art is Worship', *The Standard*, April 23, 1943.
'Two Sides of the Picture', *The Standard*, April 30, 1943.
'The Road to Nowhere', *The Standard*, May 14, 1943.
'The Anglo-Irish Mind', *The Standard*, May 28, 1943.
'Davis Says to Me', *The Standard*, August 31, 1945.
'Tailor and Ansty', *The Irish Times*, September 18, 1945.
'Diary', *Envoy*, December, 1949 to July, 1951.
'I Sing the Praise of Farney', *Ireland of the Welcomes*, March, 1952.
'Sex and Christianity', *Kavanagh's Weekly*, May 24, 1952.
'Moments As Big as Years', *Creation*, July, 1957.
'Bachelorhood is Tragedy', *Creation*, October, 1957.
'The Shoemaker Who Didn't Stick to his Last', *Irish Farmers' Journal*, December 6, 1958.
'The Lilies of the Field', *Irish Farmers' Journal*, May 16th, 1959.
'A World of Sensibility', *Irish Mythology: A Dictionary*, by Peter Kavanagh, Newbridge, Ireland: The Goldsmith Press, Ltd, 1988 (1959), pp. 1-5
'The Bard of Callenberg', *Irish Farmers' Journal*, February 4, 1961.
'I'll be a Camera', *Irish Farmers' Journal*, May 6, 1961.
'Poets on Poetry', *X Magazine*, June, 1960.
'The Wonder of Easter', *Irish Farmers' Journal*, April 1, 1961.
'The House the Hens Built', *Irish Farmers' Journal*, February 17, 1962.
'Carleton the Voice of the People', *Irish Farmers' Journal*, June 30, 1962.
'Poems of Childhood', *Irish Farmers' Journal*, July 21, 1962.
'Schoolbookery', *Irish Farmers' Journal*, June 17, 1966.

For a more complete bibliography of Patrick Kavanagh material see:

Kavanagh, Peter, *Garden of the Golden Apples*, New York: The Peter Kavanagh Hand Press, 1972.
    – 'An Annotated Bibliography of Patrick Kavanagh', *Patrick Kavanagh: Man and Poet*. Newbridge, Ireland: The Goldsmith Press, 1987, pp. 393-450.
Nemo, John, 'A Bibliography of Writings by and about Patrick Kavanagh', *Irish University Review*, III (Spring 1973), pp. 80-106.

SECONDARY SOURCES

1. Works of Biographical interest:

Byrne, Michael, *Tullamore Catholic Parish: A Historical Survey*, Printed by the Leinster Leader for the Tullamore Parish Committee, Tullamore, 1987.

Dunn, Peter, 'An Irish Poet not Going Gentle into that Good Night', *London Independent*, October 7, 1989.

McArdle, Patsy, 'Dr Kavanagh Airs his Views to "NS"', *The Northern Standard*, September 14th, 1989.

Kavanagh, Peter, *Beyond Affection: An Autobiography*, New York: The Peter Kavanagh Hand Press, 1977.

   – *Love's Tortured Headland*, The Peter Kavanagh Hand Press, 1978.

   – *Patrick Kavanagh Country*, The Goldsmith Press, 1978

   – *Sacred Keeper: A Biography of Patrick Kavanagh*, The Goldsmith Press, 1979.

   – 'Bernard Canon Maguire: Parish Priest of Inniskeen 1869-1948, A Reminiscence by Peter Kavanagh', *Dundalk Democrat*, May 19, 1973, p. 23

2. References Works: Literature

Barry, Michael, *By Pen and Pulpit: The Life and Times of the Author Canon Sheehan*, Cork: Saturn Books, 1990.

Blake, William, *Poetry and Prose of William Blake*, Geoffrey Keynes (ed), Bloomsbury: The Nonesuch Press, 1927.

Brady, Anne, M. and Brian Cleeve, *Biographical Dictionary of Irish Writers*, Mullingar: Lilliput Press, 1985.

Carroll, Paul Vincent, *Shadow and Substance*, New York: Random House Inc, 1937.

Carleton, William, *Traits and Stories of the Irish Peasantry* with preface by Barbara Hayley, 2 Volumes, Gerrard's Cross: Colin Smythe Ltd., 1990 (1842-44).

Corcoran, Father SJ, *Intermediate Poetry Book*, Dublin: Educational Company Ltd, n.d.

Corrigan, D. Felicitas, *Helen Waddell: A Biography*, London: Victor Gollancz, 1990.

Cronin, Anthony, *Dead as Doornails*, Dublin: Poolbeg Press Ltd, 1980.

Cross, Eric, *The Tailor and Ansty*, Dublin: The Mercier Press, 1970 (1942).

Danaher, Kevin, *Gentle Places and Simple Things*, Cork: The Mercier Press, 1964.

Dilliard, Annie, *Pilgrim at Tinker Creek*, Toronto / New York / London: Bantam Books Inc, 1974.

Dostoyevsky, Fyodor, *The Idiot*, trans. David Magarshac, London: Penguin Classics, 1955.

Eliade, Mircea, *Symbolism, the Sacred, and the Arts*, Diane Apostolos-Cappadona ed., New York: Crossroad, 1986.

– *The Sacred and the Profane*, New York: Harper and Row, 1961.

– *The Forge and the Crucible*, trans. Stephen Corrin, New York: Harper and Brothers, 1962.

Finlay, Thomas. A. SJ (ed), *The School and College Readers*. Glasgow /Dublin /London /Belfast: Commissioners of Education Publications, 1898.

– (ed), *The New School and College Readers*, (Various School Publishing Houses), Dublin, 1900 onwards.

Foster-Damon S., *William Blake: His Philosophy and Symbols*, Gloucester, Mass: Peter Smith Publications, 1958.

Friel, Brian, 'Faith-Healer', *Selected Plays*, London: Faber and Faber, 1984, pp. 327-76.

Gailey, Alan, *Irish Folk Drama*, Cork: The Mercier Press, 1969.

Garratt, Robert F., *Modern Irish Poetry: Tradition and Continuity From Yeats to Heaney*, University of Los Angeles: California Press, 1989 (1986).

Gibbon, Monk (ed), *The Living Torch: AE*, London: Macmillan and Co, 1937.

Harmon, Maurice, *Anglo-Irish Literature and its Contexts*, Dublin: Wolfhound Press, 1979.

Heaney, Seamus, *Government of the Tongue*, London: Faber and Faber, 1988.

– *Preoccupations: Selected Prose, 1968-1978*, Faber and Faber, 1980.

– *Seeing Things*, Faber and Faber, 1991.

– *Sweeney Astray*, Derry: Field Day Theatre Company, 1983.

Heidegger, Martin, *Poetry, Language, Thought*, tr. Albert Hofstadter, New York/London: Harper and Row Publishers, 1971.

Hopkins, G.M., *Poems and Prose*, W.H. Gardner (ed), Baltimore, Maryland: Penguin Books, 1953.

Jeffares, A.N., *Anglo-Irish Literature*, Dublin: Gill and Macmillan, 1982.

Johnston, Dillon, *Irish Poetry After Joyce*, Indiana: University of Notre Dame Press, 1985.

Joyce, James, *A Portrait of the Artist as a Young Man*, Middlesex, England: Penguin Modern Classics, 1960.

– *Stephen Hero*, Theodore Spencer (ed), A Triad Grafton Book, London, 1977.

Kavanagh, Peter, *Irish Mythology*, The Goldsmith Press Ltd, 1988 (1959).

Kennelly, Brendan (ed), *Penguin Book of Irish Verse*, London: Penguin Books, 1970.

Kierkegaard, Soren, *The Point of View for My Work as an Author*, Walter Lowrie tr., New York: Harper Torchbooks, 1962.

Kilroy, Thomas, *Talbot's Box: A Play in Two Acts*, Dublin: Gallery Press, 1979.

Kinsella, Thomas (ed), *The New Oxford Book of Irish Verse*, Oxford /New York: Oxford University Press, 1986.

Lee, Joseph (ed), *Ireland: Towards a Sense of Place*, Cork University Press, 1985.

Lucy, Sean (ed), *Irish Poets in English: The Thomas Davis Lectures in Anglo-Irish Poetry*, Cork and Dublin: The Mercier Press, 1973.

Martin, Augustine, *Anglo-Irish Literature*, Dept. of Foreign Affairs, Dublin, 1980.

Mason, Eugene, *Aucassin and Nicolette and Other Medieval Romances and Legends*, New York: E.P. Dutton and Co, 1958.

McMahon, Sean, *The Best from the Bell: Great Irish Writing*, Dublin: O'Brien Press, 1983 (1978).

Melville, Herman, *Moby-Dick: or the Whale*, Harold Beaver (ed), London: Penguin Classics, 1972.

Molloy, M .J., *Three Plays: The King of Friday's Men, The Paddy Pedlar, The Wood Whispering*, Newark, Delaware: Proscenium Press, 1975.

Murphy, Daniel, *Imagination and Religion in Anglo-Irish Literature 1930-1980*, Dublin: Irish Academic Press, 1987.

Nemo, John, *Patrick Kavanagh*, Boston, Mass: Twayne Publishers, 1979,
 – (ed), *The Journal of Irish Literature: 'A Patrick Kavanagh Number'*, Volume 7, Special Issue, 6 January, 1977.

O hÓgáin, Daithí, *Myth, Legend and Romance: An Encyclopaedia of the Irish Folk Tradition*, London: Ryan Publishing Company Ltd, 1990.

O'Loughlin, Michael, *After Kavanagh: Patrick Kavanagh and the Discourse of Contemporary Irish Poetry*, Dublin: Raven Arts Press, 1985.

Quinn, Antoinette, *Patrick Kavanagh: Born Again Romantic*, Dublin: Gill and Macmillan, 1991.

Royal Readers Series, 'The Sixth Reading Book', Dublin: Alex Thom and Co Ltd, 1889.

Ryan, John, *Remembering How We Stood: Bohemian Dublin at the Mid-Century*, Dublin: Gill and Macmillan, 1975.

Sheehan, Canon P. A., *Luke Delmege*, Dublin: The Phoenix Publishing Company Ltd, n.d. (1902).
 – *My New Curate*, Dublin: The Talbot Press Ltd, 1928 (1899).

Steiner, George, *Heidegger*, London: Fontana Press, 1978.

Thoreau, Henry David, *Walden and Civil Disobedience*, A Signet Classic, New York, 1960.

Warner, Alan, *Clay is the Word: Patrick Kavanagh 1904-1967*, Dublin: The Dolmen Press, 1973.

Wilde, Oscar, *The Fairy Stories of Oscar Wilde*, illustrated by Harold Jones, London: Victor Gollancz Ltd, 1990.

Yeats, W.B., *Collected Poems*, Augustine Martin (ed), London: Arrow Books Ltd., An Arena Book, 1990.,
 – *Essays and Introductions*, London: Macmillan and Co.,Ltd, 1961.

2(a). Articles in Books, Newspapers and Periodicals.

Anonymous, 'Profile: Patrick Kavanagh', *The Leader*, October 11, 1952, pp. 8-12.

Boland, Eavan, 'Tragedy into Comedy', *The Irish Times*, June 5, 1971.

Egan, Desmond, 'Homer's Ghost', *Kavanagh: Man and Poet*, The Goldsmith Press, 1987, pp. 197-213.

Erving, St John, 'AE, the Man and the Writer', *John O'London's Weekly*, August 9, 1919.

Heaney, Seamus, 'From Monaghan to the Grand Canal: The Poetry of

Patrick Kavanagh', *Preoccupations: Selected Prose 1968-78*, London: Faber and Faber, 1980, pp. 115-30.

– 'The Placeless Heaven: Another Look at Kavanagh', *The Government of the Tongue*, London: Faber and Faber, 1988, pp. 3-27.

Houston, Douglas, 'Landscapes of the Heart: Parallels in the Poetries of Kavanagh and Auden', *Studies*, 77 (Winter,1988), pp. 445-59.

Jordan, John, 'A Few Thoughts About Patrick Kavanagh', *Poetry Ireland*, 4 (Summer, 1964), pp. 123-26.,

– 'Mr Kavanagh's Progress', *Studies*, 49 (Fall, 1960), 295-304.

– 'P.K.'s Point of View', *Hibernia*, 22 October, 1971.

– 'Tribute to Patrick Kavanagh', *Hibernia*, January, 1968.

Jenkes, Norma, 'The Rocky Road to Dublin: Patrick Kavanagh's Apprenticeship, 1930-39', *Patrick Kavanagh: Man and Poet*, The Goldsmith Press, 1987, pp. 371-81.

Kennelly, Brendan, 'Patrick Kavanagh', *Ariel 1* (July, 1970), pp. 7-28.

Liddy, James, 'A Memoir of Parnassus', *Patrick Kavanagh Man and Poet*, The Goldsmith Press, 1987, pp. 295-300.

Martin, Augustine, 'The Apocalypse of Clay: Technique and Vision in "The Great Hunger"', *Patrick Kavanagh: Man and Poet*, The Goldsmith Press, 1987, pp. 285-93.

Morrow, Larry, 'Meet Mr Patrick Kavanagh', *The Bell*, April 19, 1948.

Nemo, John, 'A Joust with the Philistines: Patrick Kavanagh's Cultural Criticism', *The Journal of Irish Literature*, 4 (May, 1975), pp. 65-75.

– 'The Green Knight: Patrick Kavanagh's Venture into Criticism', *Studies* (Autumn, 1974), pp. 282-294.

O'Brien, George, 'Fr Thomas A. Finlay, SJ, 1848-1940', *Studies* (March, 1940), pp. 27-40.

Payne, Basil, 'The Poetry of Patrick Kavanagh', *Studies* (Fall, 1960), pp. 279-94.

Rafroidi, Patrick, 'A French Tribute', *Patrick Kavanagh: Man and Poet*, The Goldsmith Press, 1987.

Ryan, John, Obituary, *The Sunday Press*, Dublin, December 3, 1967.

Sheedy, Larry, 'How Kavanagh Told His Story', *Irish Farmers' Journal*, August 18, 1962.

Wright, David, 'Patrick Kavanagh, 1905-1967', *London Magazine*, New Series, 8 (April, 1968), pp. 22-29.

3. Manuscripts
Manuscript 3220, 'Family Record Book', National Library of Ireland.
Manuscript 3218, 'Note-Book', National Library of Ireland.

4. Reference Works: Religion, Mysticism and Spirituality
Anonymous, *The Cloud of Unknowing and the Book of Privy Counseling*, William Johnston (ed), New York: Image Books, 1973.

Abbott, Walter M. SJ (ed), 'Pastoral Constitution on the Church in the Modern World' (*Gaudium et Spes*), *The Documents of Vatican II*, London/Dublin: Geoffrey Chapman, 1966.

Boff, Leonardo and Clodovis, *Salvation and Liberation*, Robert R. Barr tr.,
   New York: Orbis Books, 1984.

Bouyer, Louis, *A History of Christian Spirituality*, 3 Vols, London: Burns
   and Oates, (1965) 1969.

Bremond, Henri, *Prayer and Poetry*, Algar Thorold tr., London: Burns
   Oates and Washbourne Ltd, 1927.

Campbell, Roy, tr., *The Poems of St John of the Cross*, with preface by
   M. C. Darcy SJ, London: Harvill Press, 1951.
   – (trans.), *Collected Poems*, 3 Vols, The Bodley Head Ltd., London,
   1960.

Corish, Patrick, *The Irish Catholic Experience: A Historical Survey*, Dublin:
   Gill and Macmillan, 1985.

Egan, Harvey D. SJ, *Christian Mysticism: The Future of a Tradition*, New
   York: Pueblo Publishing Company, 1984.
   – *What are the Saying About Mysticism?*, Paulist Press, New
   York/Ramsey, 1982.

Eliot, T. S., *Four Quartets*, Harcourt, Brace and the World Inc., New York:
   A Harvest Book, 1943.

Fox, Matthew, *Original Blessing: A Primer in Creation Spirituality*, New
   Mexico: Bear and Co. Inc, 1983.

Hardy, Daniel W. and David F. Ford, *Jubilate: Theology in Praise*,
   London: Darton Longman and Todd, 1984.

St John of the Cross, *The Complete Works of Saint John of the Cross*, Kieran
   Kavanaugh and Otilio Rodriguez tr., Washington Institute of
   Carmelite Studies, Washington DC, 1973.

Johnston, William, *The Inner Eye of Love*, London: William Collins Sons
   and Co Ltd, 1978.

Knox, Ronald, *Enthusiasm*, London: Clarendon Press, 1950.

Leclerq, Jean, *The Love of Learning and the Desire for God*, Catherine
   Misrahi tr., New York: Fordham University Press, 1961.

Macquarrie, John, *Paths in Spirituality*, London: SCM Press, 1972.

Maher, Michael (ed), *Irish Spirituality*, Dublin: Veritas Publications, 1981.

Martz, Louis L. *The Poetry of Meditation: A Study in English Religious
   Literature of the Seventeenth Century*, New Haven/London: Yale
   University Press, 1962.

Mercy, Sisters of, *The Catholic Child's and Youth's Bible History*, (New
   Testament Part), M. H. Gill and Son, Dublin / Brown and Nolan Ltd,
   Belfast, 1949 (1898).

Ó Laoghaire, Diarmuid SJ, *Ár bPaidreacha Dúchais,* Baile Átha Cliath:
   FÁS, 1975.

Otto, Rudolph, *The Idea of the Holy*, John W. Harvey tr., London:
   Oxford University Press, 1950.

Pine-Coffin, R.S., tr., *Saint Augustine: Confessions*, London: Penguin
   Classics, 1961.

Purcell, Mary, *Matt Talbot and His Times*, Alcester/ Dublin: C. Goodliffe
   Neale, 1976.

Reilly, Most Rev Dr, *A Catechism of the Christian Doctrine*, Dublin: Printed by C. M. Warren for Duffys, 1855.

Saward, John, *Perfect Fools: Folly for Christ's Sake in Catholic and Orthodox Spirituality*, Oxford University Press, 1980.

Stace, Walter T. (ed), *The Teachings of the Mystics*, New York: A Mentor Book, 1960.

Tynan, Michael, *Catholic Instruction in Ireland 1720-1950: The O'Reilly/Dunlevy Catechetical Tradition*, Dublin: Four Courts Press, 1985.

Underhill, Evelyn, *Mysticism: A Study in the Nature and Development of Man's Spiritual Consciousness*, New York: E.P. Dutton and Co Inc, 1961 (1911).

– *Practical Mysticism*, New York: A Dutton Paperback, 1915.

4(a) Periodicals, Journals, etc.

Browne, Dr Noel, 'Church and State in Modern Ireland', (extracts), *The Irish Times*, March 21 and 22, 1991.

Carroll, Denis, 'Creation', *New Dictionary of Theology*, J. A. Komonchak, Mary Collins and Dermot A. Lane (eds), Dublin: Gill and Macmillan, 1987, pp. 246-58.

Daly, Gabriel OSA, 'Modernism', *New Dictionary of Theology*, etc. Gill and Macmillan, 1987, pp. 668-70.

Davies, John H., 'Mysticism, Nature', *A Dictionary of Christian Spirituality*, Gordon S. Wakefield (ed), London: SCM Press Ltd, 1983, pp. 274-5.

Hackel, Sergei, 'The Eastern Tradition from the Tenth to the Twentieth Century: Russian', *The Study of Spirituality*, Cheslyn Jones, Geoffrey Wainwright and Edward Yarnold SJ (eds), London: SPCK, 1986, pp. 259-276.

Larkin, Emmet. 'The Devotional Revolution in Ireland, 1850-75', *American Historical Review*, 77 (1972), pp. 625-52.

McRedmond, Louis. 'The Church in Ireland', *The Church Now: An Inquiry into the Present State of the Catholic Church in Britain and Ireland*, John Cumming and Paul Burns (eds), Dublin: Gill and Macmillan, 1980, 35-45.

O'Donoghue, Fergus SJ, 'Fr James Cullen, Founder and First Editor of "The Messenger", *The Messenger*, January, 1988.

– 'Two Corkmen, The Editors of "The Messenger" 1929-62', *The Messenger*, March, 1988.

O'Higgins, Brian, 'Stories of the Sacred Heart', *The Messenger*, 1920-21.

Russell, George (AE), *Editorial*, *The Irish Homestead*, 1 (March 9, 1895).

Ryden, Lennart, 'The Holy Fool', *The Byzantine Saint*, Sergei Hackel (ed), A Special Number, Sobornost Inc., *Eastern Churches Review*, London: Bemrose Press Ltd, 3, (1981), pp. 106-113.

Veale, Joseph SJ, 'Ignatian Spirituality and Devotion to the Sacred Heart', *Milltown Studies*, 24 (Autumn, 1989), pp. 66-82.

5. Other Reference Works

Albert Agricultural College Centenary Souvenir 1838-1938, in NLI and
  UCD Archives. Census of Ireland, 1901 and 1911, for Tullamore,
  Easkey and Inniskeen.

Farragher, Sean P., *Dev and His Alma Mater: Eamon De Valera's Lifelong
  Association with Blackrock College 1898-1975*, Dublin: Paraclete Press, 1984.

Livingstone, Peadar, *The Monaghan Story*, Enniskillen: Watergate Press,
  1980.

Oram, Hugh, *The Newspaper Book: A History of Newspapers in Ireland
  1649-1983*, Dublin: MO Books, 1983.

Rushe, Denis, *Carolan, Historical Sketches of Monaghan*, no publisher
  given, Monaghan, 1894.
  – *Monaghan in the Eighteenth Century*, Dundalk: Dundealgan Press,
  1916.
  – *History of Monaghan for Two Hundred Years*, Dundalk: Dundealgan
  Press, 1921.

Shirley, Evelyn Philip, *Some Account of the Territory or Dominion of
  Farney, in the Province of Ulster*, no publisher given, London, 1845.
  – *The History of the County of Monaghan*, no publisher given, London,
  1879.

Short, Con ed., *The Bard of Callenberg: Ballads of Inniskeen*, by John
  McEnaney, Dundalk: Dundalk Democrat Office, 1974.

The Blackrock College Annual ,1973.

The Messenger, 1910-1930.

Titbits, Publication ongoing, Stampford Street, London.

6. Unpublished Material

Bardwell, Leland, 'One Autumn Day: Women in Kavanagh's Work and
  Life', paper read at Kavanagh's Yearly, Carrickmacross, 1986.

Cronin, Anthony. 'Kavanagh from Patmos', keynote address given at
  Kavanagh's Yearly, November 24, 1989.

Deane, Raymond, 'November Songs', based on six poems by Patrick
  Kavanagh first sung by Ms Collete Mc Gahon, Kavanagh's Yearly,
  November 24, 1990.

Deane, Seamus, 'Kavanagh: Naming the Place', keynote address given
  at Kavanagh's Yearly, Carrickmacross, November 23, 1990.

Durcan, Paul, 'The Mystery of Lough Derg', Poetry reading and commentary given at Kavanagh's Yearly, November 23, 1985.

Eliade, Mircea, 'Personal Notes' taken at Lecture sponsored by the
  Psychology Dept., Duquesne University Pittsburgh, February, 1973.

Harding, Michael, 'When the Angel Woos: The Movings of Mystery
  through a Writer's Work', paper read at Kavanagh's Yearly,
  Carrickmacross, November 28, 1987.

Howlett, Michael, *The Human Condition in The Writings of Patrick
  Kavanagh (1904-1967): A Theological Exploration*, Unpublished
  Doctoral Thesis, Gregorian University, Rome, October, 1990.

Jordan, John, 'A Biographical and Bibliographical Reminiscence of the Poet', keynote address at Kavanagh's Yearly, November 23, 1984.

MacIntyre, Tom, and Patrick Mason, 'Staging the Great Hunger', talk given at Kavanagh Yearly's, Carrickmacross, November, 1984.

Martin, Augustine, 'The Brothers Kavanagh: The Kavanagh Archives in New Jersey, USA', lecture given at Kavanagh's Yearly, November 23, 1985.

O'Loughlin, Michael, 'The Sense of Place and the Place of Exile in Irish Literature', introductory talk to symposium held during Kavanagh's Yearly, Carrickmacross, November 26, 1989.

O'Toole, Fintan, Introductory Talk: 'Lilacs in the City', A Symposium on Kavanagh's work and themes, Kavanagh's Yearly, Carrickmacross, November 29, 1987.

Ryan, Liam, 'The Sociological Aspects of Popular Devotion to Christ', Paper given at Miltown Institute of Philosophy and Theology, June, 1988.

Stack, Thomas G., *Ordinary Plenty: Patrick Kavanagh and the Catholic Imagination*, Unpublished M. Theol. Thesis, Harvard University, May, 1986.

OTHER RESEARCH USED

1. Public Records and Archives:

The National Archives, Bishop Street Dublin, Educational Registers, Salary Books and Registry of Wills.

Civil Records (Births, Marriages, Deaths), 8-11 Lombard St, Dublin 2.

Minute Books of the Board of Guardians of Tullamore, Offaly County Library, 1839-1921 (not complete).

Reports from Commissioners of the Board of Education, 1903-4.

Inniskeen Folk Museum, Curator: Clinton O'Rourke, Inniskeen, Co Monaghan.

Inniskeen Parish Records, (1837-) on Microfilm in National Library.

Irish Jesuit Province News, July, 1951.

Kednaminsha School Registers, 1877-1930, kept at Inniskeen NS, Co Monaghan.

Mc Kenna, James E., Parishes of Clogher: Parochial Records. 2 Vols. Fermanagh Herald Office, Enniskillen, 1920.

Redemptorist Archives, Archivist, Fr O'Donnell CSSR, Marianella, Orwell Rd, Rathgar, Dublin 6.

Redemptorist Annals, St Josephs, Dundalk.

The Irish Catholic Directory, published yearly for the hierarchy of Ireland, (1870-)

The Kavanagh Papers, UCD.

Griffith's Valuation of Rateable Property, 1850-60, National Library of Ireland.

Sick-Call Book, Westland Row, Dublin 1.

UCD Archives.

2. Personal Interviews

Mary Kavanagh (poet's sister) d.1991

Josephine Markey (nee Kavanagh) (poet's sister).

Peter Kavanagh (poet's brother) April, 1991.

Kieran Markey (poet's nephew), January, 1991.

Mrs Jennie Uí Chléirigh, (Fr Bernard Maguire's niece) July 1988 and February, 1991.

Annie McEnaney (daughter of the Bard of Callenberg), Shelagh, Dundalk.

Art and Helen Agnew (PROs for Kavanagh Society and Kavanagh Yearly) Ardross Avenue, Carrickmacross, Co Monaghan.

Father Basil OSB, Glenstal Abbey, Co Limerick.

Katie Kirke-Campbell (nee McGeough), December 1989, January 1990.

Mrs Annie Fitzpatrick, Inniskeen village, Co Monaghan, November,1989.

Mr Tom Fitzpatrick, Drumboat, Inniskeen, March 1991.

Sr Mary Lonan SSL, Dundalk, December 1990.

Mary Mulholland, August 1987, September 1989 and May 1991.

Bishop Mulligan, March 1989, (d.1990)

Fr McDermott, Glaslough, Co Monaghan, March 1989.

Srs Ethna and Nuala McCluskey SSL, January 1989, May 1989.

Kevin McKeown, Magoney, Inniskeen, March 1991.

May O'Flaherty, Parsons' Bookshop, Baggot St, October 1986.

Richard Riordan, (groom's man at Patrick Kavanagh's wedding) October1986 and November 1989.

Leland Bardwell, November 1990.

John Jordan, January 1986, November 1986 and January 1987.

Fr Sean Farragher, Archivist, Blackrock College, November 1989.

Philip McArdle (grandnephew of Fr Pat McConnon) Ballybinaby, March 1991.

Mrs Minnie Gorman, (nee Mc Ardle) (grandniece of Fr Pat McConnon) Shanmullagh, Co Louth, March 1991.

Paddy Kierans, Annavackey, Dundalk, September 1989.

Paul Murray OP, Dominican Priory, Tallaght, Co Dublin. October 12th 1990.

Benedict Kiely, Morehampton Rd, Dublin 4, April 8th 1991.

Mrs Briege Mc Caughan (daughter of 'Miss Moore'), Grand Parade, Dublin.

Patrick and Mary Hamill, Knockbridge, Co Louth, May 1991.

May Treacy, Shortstone, Dundalk, April 1991.

Charles Cassidy, Castleknock, Co Dublin, October 1990.

Terence Lennon, Hackballscross, Dundalk, August 1990.

Elizabeth Gregory, (nee Cassidy), Gortin, Inniskeen, Co Monaghan (consulted on several occasions between 1985 and 1991).

Gretta Agnew, Courtbane, Hackballscross, Dundalk (teacher at Inniskeen NS 1929-34) (consulted frequently between 1985-1991)

Sr Helena O'Tierney, St Louis Convent Rathmines, Nov. 1990, d. 1998.

Mrs Annie Callan, Merrion Rd., Dublin 4 (former teacher at Kednaminsha NS 1918-1922), June 1991.

3. *Letters received from:*

Fr Drumy PP, Swords, Co Dublin, November 1989.

Florence Foley (nee Connaughton), New Jersey, USA.

Fr Roland Burke-Savage, Clongowes Woods, October 12th 1989.

Fr Seamus Morris, Presbytery, Carrickmacross, January 12th 1987.

Sr Raymond O'Mahony PBVM, Presentation Convent, Isle of Wight, October 7th and November 4th 1989.

Fr Patrick O'Donnell CSSR, (Archivist), St Gerards, Antrim Rd, Belfast.

Mary Purcell, 32 Gardiner Place, Dublin 1, March 9th 1987.

Michael Mc Hugh, Easkey, Co Sligo. (Correspondence October 1989-June 1991)

Enda Waters, CSSP, Kimmage Manor, Dublin.

Index